THE COMPASSIONATE-MIND GUIDE TO

ENDING OVEREATING

using compassion-focused therapy to
overcome bingeing & disordered eating

KEN GOSS, DClinPsy

New Harbinger Publications, Inc.

Publisher's Note

Distributed in Canada by Raincoast Books

Copyright © Ken Goss 2010. First published in the UK by Constable, and imprint of Constable & Robinson, Ltd. 2010.

The eatwell plate was produced by the Food Standards Agency of the UK. © Crown copyright material is reproduced with the permission of the Controller of HMSO and Queen's Printer for Scotland.

Copyright © 2011 by Ken Goss
    New Harbinger Publications, Inc.
    5674 Shattuck Avenue
    Oakland, CA 94609
    www.newharbinger.com

Cover design by Amy Shoup
Acquired by Tesilya Hanauer
Edited by Nelda Street

Printed in the United States of America

Distributed in Canada by Raincoast Books

FSC
Mixed Sources
Product group from well-managed
forests and other controlled sources

Cert no. SW-COC-002283
www.fsc.org
© 1996 Forest Stewardship Council

Library of Congress Cataloging-in-Publication Data

Goss, Ken.
  The compassionate-mind guide to ending overeating : using compassion-focused therapy to overcome bingeing and disordered eating / Ken Goss ; foreword by Paul Gilbert.
    p. cm.
  Includes bibliographical references.
  ISBN 978-1-57224-977-6 (pbk.)
  1. Compulsive eating--Psychological aspects. 2. Emotion-focused therapy. 3. Compulsive eaters--Psychology. I. Title.

RC552.C65G67 2011
616.85'26--dc22

2011007091

13   12   11

10   9   8   7   6   5   4   3   2   1

First printing

Contents

Foreword

We humans have always understood that compassion is very important for our well-being. Recent advances in scientific studies of compassion and kindness have greatly increased our understanding of how compassionate qualities of the mind really do influence our brains, bodies, and social relationships, as well as affect our health and well-being. Yet despite this ancient wisdom and modern knowledge, we live in an age that can make it difficult to have compassion for ourselves and others. This is the world of the competitive edge; of achievement and desire; of comparison, dissatisfaction, and criticism. Research has now revealed that such environments actually make us unhappier and that mental health issues are on the rise, especially in younger people (Twenge et al. 2010). These issues are particularly pronounced in those of us who have difficulties with our eating habits, weight, or both. As Ken Goss helps us see, we are surrounded by a food industry that wants us to eat more and more, and deliberately manipulates taste, texture, and aesthetic appeal, and also by a culture that is highly critical of overweight people. Caught between the two, the more we criticize ourselves and feel down about our difficulties with eating, the more we eat. Learning to have compassion—particularly for ourselves—offers a path out of this cycle.

Another aspect of our society is a habit of attaching blame to people if they do not seem to come up to the mark or behave in prescribed ways. However, as Ken Goss makes clear, we can have significant difficulty with eating and weight through no fault of our own. We are a species on a long and continuing evolutionary journey. We didn't design the human brain, with its various capacities for emotions like anxiety and anger, and its desires for sex or a lovely tasty meal—this is just how the brain is. Nor did we design our bodies to seek out foods that are high in fat, sugar, and calorie content—that's just how they've evolved. We developed few natural regulators in our minds to limit our intake of such foods, because we didn't need them on the savannas of prehistoric Africa, where these foods are very scarce. Today, though, it's tricky when you can go into a supermarket and find highly manufactured foods that can light up your brain's "wanting and appetite" areas like a Christmas tree.

What are we to do, then? First, we can learn to pay attention to how our minds function, and become mindful and observant of the feelings associated with eating. Ken Goss shows in helpful detail how people have learned to pay attention to their feelings rather than simply reach for the fridge.

If your relationship with yourself is critical and harsh, then your inner world is not a comfortable place to be in. Feeling ashamed and being self-critical, self-condemning, or even self-loathing can undermine our confidence, make us feel bad—and tempt us to eat more! In contrast, self-compassion is a way of being with ourselves in all our emotions, uncomfortable as they may be, without self-condemning, but rather supporting and encouraging ourselves. Research shows that the more compassionate we are toward ourselves, the happier we are and the more resilient we are when faced with difficult events in our lives (Neely et al. 2006; Leary et al. 2007). In addition, we are better able to reach out to others for help and more compassionate with others too.

Compassion is sometimes viewed as being a bit soft or weak, letting your guard down and not trying hard enough. Quite the contrary, compassion requires us to be open to and tolerate our painful feelings, to face up to our own difficulties and those of others. Compassion is not turning away from difficulty or discomfort, or trying to get rid of it. It is not a soft option. It requires courage, honesty, and a commitment to do what we can to alleviate unhappiness and pain of all kinds. It teaches us to do things to and for ourselves that help us to flourish and take care of ourselves—not as a demand or requirement but to enable us to live our lives more fully and contentedly.

In this book Ken Goss draws on his many years of experience heading the National Health Service (NHS) eating disorders service in Coventry, United Kingdom. In particular he has developed compassion-focused therapy for people with eating disorders and disordered eating. Here he outlines a compassionate way of thinking about our evolved and complex relationships with food, and provides a number of steps and exercises that enable you to develop a compassionate approach to those difficulties. You will learn about the nature of compassion and how to develop compassionate attention, compassionate thinking, and compassionate behavior. You will learn about the potential power of developing compassionate imagery and the compassionate sense of self, and how to use them when things get tough. Compassionate images can be either visual or aural (for example, imagining a compassionate voice speaking to you when you need it) and can be especially useful in enabling us to get in touch with our internal compassionate feelings and desires.

The compassionate approach outlined here draws on many other well-developed approaches, including those of Eastern traditions, such as Buddhism, and Western therapeutic approaches, like the various cognitive behavioral therapies. Recognizing that you have a difficult, sometimes love-hate, relationship with food and eating is a first step toward change; the next is to think about what would be helpful, followed by moving on with a program of clear, practical steps toward change. This book provides such a program. The benefit of a compassionate approach is that when you identify the steps, you begin to walk the path in a friendly, supportive, kind, and encouraging way, recognizing that from time to time you will trip up, things will not go as you wish, and you will have setbacks and relapses but that every time kindness, compassion, and support will help you through. You will learn to develop an inner voice that conveys a sense of understanding, encouragement, and warmth for you. If, by the end of this book, you have learned only how to speak kindly to yourself, you will have gained a valuable skill.

Many people suffer silently and secretly with eating and weight—some ashamed of or angry with it, others sometimes fearful of it. Sadly, shame stops many of us from reaching out for help. But by opening your heart to compassion for your eating, you can take the first steps toward dealing with it in a new way. Our compassionate wishes go with you on your journey.

—Paul Gilbert, Ph.D.
August 2010

Acknowledgments

My first thanks go to all those clients who have been willing to share their experience of overeating. Their insights have been invaluable, while their courage and commitment to learning ways to deal with their experiences and feelings have inspired my work for over twenty years.

This book would never have been written without the support and encouragement of Professor Paul Gilbert. I have had the privilege of working with Paul for almost my entire professional career. His influence has been profound in both my personal and professional lives. He has pioneered the development of compassion-focused therapy, and his commitment to developing, researching, and promoting this new approach has moved compassion into the mainstream of scientific thinking and clinical practice. I will always remain grateful for his help and for his encouragement to take responsibility for bringing the developments I have made in working with people with eating disorders to a wider audience. Without his faith in my ability to complete this work and his compassionate encouragement throughout the process of writing, I would never have finished.

I would like to thank my family, Gill, Adam, and Tasha, for their patience and encouragement in completing this book. Books take time to grow, and this one has taken several years! It's my greatest hope that they will always receive compassion from others and from themselves.

Finally, I would like to thank you, the reader, for taking the time to consider a different way of dealing with food and eating. I hope this approach can help you to find new ways to care for yourself and manage the challenges of life.

Introduction

This book consists of two intertwined elements: an outline of the compassion-focused approach to human psychology, specifically as it relates to our relationships with food, eating, and our bodies, and a practical program of staged tasks that will help you relate these ideas to your own life and your own habits, thoughts, and feelings around food and eating.

Throughout the book from chapter 5 onward, you will find exercises you can do and worksheets you can use to keep records. Try the exercises in your own time and at your own pace. Blank copies of the various worksheets are provided at http://49776.nhpubs.com; you can download as many of them as you need, and you may wish to adapt them to make them personal to you. You may also find it useful to have a notebook and pen with you as you work through the book so that you can make your own notes on things you find particularly useful or challenging.

This book contains a lot of ideas, and on first reading, it may seem to you that the prospect of change is too complex, difficult, or overwhelming. The key is to go one step at a time: try things out for yourself, see what you can use, and if you only change one or two things, that's still helpful. Few of us follow manuals or recipes to the letter, if we're honest. But we also know that if we want to get fit, play the piano, or learn a foreign language, the more we practice, the better we'll get.

CHAPTER 1

Understanding Your Relationship with Food

Food can be a pleasure or a curse. Without it, we die, but with too much, we have a whole range of health problems. We eat for a host of reasons: because we're hungry, to be sociable, because we're miserable, or because we just like the taste and the pleasure of putting things in our mouths. We enjoy our food because of its tastes and textures. For most of us, chocolate cake and ice cream are an awful lot more desirable than turnips and spinach. Unfortunately, the latter are much better for you. Although over half the world does not have enough to eat, many of us in the West have the opposite problem: managing the availability of relatively cheap and appetizing food. The abundance of easily accessible processed foods brings with it serious difficulties relating to how we manage our desire for food and regulate our appetites and weight. In the modern Western world, we are surrounded by enticements to buy and eat more. If we follow these cultural demands, we are pretty likely to put on weight, but then we often become the target of moral and medical condemnation, feeling guilty or ashamed about our eating. Simply telling ourselves not to eat too much is not a great deal of help. Indeed, it tends to make things worse, because we then feel depressed and consequently eat more to feel better. Sometimes it can feel as if you just can't win!

WHAT IS MEANT BY A COMPASSIONATE APPROACH?

Understanding this difficulty is actually the first step toward developing a compassionate approach to food and eating. When we look more closely at overeating, we come to understand how complex it is and to realize that it's not our fault so many of us struggle to regulate our eating behaviors and weight.

It turns out that the human brain has evolved to be attracted to foods that are high in fat and sugar, and our bodies have evolved to store excess energy (in the form of fat) for leaner times. Your brain is not really designed to regulate your eating, because for much of the time over which mammals have evolved, it didn't need to: food was hard to find, so we had to make the most of it when it was available.

Once we give up blaming ourselves for the problems we have with our diets and our weight, we become less ashamed and more open to taking responsibility for finding ways to eat and exercise that are appropriate and helpful for us. This is a hard task, but it's even more difficult to tackle it if we are swamped by self-critical feelings.

So a compassionate approach starts with understanding what we're up against. This means understanding how and in what conditions the human brain evolved to give us certain desires and passions, and how modern environments can make life both easier for us in some ways and very difficult in others.

UNDERSTANDING THE PROBLEM: WHY WE LOVE TO EAT

Let's go back a million years or so and consider how our ancestors lived. They would have spent much of their time foraging for food, because it was usually in short supply and they were not as good at hunting as other meat-eating animals, such as lions, wolves, and hyenas. Foraging animals eat as often as they can, because food is often hard to find. Seeking it out requires a lot of time and energy, and foragers are constantly on the move. Most accounts of *our* ancestors suggest that this was the way they lived for many thousands of years.

In this environment, the human brain did not evolve mechanisms for self-restraint because it did not need them: our eating was constrained by the relative shortage of food and our foraging habits. We evolved for the "see-food" diet: "see food and eat it"! Actually, many mammals are like this; you may recognize the tendency in your family dog. It's not our fault that our brains and bodies did not evolve with effective mechanisms for self-restraint in eating, but the fact that they didn't can make life very difficult for us in the modern world, where many of us have easy access to cheap, nutritious food and tend to be far less active than in former times.

What about the food itself? Well, most of the food our ancestors would have foraged for would have been pretty low in calories, so they needed to eat a lot of it. It is true that we also became hunters of meat and could bring down large game, particularly when we operated in (mostly male) teams. However, hunting tends to be a pretty hit-and-miss affair: even the most successful carnivores actually make a meal out of only about one in ten of their intended prey. So although meat was an important part of our ancestors' diet, for the most part they would have relied on nuts, berries, root vegetables, and other plants; meat and fish would have been a bonus!

Looking at groups around the world who have a more basic way of life than us in the developed West, we find that they tend not to be big meat eaters. Their diets consist mainly of foods that can be gathered, often by women: roots, nuts, and vegetables. Also, many plants evolved fruits and seeds that herbivores found palatable so that they would eat them and spread the seeds; so when the plants were ripe, they tasted sweet due to a high sugar content that made them both appetizing and naturally high in calorie (energy) content. In fact, the sugary taste is how we know plants are ripe: plants that are poisonous or unripe tend to have a sour taste. Therefore, we evolved with a sweet tooth!

Other energy-dense foods (like fish or meat) tend to be higher in fat and protein. Though harder to obtain, they keep us fuller for longer, compared to roots, vegetables, and berries. A diet rich in meat and fish thus gave hunters an evolutionary advantage in times of famine. In more bountiful times it also meant that, rather than having to constantly forage, humans had time between hunting expeditions for thinking and making things. This led to an explosion in human development, as we became toolmakers and planners.

So our desire for high-fat and high-sugar foods, together with an increasingly intelligent brain with which to find them and interest in sharing them with other group members, gave us a huge evolutionary advantage. However, because these foods were in short supply, we never had to develop the means to restrain our appetites or our weight; we simply didn't need the brain that would do this! We needed the see-food-and-eat-it (particularly sweet or fatty food) brain. The trouble is that now, for a relatively small proportion of the human population—those who live in rich industrialized societies, where sweet and fatty foods are plentiful and cheap—the see-food-and-eat-it brain is no longer helpful. Indeed, it's becoming a major problem for many of us, who are eating much more than our ancestors and doing far less exercise, and developing unhealthy eating habits and becoming overweight as a result.

To make matters worse, we, like most animals, also evolved to be an energy-conserving species. This means that when we have eaten enough to meet our energy needs, we tend to become less active. We only get more active when we need to go and find more food because we are hungry. So we have an inherent tendency to become couch potatoes!

There is another interesting aspect to our story. We don't know exactly when humans evolved, but the process began around two million years ago. What we do know is that along the way, humans became a strongly cooperative species, wanting to share a whole range of resources and information with one another. Indeed, language would not have evolved had we not taken an interest in communicating with each other. Hunting relied on social cooperation and the subsequent sharing of the meal. The most successful hunters (those lions, wolves, and hyenas) are very sociable within their own groups; they follow very specific rules about eating after a kill to ensure that those who are most valuable to the group all receive a share. We think that these habits also developed among our human ancestors, so getting food and sharing it became strongly linked to our social lives. Even today, one of the most important ways we entertain each other is to cook for each other, and we love going out for meals together. In many non-Western societies we see the same basic preference for eating together and sharing food. For the most part, eating is a highly social event, associated with pleasurable feelings of togetherness and security.

Being fed has always been a comforting experience for humans. Breastfeeding has calmed and soothed babies and young children the world over for millennia. Feeding can be soothing—understandably, as it signals the physical closeness of a caregiver and the safeness this offers. Eating in social groups has also been with us for thousands of years, and still today, eating together and sharing our food solidifies our relationships with others. Where resources are scarce, it helps us manage their use effectively. When they are more plentiful, we want to share high-quality food, to be seen as generous and as good cooks. Thus eating together can be a source of both pleasure and social comfort. So there is nothing wrong with deriving comfort from food; indeed, it is a very natural way of being soothed by others. However, at most times in human history, the comfort derived from food was self-limiting: mothers can only produce so much milk, and social groups often struggled to find enough to eat.

Our natural preference for sweet foods can easily be used to train us to behave in certain ways, and such foods may actually soothe us (as we will explore in chapter 3). The link between sweet foods and rewards, or even approval—being a "good" boy or girl—is made early if sweets are given as a reward for behaving in a particular way. For example, imagine that you are in a crowded supermarket, your children are crying, and you know you will be stuck in line for at least another twenty minutes. It's pretty easy to see how we could end up giving our children sweets, both to take their minds off their distress and to comfort them—and of course, parents learn that it can work! So they do it again and again. So what do we do when we are upset as adults? We do what we have learned to do, of course—where's that chocolate? What do we do when we feel we want a reward or want to celebrate? Yep, go for the food and drink, the night out, or a raid on the fridge. We sometimes find that people with eating problems as adults were often soothed with food as children, rather than with hugs or by talking things through and learning how to manage emotions. Indeed, some people are not aware of the link between their emotions and eating.

Of course, in most parts of the world, and until recently in the West too, cakes, chocolate bars, french fries, and potato chips weren't available for parents to use as treats and pacifiers. But today, from the day we are born to the day we die, food is linked in our minds to enjoyment, treats, celebrating, socializing, having friends, caring, calming difficult emotions, and a sense of deserving—and much more. It's unlikely that there has been any time in our history where food has had such complex and multiple associations and meanings.

In a world where we all have less and less time to care for ourselves and others, where many of us are working two or more jobs just to keep up, food (and, of course, drink) has become one way in which we have learned to reward ourselves, manage our feelings, or comfort those around us. So it's not surprising that those of us who have grown up in the last century have increasingly associated food with comfort and soothing of distress on the one hand, and with rewards and having a good time on the other.

We have to be honest, too, in acknowledging that sometimes our problems with food relate to quite complicated emotional difficulties. We know that some children are relatively neglected or come from difficult and abusive families. Having never really felt loved, connected, or worthy, they can spend a lot of time as adults trying to cope with difficult emotions with roots in their childhoods. Food can get caught up in all that. Someone who tended to binge-eat once told me that it was like a rebellion: she could do it, and no one could stop her. It was also a way of keeping down painful feelings of loneliness and anger, which at times came close to overwhelming to her. "Food—" she said, "thinking about it, imagining it, planning to eat, and enjoying it is a way of distracting myself from the pain in my life. Problem is, after I finish bingeing, I feel disgusted with myself, so the whole cycle starts up again, fueled by anger that I can't do anything about."

Some people struggling to cope with emotional difficulties in this way develop serious eating disorders, such as bulimia or anorexia. These disorders are usually best tackled with professional support, though self-help certainly can have a part to play. However, many people who do not develop these grave illnesses still struggle with their eating habits and often feel angry, ashamed, and anxious as a result. If you're one of them, this book is for you and all those like you, from those who just overdo it at Christmas to habitual binge eaters, from those who raid the fridge when they're upset to those who find it hard to stop eating once they've started. If any of these descriptions ring a bell, and if you want to develop a healthy relationship with food and to do so in a way that will care for your real needs, both physical and emotional, then this book is for you.

It's important to recognize and have compassion for the complexity of our relationship with food, eating, and weight. Sometimes we lose control of our eating because we're going through a very unhappy time in life, and our relationship with food is caught up in all that. If we are gentle with, and kind to, ourselves, if we recognize and accept this complexity and the pain that can be hidden behind the food problem, we have a better chance of working with these issues. All the time, keep in mind that if you're struggling with food, there are reasons for it that have to do with how *all* humans have evolved, which is hardly something you can blame yourself for! Once you come to understand this, and then free yourself from the shame and blame that so often go with overeating, you can then move on to think about what will really help you, what's really in your best interests, and how you can look after yourself and urge yourself to be your very best. And yes, you do deserve that, even if a little voice in your head says, *Oh no, you don't.*

THE PERILS OF MODERN SOCIETIES AND SUPERMARKETS

As the human brain evolved, so did its intelligence, and it wasn't far along the road of human evolution that we worked out that you don't need to look for food—you can make food come to you. Humans became farmers, planting our crops rather than going out to gather them, and herding and breeding livestock rather than roaming the plains looking for animals to kill. No longer did we have to spend our time firing arrows that missed the buffalo by a mile and getting back to the camp exhausted; we simply went to the pen and knocked one on the head. It wasn't quite the big-box store down the road yet, but we were on our way. Over time, of course, barter and then money came into the equation, and food became a commodity to be traded like many others; so, over the last few thousand years, we have trudged down the trail toward modern capitalist societies, where we get our food in a totally different way from how we evolved to find and eat it. It is all much easier, of course, but has created new problems.

Modern Western societies have allowed industries to exploit that old evolutionary see-food-and-eat-it drive in our brains and those deep and powerful associations among food, pleasure, and security. The food industry spends billions of dollars artificially enhancing the taste, texture, and look of foods to tempt us to buy them *and* to associate them in our minds with having a good time, being surrounded by happy people, such as family and friends. Sometimes foods are advertised as "secret pleasures," but usually the subliminal message is that eating high-fat and high-sugar foods goes with social pleasures, such as enjoying family outings or parties.

Not only are the foods themselves tempting to our see-food-and-eat-it brains, the ways the foods are packaged and displayed in supermarkets are designed to tempt us even more. Supermarkets employ psychologists to help them find the most effective ways to do this. For example, that smell of freshly baked bread stimulates your appetite, and the sight of the cream cakes and two-for-one offers encourages you to buy more than you might have planned. Sweets are placed near checkout stands, where stressed shoppers, accompanied by bored children, can easily reach them.

Another worrying development is the increasingly widespread use of a wide range of fertilizers, chemicals, and preservatives in farming and food processing. We're not entirely sure what many of these substances do. There is increasing evidence that some preservatives can have significant effects, for example on children's moods. We simply don't know the effects on people who overeat, especially if they eat a lot of processed foods and are taking in lots of these chemicals. Is it affecting their moods?

Of course, this isn't to cast supermarkets as out-and-out villains: they're not deliberately trying to cause problems, and they also provide us with good-quality fresh food, including a wide range of fruits and vegetables that, even a few years ago, were not readily available to most people. However, while they're not deliberately trying to cause problems, they're not in business to help us manage our eating either. They are in business to provide what we are prepared to buy, and to entice us to buy and consume as much of it as possible. It's only sensible to recognize that the food industry is not set up to provide us with the healthiest foods or to help us limit our diets sensibly; it's set up to provide us with as much as we will buy of the foods we will pay for, and we evolved to have a preference for sweet and fatty foods.

Modern Western societies have a rather damaging tendency to blame the individual for problems that are, in fact, side effects of our new ways of living and to see them as an individual, rather than collective, responsibility to sort out. But it's really difficult for most of us to understand how our brains and bodies, which evolved in a very different environment over many thousands of years, are responding to the demands and enticements of a modern world that has come into being over mere decades—or at the most, a couple of centuries. So, rather than see the problem clearly, we, as individuals, get squeezed in the middle between the pressures to overeat and the warnings that we shouldn't; and it's all too easy for us to end up taking the blame for problems we didn't cause. As a result we end up feeling inadequate, ashamed, helpless, and hopeless at managing our eating and weight. These feelings, in turn, completely undermine our ability to cope with our difficulties. So it is not surprising that we turn to the diet industry for ready-made answers and hope, and then blame ourselves yet again when these solutions do not work.

OUR NEED FOR COMPASSION

It doesn't take long to begin to understand the problems we face and to see that in trying to deal with our eating habits, we are actually dealing with complex relationships among our current diets, our weight, and our feelings about ourselves. It's all a bit tricky. We may eat because we are happy, we're just enjoying eating, we're celebrating (speaking personally, feel-good times are actually my danger times), or any combination of these reasons; we may eat because everybody else is eating, and we just go with the flow; we may eat because we feel unhappy, miserable, and alone; and we may eat to distract us from the unhappiness and difficulties in our lives.

As I've already said, our compassionate journey toward a healthy relationship with food must begin with a clear understanding that this relationship is a complex one. The way our brains have evolved has set us up to have problems that our modern society has simply added to—and we're not responsible for either ancient evolution or modern society! The moment you begin to move away from self-blaming and self-criticism, to take shame out of the complicated web of feelings associated with eating, you will be free to think about how to help yourself in a more compassionate and responsible way. Rather than fight against temptations, you can learn to work with them.

So the key message of this book is this: your overeating is not your fault, but you *can* take responsibility for it—and gain control over it, too, *if* you are supportive and kind to yourself along the way. As the book progresses, particularly in chapter 4, we will investigate more thoroughly what being kind to yourself means. A TV ad may tell you that being nice to yourself is treating yourself to cream cakes and boxes of chocolates, but if you eat too many of them, you may give yourself health problems. It's actually much kinder, much more compassionate, to learn how to acknowledge and respond to your real needs, rather than let yourself be easy prey to tempters who really just want you to spend money on their products!

Physical and psychological health professionals also need to understand this message very clearly. I see many clients who tell me that their conversations with professionals have left them feeling rather ashamed and criticized. There has been an undertone that being overweight is simply about greed or laziness, about lack of willpower, lack of control, lack of effort—well, lack of everything, really. Having been shamed, blamed, and stigmatized, of course, people then simply turn off, tune out, get depressed, withdraw, and take solace in the only thing that can be guaranteed to give them a little pleasure: food! They may also feel a certain amount of anger and rebelliousness: one person whom a professional had told off went back home and thought, *How rude you are, how unkind, and how little you understand me! Well, to hell with you then*, and raided the fridge.

MOVING AWAY FROM MORAL JUDGMENTS ABOUT EATING

Most of us who overeat will diet at some point as a way to manage our weight, our appetite, or both. All weight-loss diets aim to restrict our eating below the level of energy our bodies need, but we may also try to limit some types of food because they may be in some way unhealthy for us. For example, until relatively recently, diabetics were required to cut out all sugary foods to manage their conditions (although more recently, these very strict eating rules have been relaxed as the medical profession has recognized that such a restrictive diet is not usually necessary and that clients find it very difficult to maintain anyway).

Anyone who has tried to diet will be only too well aware that television programs, magazines, and diet books are full of conflicting advice and pseudoscience. The diet industry is worth billions of dollars worldwide, and hardly a week goes by without some new fad or diet being launched, or some celebrity telling us how she lost ten pounds in a week! And yet, despite all this advice, the Western world is plagued by obesity and obesity-related diseases, by eating disorders and eating problems, some of which can have profound psychological and physical consequences. With so many conflicting messages, we can feel damned if we do diet and damned if we don't.

Many of these diets and diet programs also contain hidden messages, for example, that if you have a weight problem, then it's because there's something wrong with *you*. How many actually tell you that you have been surrounded by foods that the food industry has deliberately made difficult to resist? They imply that if you are a reasonable person, you will *want* to lose weight by controlling your eating; so if you don't control your eating or you struggle to lose weight, then somehow you must be an unreasonable or weak-willed person! A lot of diet plans also imply that with a little willpower and, of course, *their* diets, actually controlling your eating and losing weight is really not so difficult. Therefore, if you're having a tough time, if you have a few successes but then put the weight back on again, that is, again, because there's a problem with *you*. No wonder many people who are overweight or struggling with their eating feel ashamed!

There are even competitive reality TV programs that follow members of the public and celebrities as they struggle to manage their weight. These programs entice us to pass judgment on those who are succeeding or failing in their battles with food and the scales. People are asked to leave, are *rejected*, if they don't lose as much as others or don't seem to be putting enough effort in. We don't yet know for sure what the effects are on participants' self-esteem or confidence, but it seems highly likely that they aren't positive. These rather cruel programs feed, and feed on, our fascination with people's struggles, but also invite us to treat those "contestants" who don't make it, at best, dismissively and, at worst, with contempt and ridicule. We are not encouraged to feel sympathy for them, to understand the complex reasons for their relationships with food and their bodies, to hear of possible stories of early emotional neglect or the sadness and loneliness of being bullied in childhood. Nor are we invited to follow the longer-term journey these people take, including those who "win" but regain weight later.

Current evidence suggests that only one dieter in twenty who loses a significant amount of weight will maintain this loss in the long term (National Heart, Lung, and Blood Institute Obesity Education and Innovation Expert Panel 1998). Even people taking part in research trials, with a high degree of professional support, are unlikely to lose more than nine to twenty-two pounds and maintain this for at least a year. If we are overweight, only a moderate amount of weight loss (approximately 5 to 10 percent) is necessary to provide some improvement in health, and anything more than this tends to be impossible to maintain in the long run. Yet most diet programs promote a far higher level of weight loss than this and suggest that the results can be maintained forever if only we follow their advice.

Television is entertainment, and such programs need winners and losers, heroes and villains, to maintain the drama of the story. Like the old Roman gladiatorial games, they manipulate our feelings, discouraging us from sympathizing with the losers. After all, the very format is not designed for us to have compassion for *everybody* in the program; if we did, there would simply be no drama. However, this way of viewing the world also fits in with, and reinforces, our cultural perceptions of those who struggle with eating, and often even our own feelings about our relationships with food and our bodies. Winner or loser, hero or villain, triumphant achiever or abject failure, compassion and sympathy or contempt and ridicule—these are just some of the complex oppositions that those who have dieted may recognize in their relationships with their food and their bodies. No wonder such programs make compulsive viewing for so many people.

Of course, anyone who has ever been on a diet (and this includes me) will know that losing weight and keeping it off is actually pretty tricky. However, when we run into obstacles in our quest to control our eating and weight, it's common for us to blame ourselves, a tendency that many diet regimens support. For example, negative attitudes and moral judgments about food and eating are often reflected in the language used: in some diets, certain foods are seen as a "sin" or a "treat"; in others, certain foods are given "points," values that are to be earned. Being weighed in front of others at a weight loss center can be seen as a supportive gesture, but also as a way of putting pressure on participants through the potential for ritual humiliation in front of the group. Many of these diets and clubs focus on successes with weight loss, holding them up as positive motivation, but what about those who feel too ashamed to reach out for help or who wander off because they feel they are failing?

I work with many people who have come to see eating as bad, a sin, or something they have to earn, rather than something their body needs to do to function—people who report having binge-eaten after being weighed publicly, either as a treat for their success in losing weight or a punishment for not losing any or enough weight. A compassionate approach to managing our weight moves away from such moral judgments and their inherent criticism of our need and desire to eat. It requires us to support the changes in eating behavior we wish to make without attacking and criticizing ourselves when we struggle, as we inevitably will when finding ways to manage our see-food-and-eat-it brain and complex emotional system. We also need to learn to focus more on our health and well-being, and less on the feelings of success or competition associated with seeing the numbers on the scales go down, and to learn other ways to feel a sense of success and to be comforted when we are distressed. This means putting food back in its place, as an important and enjoyable part of our lives, something that can be shared with others, not a threat to our health or sense of personal well-being.

HOW THIS BOOK WORKS

In this book we will explore some of the contradictions involved in trying to change our weight and some of the obstacles we meet. This will include looking at how our bodies have evolved to eat and drink, and to regulate our appetite. We will also look at how our bodies manage our attempts to eat too much or too little food. You will see how attempting to alter your body's natural mechanisms for managing your shape and weight can significantly affect your ability to let your body maintain its weight. We will explore how to find out what your personal healthy weight is—and this doesn't mean an "ideal weight" according to weight charts and diet books (whose prescriptions, by the way, change quite dramatically over the years), but a weight that's ideal for you to function healthily.

Sadly, many of us never really discover what our naturally healthy weight is. There are a number of reasons for this, including the recent availability of calorie-rich foods, our generally more sedentary lifestyle, changes in the way we eat (including eating on the go rather than savoring and enjoying mealtimes), and an increasing link between eating, or not eating, and regulating our emotional lives.

I hope that as you read through this book, you will find ways to get back in touch with your body. You will learn to respond to the need for food and drink, and to manage some of the complex challenges that our new ways of producing and consuming food pose to letting our bodies reach a naturally healthy weight. As you discover more about the complex links between food and our emotional lives, and find ways to disentangle the two, you can let your body do what it's designed to do (keep healthy) and find other ways to manage your thoughts and feelings instead of using food to do this.

Self-criticism is incredibly common in people who diet. This is often one of the most important factors in lowering our moods and isolating ourselves from others. Moreover, constantly criticizing ourselves when our diets don't work or when we break our self-imposed rules for what to eat, when to eat, how to eat, and why to eat is almost bound to lead to failure in our attempts to manage our eating. The new understandings and skills you will learn in this book will help you develop a new relationship with food and eating, free you from unhelpful self-criticism, and increase your chance of letting your body find a weight that's healthy and sustainable for you. Take some time now to consider whether you tend to criticize yourself a lot, particularly around issues of size, shape, weight, and eating. If you do, this book will probably be useful to you.

The key to the approach set out in this book is learning to have compassion toward ourselves and others. As I've said already, compassion begins with understanding, and the early chapters of this book aim to help you come to a better understanding of how our brains and bodies work. This is not another diet book, although it will help you find ways to manage your food intake and energy output that are more in tune with your body's needs. Instead, it offers you a different approach to learning to live in a complex body, in a world it was not evolved to live in, with a mind that also wasn't really evolved to deal with all these problems in the first place! It could help you find new ways to deal with the very complex challenges we all face as human beings, particularly in a rich country, where food is plentiful. These challenges include learning to:

* Regulate our eating in ways that are best for both our physical health and psychological well-being

- Accept and live comfortably with the notion that there are normal variations in human size, shape, and weight, and that the shape we might wish to have might not be the size or shape we are biologically designed to have

- Accept and value human beings, including ourselves, regardless of their, and our, weight and shapes

- Manage our feelings without using food as our main or only way of coping with distress

Many chapters contain exercises to help you explore these issues and make sense of your own relationship with food and eating. You may well come to think, as I have, that our bodies are pretty tricky things and that managing them can be hard work, but I hope you will also come to believe, as I have, that it's possible to do so without constantly criticizing ourselves or feeling pressured and without "going on a diet." We will explore a different approach to eating that involves learning to respond to our bodies' needs. This approach is more likely to lead to long-term weight change and stability than following any of the myriad dietary fads, which, although initially appealing, usually end in failure.

In chapter 2, we will explore *set-point theory*: the idea that your body evolved to keep you at a healthy weight (your *set point*) if you feed it enough energy on a regular basis. We will also explore the various ways in which you can affect your body's set point, including eating too much or too little, your eating pattern, other substances you take into your body, and, of course, your emotional life.

In chapter 3 we will explore the complex relationship between eating and feeling: how eating relates to our thoughts, emotions, and relationships. We will also explore the impact that dieting, or denying ourselves foods, can have on our feelings and how, in turn, this can lead us to feeling self-critical and ashamed.

In chapter 4 we will explore the meaning of compassion in relation to our overall emotional and mental makeup, and our attitudes to food. We will explore some of the mind-sets that lead us to overeat, and consider how a more compassionate mind-set can help us manage our relationships with food and eating, and our emotional lives in more effective ways.

Chapter 5 introduces the first exercises, as you begin to work on developing your compassionate mind, particularly through the use of compassionate imagery. Many people who overeat find this difficult, but as you will see, through gentle practice and persistence, you can train your mind to work in this different way.

We expand on these skills in chapter 6, concentrating on developing the skills of self-compassion, which includes learning new ways of activating the "affiliative soothing system" we all have in our brains to help manage our feelings without using food to do so. We will also explore ways to manage when your feelings become overwhelming, and the benefits of learning to tolerate these feelings so that you can come to understand them without resorting immediately to eating more than you need. Finally, we will explore new ways of thinking and acting from a self-compassionate perspective that can help you move away from the mind-sets and behavior patterns that so often lead to overeating.

In the later chapters of this book, we will work on understanding how your overeating developed and what keeps it going now. Chapter 7 outlines the compassionate approach to understanding the influences on your overeating, including the key threats it may have helped you to deal with, and how the unintended consequences of overeating may have made you likely to carry on overeating. Chapter 8 provides you with some skills for exploring your overeating in the here and now, in particular, using diaries to help you become more mindful of what, why, and how you eat, as well as of the things that help you to avoid overeating. Chapter 9 brings all this information together to help you develop your own personal formulation of how overeating works for you, so that you can use it as a basis for helping you resolve your overeating for good.

The next few chapters are all about changing the way you relate to food and your feelings. We begin chapter 10 by looking at the process we all go through, in one way or another, when making changes in our lives and how this is likely to affect the changes you will make in tackling overeating. This chapter also provides exercises to help you explore, maintain, and increase your motivation, and to help you manage setbacks with compassion.

In chapter 11 we explore how to work out what your body needs in terms of energy and nutrition, so that you can use this as a basis for changing your eating. In chapter 12 we outline the steps to a healthy relationship with food and eating based on and maintained with compassion, starting with eating more regularly and managing foods that can trigger overeating. In chapter 13 we build on this foundation to help you plan to meet your nutritional needs, as you learn to recognize and respond to feeling hungry and full, to care for your body, and, finally, to actually enjoy eating!

Chapter 14 brings together all the new understanding and skills you will have learned in developing self-compassion and working on overeating, using an exercise called "Compassionate Letter Writing." Chapter 15 sets out a brief summary of the key points of this approach. At the end of the book are useful resources that may be helpful as you work through this book and in the future.

Because I have used examples of a number of clients in this book, you will meet Jane, David, Alison, and Kerry as we go along. Though these are fictitious characters, their histories and the problems they face are typical of many people I have worked with. None of them is based on any particular person but has been developed to help you explore particular mind-sets that can drive overeating.

This book is designed for the majority of us who overeat, and many people will be able to work through it happily and productively on their own. You may, however, find that you want some more support to help you tackle overeating. I have written the book with this in mind so that you can use it on your own, with the help of a friend, or in collaboration with a professional therapist. Also, if you are pregnant or have a serious physical illness, it would be a good idea to consult a physician or dietitian as well as read the book, because the broad guidelines about your energy needs may not be specific enough for your particular circumstances.

If your overeating is accompanied by feeling very depressed, if you deliberately vomit or use laxatives to help you manage your feelings about eating or your size and shape, or if you hurt yourself in other ways, you may need to seek professional help rather than use this book on its own. It is also important to note that if you are significantly underweight (if your body mass index [BMI] is under 18; see chapter 2 for how to determine your BMI), then you should seek medical support, either through your general practitioner or from a professionally trained therapist. You can use some of the websites in the "Useful Resources" section to help you find advice.

As you work through this book, you will discover various examples of the complex relationships we can have with food. We will explore how a compassionate approach can help you to understand your relationship with food, to move toward a nondieting life and gradually accept yourself for who you are, including your size and shape. Moreover, this approach will help you move toward a place in the world where you can find fulfilment and happiness, and cope with life's inevitable ups and downs without the highs and lows depending mainly on your relationship with food and your body.

CHAPTER 2

Making Sense of Overeating, Part 1: How Your Body Works

WHEN SURVIVAL SKILLS BACKFIRE

As we saw in chapter 1, our see-food-and-eat-it brain gave us a massive evolutionary advantage in times of unpredictability, shortage, or famine. So we have bodies that are very good at storing energy (as fat, muscle, and glycogen) and able to survive for weeks at a time with a poor food supply, though some people's bodies do this more easily than others. Indeed, our bodies can even boost their immune systems during periods of famine by absorbing essential minerals from our bones. Our bodies help us survive until food becomes available by slowing down the reproductive system and the rate at which we burn energy. The body even gives us a natural high to help us manage the distress caused by hunger; this gives us an extra burst of energy and stops us from sleeping until we find the next available food source. People who diet can become somewhat addicted to this high.

These remarkable survival skills first became potentially problematic when we moved from nomadic hunter-gatherer groups into agricultural economies. It then became a little easier to obtain a more regular supply of protein (from the meat of domestic animals or their products, such as milk, eggs, or cheese). All the same, even in these early economies, food supplies could still be unreliable because they depended, to a large extent, on nature, so our evolved bodies still provided us with an evolutionary advantage.

The problems we face now with eating habits and obesity only really emerged as we became more efficient at producing reliable and sustainable supplies of energy-dense and good-tasting food. As this happened, over the last two hundred years, we have moved away from the diet we evolved to eat (primarily fruits and vegetables with a small amount of protein from fish and meat) to one of highly processed protein and carbohydrate with only a relatively small proportion of fruits and vegetables; and at the same time we have significantly reduced the energy we use in day-to-day life.

As we saw in chapter 1, we also evolved with a sweet tooth and a strong disgust response to food that might be contaminated or poisonous. Experiments with rats and humans clearly show that when good-tasting foods are available, we tend to prefer them over bland foods and eat more of them than we actually need. One of the consequences of eating sweet or sugary food is that it forces our bodies to increase production of a hormone called *insulin*, which is designed to sweep up excess glucose in the blood. Once the extra insulin has gone to work, the level of sugar in the blood, known as our *blood sugar level*, drops, and our bodies interpret this as hunger. The longer this cycle goes on, the more likely we are to want to eat more food than we need and the more likely it is that this food will be stored as fat (Logue 2004). It may take several more thousands of years for our bodies to evolve further to make it easier for us to regulate our eating. In the meantime we need to learn to manage our bodies and brains. This chapter and the next are designed to provide you with the information you need to begin to do this and, in particular, to help you manage the complex relationship among your emotions, body shape, weight, and eating.

BODY ISSUES

Although we all share an evolutionary history, it's pretty obvious that we are not all the same. There are lots of ways in which we differ, for example, in height, hair color, athletic talent, and intellectual abilities. It's important to recognize that our bodies are not all the same when it comes to eating and weight gain either. There are several important differences we need to take into account when considering these issues.

The ease with which we put on weight is linked to basic physiology. For example, there are cells in your body—called *brown fat cells*—that regulate how much fat you lay down. Some ethnic groups tend to put on weight faster than others, because their bodies are better adapted to survive in environments where food is scarce. We all know people who seem to be able to eat loads but don't put on weight. Some of these people will have a faster metabolic rate, so they tend to burn the food they consume more quickly than others; some are more active (even when resting, they fidget more!), which both increases their metabolic rate and means they are using up more energy than less-active people.

How easily we are satisfied by food also seems to vary among individuals. Some people, even when they are physically full, don't seem to experience the feeling of fullness. Many of us still feel able to put in a little bit more, having just an extra cracker or bit of cheese. But for some people, it's more serious: they are constantly hungry. The scientific reasons for this are still being investigated, so there remains much to learn about hunger, appetite, and craving regulation.

As we've already seen, regulating our eating isn't just a matter of willpower, as many diet gurus try to tell us, but yes, there are some people who seem to find it easier to control their desires than others. Why this is so is also still a matter of scientific debate. We do know, however, that there are many things that can undermine willpower, for example, a lack of opportunities to learn to cope with our feelings, or unhelpful rules about how and what we are "allowed" to eat. So although there are probably biological reasons why some people find it easier than others to control their eating, psychological studies also suggest that we can learn to develop willpower by creating helpful conditions for our efforts.

So it's important to note that the differences among us in terms of appetite and weight gain, our abilities to recognize when we're full, and even our willpower are in large part biologically determined and thus out of our hands. We may be able to learn to manage them differently, but we are not responsible for how and why they occurred in the first place.

Different cultures find different body shapes and sizes attractive. There are cultures where women seek to put on weight, because plumpness signals possession of resources and status. Sumo wrestlers try desperately to put on weight, because this is culturally attractive and gives them an advantage in the wrestling ring. There is nothing intrinsically attractive or unattractive in being large. However, in most Western cultures, slimness is now the culturally desired shape for women, and a flat stomach and well-defined muscles are the desired shape for men.

Researchers have wondered why so much emphasis is placed on slimness in our society, and there are potentially many reasons; one is that slimness and a high hip-to-waist ratio has come to indicate youth and health. There has certainly been an extensive change in preferred body shapes in the last fifty years. For example, the most widely admired film stars of the 1950s were women such as Jayne Mansfield and Marilyn Monroe, with notably curvaceous bodies (a low hip-to-waist ratio). These are very different figures from those of more recent pinup models, such as Twiggy or Kate Moss. These almost prepubescent images highlight the competition to present ourselves not only as thin but also as young, and indeed, considerable fortunes are spent on trying to make our bodies appear young. Interestingly, however, most men actually prefer larger women, and some researchers think this drive for thinness has more to do with women competing among themselves than with competition to please or attract men. There is an old saying: "The men watch the women; the women watch each other."

This competing to show ourselves to be slim *and* young looking has arisen largely within capitalist societies in the last fifty years. It's difficult to find any other culture or time in history when this was so. Why should it have happened here and now? There's no doubt that it has been driven partly by clever advertising to operate on people's anxieties about social acceptance. We live in a society that has become highly focused on how people look, including facial appearance, body size, and clothes. So, again, a drive for a slim and young-looking body shape is partly linked to social and cultural definitions of what's attractive, and these, in turn, both feed off and are fed by consumer industries whose business is selling things.

Although the diet and fashion industries are very largely aimed at women, men have not escaped this cultural onslaught on body size and shape. Again, if you look at stars of the 1950s, very few have a Brad Pitt physique. Many of Mr. Pitt's contemporaries, however, do, and many more men today would like to. (I had to give up on that idea ages ago!)

If we cannot meet these goals, we—men and women alike—often feel inferior and ashamed, and fearful of being rejected, so we push ourselves to change our eating habits and our bodies to get closer to what we *think* is the ideal. And when, as is so often the case, we can't reach our unrealistic goals, we can also become very self-critical.

HEALTH ISSUES

More pressure to eat less and weigh less has come from an entirely different source. Medical science has recently shown that there's a link between weight and health. People with a body mass index above a certain level are more likely to suffer from significant difficulties with blood pressure, vulnerability to diabetes, pressure on joints, and so forth. Indeed, some of the health problems associated with being excessively overweight can be tragic. On the face of it, it's hard to argue with the message that we should avoid being overweight if it's doing us physical harm. But part of the problem with this message is that it comes with an associated idea that healthy is *morally* good, and unhealthy is *morally* bad. So, if we are putting on weight because we can't control our eating or are eating an unhealthy diet, then there's something bad about *us*. This rather accusatory approach is reflected in the number of television programs about losing weight where overweight people are targeted. In some cases, too, there are class undertones, with barely disguised suggestions that working-class people have poor diets because they are somehow lazy or can't be bothered to eat "properly." Again, all too often, concerns about the consequences of being overweight, whether based on medical or commercial motives, have come to be increasingly associated with shame and problems of self-control.

Increasingly, a healthy lifestyle is seen as a matter of choice, and failure to adopt one as shameful and weak. Smokers and drinkers who put themselves at risk are often the targets of shaming attacks by others, including the government and health professionals. Indeed, some in the medical profession have even debated whether treatment should be withheld from such individuals because resources are scarce and, they argue, should not be "squandered" on people who don't "look after themselves." People with weight problems can similarly run into difficulties if their doctors feel they are not making enough effort to control their weight. Many of my clients have stories to tell about health professionals who have not been very sympathetic to their struggles. And yet there's plenty of evidence that it's really difficult to lose weight and keep it off in the long term, and that you don't need to lose very much weight to become healthy, even if you still don't fit social ideals.

It's hard not to feel as if you are caught between two worlds: one that tells you cream cakes are "naughty but nice" and hires popular football stars to advertise potato chips, and one populated by people in white coats who imply there's something morally suspect about you if you can't control your weight. No wonder so many people struggle with eating and weight, and criticize themselves when they can't exert perfect control over their appetites or desires for food!

It's also important to keep in mind that most of us in the modern Western world rarely use our bodies for the things they evolved to do, namely the various kinds of physical activity that filled up the vast majority of most people's lives from hunter-gatherer times to the Middle Ages. Over the past two hundred years, our working lives have become more sedentary, and manual work has become the exception rather than the norm. We are far more likely to travel by car or public transport than by foot or bicycle, because our homes are farther from our jobs, and the fear of harm has meant that our children are less likely to walk to school, play outside, or even take part in some school or club sports, while curriculum pressures have all too often resulted in less and less time being given to formal and informal physical activity in the school week. There's now a real concern about the lack of physical activity that we and our children get, but it's only recently that our governments have awakened to the problem and tried to introduce schemes to encourage us to be more active.

But again, even if we want to be physically active, it can be difficult to fit exercise around our working and family lives. Cultural changes and constraints are no more our fault than our biological makeup is, and yet they do pose significant problems in how we manage our bodies.

I'm not suggesting for a moment that we should ignore these health issues or brush them under the carpet. Indeed, focusing on what helps you flourish is central to compassion-focused therapy. What this approach does is challenge the way these problems have been viewed as the fault of those struggling to manage their eating. It's the blaming and shaming that are wrong, because these behaviors just make us feel bad and don't encourage or inspire us to try harder if we need to. An accusatory approach based on blaming and shaming does not offer solutions, and often makes us even less likely to lose weight for the sake of our health.

Jane's Story

We can get more insight into how complex these difficulties can be, and how mixed messages can make us feel ashamed and self-critical by looking at one person's experience. Jane's story is typical of many people who have attempted to diet. It shows how something as supposedly easy as losing weight can be a very complicated and tricky business, and how this struggle can often be linked with other feelings we have about ourselves.

Though she was in the healthy weight range for her height, Jane had always felt very dissatisfied with her body. While she was growing up, she was a little overweight for her height and was often teased by her peers about her appearance. She learned to think about her body all the time, because that was the aspect of her that attracted criticism, and also to be fearful of what people thought about her. She believed that she would never meet people who would accept her as she was. She believed that the only way she could be accepted by others was to be thinner, so ever since her early teens, she has been on been on and off diets.

In some ways, Jane was a relatively successful dieter. Although her weight fluctuated in a range of about twenty-five pounds, she was able to keep it within the healthy weight range. However, she believed she needed to be constantly vigilant about what and when she ate. She had lots of rules about this and did her best to avoid eating socially so that people could not pressure her into eating things she thought she shouldn't eat.

Like many dieters, Jane often found she couldn't keep to her strict rules about eating for more than two or three months. When she gained weight after a diet (as most dieters will), she became very afraid and, after a week or two, would try to diet again. Jane felt that the best way to keep her desire for her "forbidden foods" and hunger in check was to constantly call herself names like "fatty," "pig," and "fat cow," some of which she had learned from the children who had bullied and teased her when she was young and some of which she had made up herself. Not surprisingly, Jane felt low and miserable when she called herself these names. Because Jane was fearful of her weight due to its mental association with social unacceptability and shame, whenever she felt overweight those feelings of being pointed at and shamed came back to her. Those feelings would then trigger a sinking feeling and a sense of frustration, which quickly turned into self-criticism: *What's the matter with me? Why can't I stick to my diets?* Out of this would come feelings of anger and contempt, and more name-calling.

Sometimes, when she felt low, Jane would stand in front of the mirror looking at parts of her body that she particularly didn't like and call herself even more names. At other times she would scream and shout at herself as she tried on clothes (usually the ones she could only fit in at her lowest weight), or look at pictures of herself in the past and predict future misery if she didn't lose weight. Sometimes Jane could not stand the misery that dieting caused her and would have what she called a "screw it" moment, when she would give up dieting and eat a lot of her "forbidden foods." At these times food would give her comfort and relief, but this was also a way of punishing herself.

Jane's rejection of dieting showed a more rebellious side of her that was struggling to feel free, and in some ways was vital to her moving forward. However, as you can imagine, she had a real battle going on inside herself, between the angry, "screw it" part of her and the fear-driven part that wanted to control her eating. If we are honest, we can all feel that battle in ourselves sometimes—between the angry, "screw it," "what the hell, let's just party" side and the anxious, "keep control" side.

So Jane had two problems: one was linked to her eating and weight, and the other, more serious, was about her relationship with herself, which was negative, attacking, and rejecting. Self-criticism of this type never creates confidence, encouragement, enthusiasm, or sustained or genuine efforts to take responsibility. At best it can create a temporary, fearful falling into line, which is what it did for Jane.

When I met Jane, it became clear that her relationship with food and eating had little to do with managing her physical health. Rather, it was tied up with managing her painful memories from the past and her fear of bullying and rejection. Given how horrible these events made her school years, it's understandable that Jane would try to manage her size and shape to avoid further rejection as an adult. But one of the unintended consequences of doing so was that she became a bully to herself and, instead of finding new ways to manage relationships and seeking out people who would support her rather than criticize her, got caught up in a vicious cycle of dieting, self-attack, low mood, and binge eating. This in turn left her feeling even more fearful of others' rejection and led to her weight yo-yoing by about twenty-five pounds, even though she remained in a healthy weight range.

These unintended consequences of trying to manage your see-food-and-eat-it brain and your body's size and shape can frequently lead to feeling more distressed and even to more weight gain (as we will see in chapter 3).

It is for people like Jane—like most of us, including me—that this book is written. Jane was able to use many of the skills we will explore later to help her end this vicious cycle and develop a more compassionate relationship with her eating and her body.

FOOD, EATING, AND THE NEED FOR SELF-COMPASSION

Here in the West, we live in a culture that dictates what our body sizes should be and that links this image with success in our relationships and professional lives, and self-esteem. And yet I have never met anyone, in either my professional or personal life (and that includes me) who was completely happy with his or her body size and shape. Indeed, all of us can find fault with parts of our bodies if we look hard enough. If you don't believe this, imagine standing right in front of a mirror and looking closely at a part of your body you feel happy with, trying to spot small flaws and imperfections you may not have noticed before. If you tell yourself that these things are important and will have a bearing on how other people see you or treat you, you will find an easy path to dissatisfaction with your body. In fact, when people are anxious about their looks, that's exactly what they sometimes do: stare into the mirror looking for flaws and things they are dissatisfied with. This is not a good idea. When you focus like this, your brain can easily give you a feeling of dissatisfaction, even with things you were satisfied with before!

On the other hand, we know that the numbers of people who are very overweight—that is, clinically obese, which is defined as having a BMI of 35 or over—or morbidly obese (BMI over 40) are rising sharply. In the United States 31 percent of adults are estimated to have a BMI over 30, while recent estimates suggest that over 25 percent of adults in the United Kingdom are now clinically obese, almost double the rate of ten years ago. And the picture is even worse for our children, whose overall levels of obesity and rates of increase are higher than that of their parents.

As we have already seen, there's a range of reasons why obesity has become such a serious problem, including changes to our diet, the increasing availability of food, advertising, our changing lifestyles, and the reduction in physical activity and exercise. It's very clear that the *cause* of the problem lies not in individuals but in our societies. You might think, then, that it would be best tackled by trying to develop social interventions that target the food industry and increase activity levels. In fact, quite the opposite has happened, with yet another industry growing: the diet industry.

Most of the diets marketed by this new industry tell you that significant reductions in energy intake and increases in energy output through exercise will give you complete control over your size and shape. There's also the suggestion that weight loss is both desirable and sustainable for everyone. Anyone who has been on a diet or seen friends and family dieting probably knows that things are not as straightforward as this. Indeed, the evidence suggests that most diets, particularly those involving severe or rapid weight loss, are likely to end in failure and in all probability further weight gain. Furthermore, dieting can have significant physical and psychological consequences, particularly if your weight goes up and down repeatedly, called "yo-yo dieting," or you lose weight too rapidly. There's also the psychological harm that can arise if we keep trying and failing at things, which doesn't exactly inspire confidence in ourselves or build self-esteem, and yet this is the common experience of dieters.

We need to recognize that, for health reasons, it's important to eat enough healthy food, maintain a relatively stable and healthy body weight, and provide our bodies with the degree of both physical activity and rest that they need. We also need to recognize that we must take responsibility, as best we can, for doing all these things, but that we are living in a society that doesn't really help us to do any of them. So we have to find a way of helping ourselves, which, as we will see in the rest of this book, means learning to be deeply compassionate to ourselves in tackling these difficulties so that we can feel encouraged and supported, can fail without feeling ashamed or self-critical, and can just pick ourselves up and keep going.

WHAT IS A HEALTHY BODY WEIGHT?

Now let's look more deeply into the health aspects of weight. Medical professionals today calculate a healthy body weight using something called the body mass index, or BMI, which I've already referred to. It's not hard to work out your own BMI. First multiply your height in feet by itself. Then divide your weight in pounds by this number, and the number you end up with is your BMI. (Visit this website, www.eatwell.gov.uk/healthydiet/healthyweight/bmicalculator, for help with calculating your BMI.)

For example, Jane weighs 154 pounds and is 5 feet 7 inches tall. So to work out her BMI, she would first multiply 154 by 703, giving a figure of 108,262, and then divide that figure by her height in inches squared (4,489). This gives her BMI, which is just over 24.

People with a BMI in the range 20 to 25 are believed to have a healthy body weight. So Jane could weigh from 127½ to 165 pounds, a range of 37½ pounds, and still be at a healthy weight for her height.

This BMI range, which gives people considerable scope in what their healthy weight can be, represents a move away from the old-fashioned (and unsustainable), very narrow "ideal weight" bands, which were mainly based on the dictates of fashion rather than health.

Many health professionals believe that risks to our health increase significantly if we have a BMI of over 30 or below 18. However, even this wider band—at the upper end, at least—has been questioned by some health professionals. There's now good evidence to suggest that some people with a BMI of over 30 may face significantly fewer health risks than people who are in the "healthy" weight range, if they are physically active and eat healthily according to their bodies' needs.

There are many myths around healthy body weight. As we've already seen, obesity is rising in many Western countries, and very substantial excess weight, described by medical professionals as *morbid obesity*, does pose risks to health. However, there are other statistics to be taken into account. Though we are collectively a bit heavier (about 6 to 11 pounds) than the previous generation, we are also taller (by about 1 inch on average) and are likely to live up to seven years longer.

So there's no need to panic! The key issue for our own well-being is not to let collective changes blind us to our individual needs or to automatically assume we need to lose weight. We may live in a culture where being a little taller and a little heavier than our parents is actually more likely to mean we are healthy, *if* we also eat what our bodies need and are physically active. However, if we overeat a lot, especially foods that are not particularly good for us, and are much heavier than we would be if we ate what our bodies needed, then it can only be a good thing to address this in a compassionate manner to improve our health and sense of well-being.

So we know that our bodies can be healthy in a relatively wide weight range. When we are at a healthy body weight, we can function to the best of our abilities, physically, intellectually, and emotionally. It's important to realize that (apart from very excessive levels, as I've already said) it's often not weight *itself* that poses risks to our health as much as *not caring for* our bodies by providing them with consistent levels of adequate nutrition and activity. Attempts to achieve rapid weight loss, often driven by dissatisfaction with our body shapes or as a way of helping us feel in control of difficult emotions, are no more likely to improve our health than rapid or prolonged weight gain. Weight does play a role in our health, but as one of a wide range of other factors.

HOW OUR BODIES REGULATE THEIR OWN WEIGHT: THE SET-POINT SYSTEM

Our bodies have evolved to maintain a set weight, which is determined by factors such as genetics and the level of nutrition received in the womb or as a child. People who do not diet or overeat very much tend to maintain a relatively stable weight throughout their adult lives. When weight changes do occur, biological mechanisms (for example, increases or decreases in appetite, or changes in body metabolism) then act to restore weight to a stable level. This *set-point system* evolved to maintain our body weight at a level that's healthy for each of us. Though it's possible to override your set point, it takes a great deal of effort to keep your weight below your set point in the long term, and doing so poses a significant risk to your health. Our bodies find it easier to maintain our weight above our set points, but again this can also affect our health.

In animals and young children, the set point is relatively easily maintained by the hunger–satiety system, whether we feel empty or full! As we grow up, our relationship with food becomes far more complex, and we can choose to ignore our hunger–satiety system, for example, by not eating when we are hungry or eating when we feel full. Our bodies are able to cope with day-to-day fluctuations in eating (for example, overdoing it at Christmas) and will normally restore our body weight through short-term changes in our appetite and metabolic rate. However, our bodies have not evolved to cope with prolonged periods of starvation, overeating, or irregular eating patterns. These patterns can override the body's natural ability to stabilize our weight. Our bodies also work on a "better safe than sorry" principle, which evolved in times when famine was a constant threat. So if we do lose a significant amount of weight and then go back to eating normally again, our set point goes up to allow us to gain more weight in defense against future "famine." This is why, on average, in the long term a person who goes on a diet ends up three pounds heavier than before beginning the diet.

The set-point system is a complex one. Our bodies regulate our weight and eating through two main mechanisms: the rate at which the body naturally uses up energy (the metabolic rate) and our experiences of feeling hungry or having had enough food (the hunger–satiety system). In addition, there are several ways to override the natural set-point mechanism, some of which involve deliberate attempts to manage our weight or feelings, while others happen without any direct intention on our part. These methods are shown in figure 2.1.

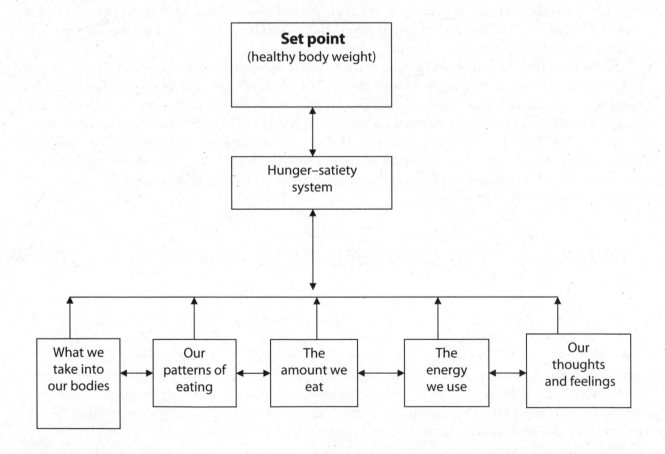

Figure 2.1   Ways to Override the Hunger–Satiety System

OVEREATING, THE SET POINT, AND THE HUNGER–SATIETY SYSTEM

In the previous section we looked at how our bodies can cope with temporary, short-term changes in our eating patterns. However, in the long term most people who overeat will deliberately or accidentally override their hunger–satiety systems and thus change their natural set points, their natural, individual healthy body weight. In this chapter we will explore how this can happen via the body's natural response to things we take into it, our eating patterns, and the amount of energy we eat and use up (the first four boxes in the bottom row of figure 2.1). In chapter 3 we will explore the complex relationship among our social relationships, emotions, and eating (the last box in the figure). We will see, in particular, how central self-criticism is to many people's attempts to manage their eating—even, in some cases, turning into self-disgust and self-loathing.

Clearly you may not do all of the things listed below. However, it's useful to explore the things you *do* do, deliberately or accidentally, that influence your body's natural tendency to keep you at your own healthy weight. Again, it's important to remember that you are not to blame for the side effects of doing these things. Many of the things you have been doing that work to override your body's set point are likely to have come from a genuine attempt to improve your physical or psychological health. The diet industry is powerful and well established, whereas much of the information you need to understand the unintended consequences of managing your weight is not yet generally available. So it's all too easy to set out with the best of intentions without realizing that some of what you are doing may actually be hindering rather than helping you.

As a result of unwittingly altering the balance of your hunger–satiety system, you are probably out of touch with, or afraid of, your body's natural response to hunger or to being overfed. This section is designed to help you understand this system and to begin to work with it, rather than against it, as you develop a healthier relationship with eating.

WHAT WE TAKE INTO OUR BODIES

Fluid

Besides air, food is the third most important thing we take into our bodies; the second most important is, of course, fluid. How much we drink can have a significant effect on our eating and our health. Many weight-loss diets advise people to drink a glass or more of water before or while eating so they will feel full, and hence eat less.

Given how important fluid is to us, it's not surprising that we have evolved powerful mechanisms for dealing with fluid intake, just as we have for hunger. However, just as in hunger, this mechanism can be pretty complex. If we eat less, we also tend to drink less, and the more we eat, the more we need to drink. So drinking a lot of water when we are eating less (as many diets suggest) can upset this mechanism. Training our bodies to drink water rather than eat when we are hungry will leave us feeling full, even bloated, but can also make it very difficult for us to know when we have had too much (or too little) food. Drinking a great deal too much, particularly without eating, can lead to imbalances in the body that can seriously affect our health and, in the most extreme cases, kill us.

Over 70 percent of our weight is made up of fluid. Rapid weight loss is often seen as desirable in diet programs, but this usually relies on dehydration, which is not sustainable in the long term: as soon as we put fluid back into our bodies, the weight tends to go back on and even increase for a while. What happens when we lose weight rapidly, through dieting or a lot of activity, is that we lose water and glycogen. Glycogen is starch, and we store one to three pounds of it in the liver and muscles. It's the body's equivalent of rocket fuel, an easily accessible source of energy. Understandably, the body does not like running out of this handy resource, and if it runs low, we are evolved to snatch it back as soon as some carbohydrate is eaten. Glycogen needs to be stored in solution, and we need one to three pounds of water to store one pound of glycogen. So if you use up one pound of glycogen, you will actually lose two to four pounds of total weight. Conversely, if you put back one pound of glycogen, you will gain two to four pounds of total weight.

Suppose, for example, that you go on a strict diet for a week before your vacation, eating very little and also exercising hard, perhaps going to the gym and jogging every day. Perhaps by the end of the week, the scales indicate you've lost eight pounds. You're delighted; now you can feel better on the beach. On your vacation, you eat normally, not excessively, and do a fair bit of walking and swimming, but nothing very energetic. You get home and stand on the scales, and are horrified to discover that not only have you put back on that eight pounds, but you've also put on another two pounds! All that happened, in fact, is that you lost two pounds of glycogen in that week of near starvation, which took another six pounds of water with it. This sudden depletion of your glycogen stores rang warning bells in your body, so as soon as you started eating some carbohydrates again on vacation, your body made sure to get back all the glycogen it could, replacing a bit more than the two pounds you lost so that, with the extra water needed to store it, you gained a little more weight than you'd lost in the first place. Not very encouraging, is it?

Alcohol and Other Drugs

It's all too easy to think that weight is all about food, and in fact we are often unaware of the effects that other things we put into our bodies can have on our eating and weight. It's not surprising, given the prejudice and stigma attached to being even a little overweight, that some people are so desperate to change that they will deliberately take legal and illegal drugs in their attempts to lose weight, including:

- laxatives

- diuretics (such as caffeine)

- amphetamines

- diet pills

- thyroxine

- insulin (necessary for diabetics, but sometimes misused)

- cigarettes

It's important to acknowledge that these substances do work for some people, at least in the short term. Some of these substances (such as diet pills) will affect appetite directly; others (such as cigarettes) are likely to be used as a food substitute or a substitute for emotional eating. All carry health risks—for example, smoking is linked to cancer, and caffeine to disturbed sleep—and most people are likely to gain weight when they stop using them. Some of these substances, such as diuretics (including caffeine) and laxatives, give the illusion of weight loss, but as we have seen in discussing glycogen, this result is usually from causing rapid fluctuations in fluid content that do not translate into long-term weight loss.

So while taking any of these drugs can often give you a sense of control over weight gain, it's likely that this result will be, at best, short lived. It may actually make things worse as we give ourselves permission to overeat, because we will later take something to get rid of the food (such as a laxative).

Other people may deliberately or accidentally stimulate their hunger by taking:

* alcohol

* antihistamines

* steroids

* some antidepressant or antipsychotic medication

* marijuana

These are substances people often take to manage difficult feelings, without recognizing the potential longer-term effects on mood, appetite, or ability to manage eating. Some people, of course, have no choice but to take medication to manage medical or psychiatric conditions; however, they are often unaware of the side effects for their weight.

Perhaps the most interesting, and certainly the most widely used, of these substances is alcohol. Most of us know that alcohol contains a lot of calories and that it reduces our inhibitions, including those about eating. More important for those of us trying to manage our eating is that it also stimulates appetite in the short term (how else could I explain the desperate need for a burger at 2:00 a.m.?). Although in the short term, alcohol can feel as if it relaxes us and helps us feel good, it can actually have a negative effect on our moods, leaving us wanting another drink when we come home at the end of a hectic evening. So we have that extra glass of wine, which reduces our inhibitions more, in turn reducing our ability to eat sensibly, leading us to raid the fridge for snacks. Then in the morning we can feel a bit annoyed with ourselves again. This is a very common cycle, and most of us never stop to wonder whether maybe our lifestyles, which send us to alcohol for relaxation, are just too stressful.

So the role alcohol plays in our weight is complex. It's linked to the amount we drink and its effect on our moods, our appetites, and our ability to resist our desires.

OUR PATTERNS OF EATING

Our eating patterns can have a profound effect on the body's natural mechanism for regulating our weight. We live in a world that all too often makes extreme and conflicting demands on us. On the one hand, often it's difficult to respond to our natural urges to eat regularly, for example, because we work in jobs that don't allow us time to take proper breaks to look after our bodies, or because we are running around looking after a house and children and rarely have time for a proper meal. On the other hand, our culture promotes the belief that exercising extreme control over our eating habits is the only way to manage our weight—or even to be happy!

There are three major eating patterns that people who overeat tend to fall into:

- the starve-eat cycle

- the starve-binge-purge cycle

- chaotic eating

The Starve-Eat Cycle

Many people will at some time deliberately attempt to lose weight, either by restricting eating, exercising more, or both. As a result *biological starvation* takes place: this is when the body uses up more energy than it consumes. The body's natural response to biological starvation is to make us want to eat. This was the pattern we evolved to help us deal with times of famine, to encourage us to go looking for more food.

In the late 1940s and 1950s, when psychologists and doctors tried to understand how to safely refeed famine and concentration-camp victims after the end of the Second World War, we learned a lot about what happens to the human body when it is deprived of adequate nutrition. In a pioneering study, Ancel Keys and his colleagues (1950) found that even at the calorie levels suggested by most diet programs, study participants experienced profound psychological and physical side effects, including:

- preoccupation with food and eating

- episodes of overeating

- low mood and irritability

- becoming obsessional

- difficulty with concentrating

- loss of interest in everyday activities

- loss of sexual desire

- feeling unsociable

- relationship difficulties

The starvation response appears to follow a specific pattern that is not confined to humans but can be found across species. It has two distinct phases: initially the body drives us to find food, and then, if these attempts fail, the body helps us to conserve its energy stores. The side effects of these responses can reinforce our attempts to lose weight, particularly in the early stages of a diet. However, the effects in phase two can often lead to weight gain and, in turn, to fear of our appetites and desires for food. It's worth going into a bit of detail here about how the starvation response works in someone who goes on a diet, because it's very important to understand this if we are to understand why attempts to manage our weight so often founder. I'm describing the most extreme forms of the various features, but everyone who diets will experience them to some degree.

PHASE 1: THE INITIAL SEARCH FOR FOOD

Weight loss is relatively easy in the early weeks of dieting, mainly because, as we saw earlier in this section when considering fluid intake, we lose fluid and glycogen first. This can help motivate us further to continue with our diets.

In these first weeks, we get an initial burst of energy and tend to be in a good mood (a "starvation high"). This response evolved to help us get up and look for food. So if we are dieting, we learn (at least in the early stages) that eating less makes us feel better. We learn to associate not eating with feeling good.

So far, seemingly so good—but the next feature of this phase often causes problems if we're dieting. Food becomes more important than anything else. We become preoccupied with thoughts of food and eating, and more sensitized to food smells or taste. So if we are dieting, we will often be more tempted by foods than usual. If we give in to this temptation and eat them, we often (wrongly) see this as a lack of willpower, which is one of the points where we can become very self-critical of our "weakness."

Another effect in this phase is that we become more emotionally detached—that is, our feelings become somewhat blunted—because when we were really starving, we could not afford to let any emotional distractions get in the way of our search for food and survival. Again, if we're dieting, it seems to us that losing weight actually does help us manage our emotions.

We also find it more difficult to sleep and may become more restless, because we cannot afford to rest when we need to look for food to survive. Problems with sleep are common in people who diet, and sleep deprivation in turn has a profound effect on our appetites. When we are tired, we tend to produce more of the hormones that make us feel hungry: we feel less full, and our appetites increase. We also become depressed and irritable. None of this is good news for those of us who are anxious about eating more or who tend to eat to manage our feelings.

As we lose weight, our bodies adjust our metabolic rates downward to conserve energy, so it becomes harder to lose more weight (this is what dieters call a "plateau"). Very frustrating for those of us wanting to lose weight, this phase often drives us to even more extreme attempts at weight loss or into the starve-binge-purge pattern we will look at next.

PHASE 2: LOSING THE HUNT FOR FOOD

Again I have outlined the more extreme forms of the various aspects of this phase, as they would have occurred in our hunter-gatherer ancestors in times of real famine; but again, everyone who diets will experience them to some degree.

As we lose more weight and cannot find food, the body starts to take emergency steps to preserve energy:

- It stops pumping blood to our fingers and toes to reduce heat loss.

- It slows down the rate at which we empty the stomach, leading to problems of constipation and bloating (so we feel very full).

- We are even less able to concentrate.

- We feel exhausted. By this point our rate of weight loss has slowed down even more; we have given up the hunt for food, and our only hope is to stop moving and survive until someone brings it to us.

- We experience mood swings, feeling increasingly detached from everyday living, and tend to isolate ourselves from others. This may be an evolved response to save us from the distress of imminent death and allow our families to leave us and carry on the hunt for food.

- Eventually the body begins literally to eat itself to survive: it gets vitamins and minerals from our bones (giving us osteoporosis), and starts to draw on our vital organs and muscles to provide calories.

- Finally, if there is still no food coming in, we die.

Of course, most of us who diet will not get to the last stage of this sequence! But there is good evidence to suggest that those who lose weight by deliberately giving the body less than it needs or to keep the body below its set point for long periods of time will experience problems with their physical and psychological health. Fortunately, as we will see in later chapters, managing your weight doesn't have to be a constant battle with your own survival instincts: the good news is that the body has very good ways of judging how much it needs to eat, and if we trust it and learn to listen to it rather than feel that we must fight our impulses, our physical and psychological health will benefit as a result.

THE EATING RESPONSE TO STARVATION

Just as our bodies have evolved a fixed set of responses to the absence of food, so they have also evolved very efficient survival mechanisms to make the most of food when it becomes available again, which affect:

- what food we eat

- how fast we eat

- how our weight changes

Our initial response to starvation is to try to eat—anything!—including things we would not normally contemplate. This can break down any cultural or food preference barriers to eating we may have. At the most extreme, this response can mean eating things that are otherwise taboo for religious or cultural reasons (including animals or even other humans). In less extreme circumstances, for example, if you're on a diet, it can mean eating things you really don't like; how many of us have found ourselves, late at night in the kitchen, gulping down unappetizing leftovers or eating cold baked beans from the can? No, I thought it wasn't just me!

Because most dieters have a lot of rules in place about what they can and can't eat, this drive to eat can cause real difficulties. We can become very self-critical when we break our rules, seeing ourselves as weak or inadequate in some way, when all we're doing is responding to the body's natural need to recover from a famine—even if it's one we have imposed on ourselves.

Also, once food is available again, we usually eat more and faster than we would normally. In evolutionary terms, this makes sense if you do not know where your next meal is coming from! For a dieter it seems that a week's "success" can be wiped out in ten minutes.

As you have been eating less, your body has already slowed down your metabolic rate to conserve energy, meaning that when you start eating again, your weight tends to rise relatively rapidly, and at first it will stabilize at a higher weight than before the "famine" began. This is the "better safe than sorry" principle in action, giving you some extra energy stores, particularly in the form of fat, in case famine returns. This can be very disappointing if you have deliberately tried to lose weight: extra weight gain is seen as a sign of failure and often sparks another round of dieting. Many serial dieters will recognize this repeated cycle of weight loss followed by weight gain. In fact if you want to gain weight, the best way to do it is to diet!

Now for the good news: Your body does not continually gain weight if food supplies are enough for your needs. Gradually your metabolic rate and eating returns to normal, and because excess energy stores are no longer necessary, you gradually lose weight to your pre-diet level—but *only* if you don't diet again. However strange this may sound to habitual dieters, if the food supply continues to be adequate and your activity levels don't exceed your need for food, then gradually, eating and weight return to normal.

The Starve-Binge-Purge Cycle

When you go without food for more than three or four hours, it becomes increasingly difficult to ignore your body's drive to find and eat food in order to survive. After this time your blood sugar falls, and you produce hormones that stimulate your appetite. If you eat, particularly foods with some fat in them, this will turn off these hormones and trigger other hormonal changes that give you feelings of fullness, so you stop eating. We have already explored the various ways we can override this system, particularly by dieting. If you were in a genuine famine, your body's drive to find food would mean that when you came across any, you would eat as much as possible to replenish your energy supplies, because of your uncertainty about when you would next be able to eat.

Eating larger amounts of food than is normal in an uncontrolled fashion is referred to as *binge eating*, or *bingeing*. However, whereas primitive men and women would relax and tuck in at the end of a famine, finding the presence of food a reason for rejoicing, people who are deliberately trying to lose weight or control their food intake tend to find bingeing a very upsetting experience. They often do not understand or are scared of their bodies' attempts to push them back to a healthy weight and an adequate food intake. They tend to experience feelings of fear (of weight gain and loss of control), guilt, shame, and panic about wanting and needing to eat.

These feelings can then lead them to the purge stage of the cycle to get rid of the food they have eaten. Purging includes any method of getting rid of calories or food itself (for example, excessive exercise, vomiting, or use of laxatives). As well as having dangerous physiological effects for the body, these reactions also make the body feel as if it's being starved even more. Most people who diet will recognize this cycle, even if only in a mild form that sends them off to the gym for an hour after eating half a package of cookies. In its most extreme form, it is the pattern associated with the eating disorder bulimia nervosa. However, most dieters are more likely to follow episodes of bingeing with further episodes of dieting, a pattern that tends to lead to weight gain, mainly because of the effects of dieting on the metabolic rate we looked at earlier.

So you can see how this pattern can become a vicious cycle of dieting, bingeing, and purging, which is emotionally very difficult to manage and can have very serious health consequences. Figure 2.2 shows how this cycle fits together.

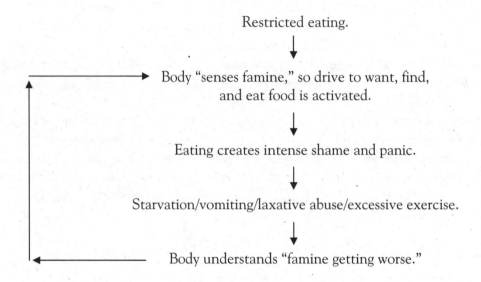

Source: Adapted from Fairburn, C. G., and P. Cooper. 1989. Eating disorders. In *Cognitive behaviour therapy for psychiatric problems: A practical guide*, ed. K. Hawton, P. M. Salkovskis, J. Kirk, and D. M. Clark, 277–314. Oxford: Oxford University Press.

Figure 2.2   The Starve-Binge-Purge Cycle

Chaotic Eating

Now, of course, most of us, when we are trying to do something about our weight, do not fall neatly into the mild versions of the starve-eat or starve-binge-purge cycles. Some of us may fluctuate between the two. Some people find that even *thinking* about beginning a diet can trigger an eating response. This may be particularly true for serial dieters. Many of us find that our eating just becomes chaotic, veering between episodes of dieting and overeating, both to varying degrees, so that we lose any sense of what it is to eat "normally." The important thing for you to remember is that if you eat chaotically, your body will tend to be on higher alert for signs of famine, so it's likely to trigger the hunger response more readily.

It's possible for your body to respond to your need to eat even if you try to stop eating. For example, some people develop what's called *night eating disorder*, a form of sleepwalking where people may not be aware of what they are eating because they do it while asleep. Others may develop a bingeing pattern but can't or don't attempt to compensate for their binges by purging or restricting their food intake, so they may put on weight. This weight gain leads to an increase in metabolic rate. So, to maintain their weight at the new level, they will initially feel hungrier than before or feel hungry even when full. This may mean that they eat more in the long term, possibly leading to further gradual weight gain.

Some dieters can keep to their strict rules most of the time, but when they break them, they have the "screw it" response. They get angry with themselves for breaking their diets, and decide that if they have broken a rule, they might as well break it properly! This behavior can lead to binge eating. Yet others may use food to punish themselves for being unable to keep to their diets.

It's important to realize that people the world over who diet follow these patterns. If you recognize any of them in your own life, remember, they are just a normal human response to trying to diet and lose weight. If you think about the number of rules you have to follow when you are on a diet, you'll see that it's impossible to keep them all, even if other people don't tempt you to break them; your natural need to eat means you will break them. Criticizing yourself or seeing your desire to eat as a sign of personal weakness may motivate you to start dieting again, but it's also likely to lead to a lifetime of struggling with your weight, eating, and mood.

THE ENERGY WE USE

Having looked at the intake side of the equation, let's now look at the output side. All the energy we get comes from food, and we use it in three ways:

- to keep our bodies functioning, for example, to keep our hearts beating, our blood flowing, and all our other vital organs functioning

- to digest the food we eat

- to fuel whatever activities we do

If you eat just the amount of food you need for these three things, you are in "energy balance." Energy in equals energy out; you do not store energy, nor are you deprived of it, and your weight remains stable. If you eat more energy than you use, it's stored as fat to be used at a later date. If you eat less energy than you use, your body interprets this as biological starvation and responds in the ways you saw in the previous section.

Functioning

The largest portion of the energy we use up every day (60 to 75 percent) is used just to keep our bodies functioning. The energy we eat is measured in calories, and as a rule of thumb, most adults need about 1,400 calories a day just to function. This would keep us alive if all we did was to lie completely still all day. The rate at which we use energy (without doing anything other than lying still) is called our *resting metabolic rate* (RMR). Our RMR increases when we eat more, and decreases when we eat less than we need, as the body tries to conserve its dwindling energy stocks. There are also small differences in metabolic rates among individuals; for example, people with a higher proportion of muscle and bone, compared to fat, tend to have a higher metabolic rate, and our metabolic rate tends to reduce a little as we get older. But the requirement of about 1,400 calories a day just to keep functioning is a pretty good rule of thumb.

Digestion

Eating and digesting food actually uses energy, but not much: on average, around 150 calories a day! So, to cover our RMR and the "cost" in energy of taking in energy, we need to consume something like 1,550 calories a day.

Physical Activity

Of course, none of us actually lies still all day, every day, so to get at the total number of calories you use, you have to add those you need to maintain your RMR, those you use up eating and digesting, and those you need to fuel whatever physical activity you do. This includes all the ordinary things, like walking to the bathroom in the morning and moving paper across your desk, as well as consciously exercising, such as playing football or going to the gym. Most people who are neither very inactive nor extremely active use between 2,000 and 2,500 calories a day.

This third area of energy use, physical activity, is the most variable. For example, people who do no physical activity (that is, sit around all day) may need to add just 100 calories to the 1,550 they need for their bodies to function and to feed themselves, whereas people who are very active may need to add 3,000 calories a day to the same basic 1,550.

Interestingly, just as the body responds to our eating too little by slowing down energy use, if we eat too much, it responds by trying to use up more. There's wide variation in how well our bodies do this, but all people tend to increase their physical activity when they eat more. Scientists have proven what I call the "Boxing Day effect," the overwhelming desire to go for a walk after eating too much on Christmas Day (Levine, Eberhardt, and Jensen 1999)! They found that humans naturally increase their physical activity after being forced to eat more than their bodies need. Much of this activity appeared to be involuntary (for example, fidgeting). So if we tune in to this mechanism, even if we do overeat, it's unlikely we will gain weight.

Much of the information the diet industry puts out does not focus on the significant effects exercise can have on metabolic rate and health, implying that restricting eating, particularly by following low-calorie diets, will do the trick. In fact, as we have already seen, because our bodies have well-established mechanisms designed to keep us healthy, the most likely outcome of severely restricting our eating is that our metabolic rates will slow down. On the other hand, even moderately increasing physical activity has a beneficial effect on both our physical and psychological health. It works with our bodies by helping them to increase their metabolic rates, which in turn will help us to avoid gaining weight, as long as we put in enough calories to stop our bodies from going into a starvation state.

Excessive Exercise and Activity

As I just mentioned, regular, enjoyable exercise and activity can improve our physical and mental health. However, some people use exercise not only as a way of keeping fit and relaxed, but also as a way to try to reduce their weight below its natural set point, to alter their natural shapes, to manage difficult feelings, or both. I'm not suggesting that exercise and physical activity are bad things—far from it! However, if we are to develop a compassionate approach to our bodies, it's important to recognize the potentially damaging effects that *too much* exercise can have on our health; for example:

- If no additional calories are taken in to compensate for those used in excessive exercise, your body will read this sustained energy loss as "famine," which can trigger the starve-eat cycle or the starve-binge-purge cycle.

- Excessive exercise can do physical damage, for example, to joints and muscles.

- If exercise becomes an obsession, this can do psychological damage; for example, you may start to get depressed, agitated, angry, or anxious if you can't exercise as much as you want to.

- Obsessive exercise can also damage your social, personal, and working lives if you get to the point of putting it ahead of other areas of life.

If you're not sure whether you might be exercising excessively, a good way to approach the question is to ask yourself if you treat your body as a professional athlete would. They have planned rest days, refrain from exercising if they are ill or injured, maintain adequate levels of food intake, and tend to enjoy what their bodies can do for them!

SUMMARY

We humans have evolved a complex system to help us manage our eating in times of famine and make the most of food when the famine passes. This system is sensitive to a whole range of deliberate or accidental changes in our eating and appetites. Sometimes we can become afraid of, or even blame ourselves for, our bodies' natural attempts to stabilize our weight at a level that's healthy for us. Learning to take a compassion-focused approach to this area of your life involves coming to understand more about the ways in which you have affected your set-point weight and getting back in touch with your body's natural system for managing your weight and eating. Many people find this very difficult, particularly because it involves ignoring the advice that many in the diet industry (and many health professionals) give and the hope it offers, that if only we could keep to a low-calorie diet, we could all be as thin was we want, which is the path to happiness!

In the next chapter we will explore how your feelings can influence your eating, and how you can learn different ways to deal with some difficult emotions.

CHAPTER 3

Making Sense of Overeating, Part 2: Eating and Your Feelings

In chapter 2 we explored the ways you can deliberately or accidentally interfere with your body's natural ways of keeping you healthy and managing your urges to overeat. Perhaps the most powerful way in which we override these natural mechanisms is in eating as a response to factors in our social environments and to our emotional states.

Now, emotions are tricky things. Our basic emotions—our capacity to feel anger, anxiety, sadness, joy, and lust—are older than our human species, having evolved many millions of years ago. Potentially easily activated, they can be powerful, because the feelings we identify as emotions are accompanied by the surge through our bodies of chemicals called *hormones*. This means that when we feel strong emotions, they arouse in us desires and urges to act: to fight, to run away, to cry, or to celebrate. Sometimes, if we have not learned to recognize, understand, or cope with our emotions, they can seem overwhelming. Sometimes we can worry that if we don't control them, we will simply fall apart.

Also, of course, we can have a conflict of emotions. For example, we can be very angry with loved ones and, because we don't want to hurt them, refrain from saying anything but still feel resentful; or we can be very angry with somebody we're frightened of and, again, keep quiet, but later become angry and berate ourselves: *Why don't I stand up for myself?* We can be criticized for being too emotional or not emotional enough. Often our feelings (or at least showing them) can be seen as a sign of weakness or a source of fear or shame. So we can feel ashamed of our feelings. Interestingly, there seem to be different rules about feelings and how to handle them for different genders and cultures. These messages can be quite confusing; for example, *Men don't cry* (but *New men should*), or *Women shouldn't show anger* (but *New women should*).

Many people use food to deal with their emotions. Sometimes as children, they were given food (chocolates, sweets, cakes) when they were upset. So instead of talking about and learning to think about their feelings, they've learned to simply try to turn them off by distracting themselves with food. As they grow up, getting rid of, avoiding, and turning off painful feelings becomes a way of life—and not doing so, but instead starting to allow themselves to feel and think about their emotions can seem very frightening. So for a host of reasons, we can be very confused about our feelings and how to manage them. In this chapter we will explore our emotions and how they can effect our eating.

LEARNING TO EAT

Having always been a social experience for humans, eating helps us to make and keep social relationships and to celebrate important events in our lives. We will begin our exploration journey by considering how feeding as infants affects our emotions.

We know that allowing infants to suckle has a positive emotional impact. Infants show a typical pattern of being soothed and relaxed while feeding, but this also requires active involvement from the person providing the feeding. If baby mammals are given food, but not physical closeness, emotional warmth, and eye contact, they become distressed when eating. They can even fail to grow and refuse to eat. So from a very early stage, we learn to associate food and eating with emotional comfort. Indeed, some psychologists have suggested that the feeding process actually provides the beginning of social and emotional development.

We have already seen that some of our food preferences, for example, our liking for sweet things, are part of our biological makeup (Booth 1994). However, we also learn a lot about the foods we like (or dislike) and when to stop eating them as we grow up. For example, by two years of age, toddlers know when they are full, but also have learned from adults what foods are supposed to be eaten for breakfast. As we grow older, we learn to express certain food preferences and will even choose what foods we will eat in different situations. Most of us will remember some foods we would eat at school but never dream of eating at home. How we eat, too, often depends on what we learn from those around us. All too often these days, meals are eaten on the go, so we have very little chance to recognize the tastes and textures of food, or the pleasure and feelings of fullness and satisfaction that taking time for a meal can provide.

As we grow older, we become more aware of the social nature of eating and how it can be used to celebrate or reward, as a distraction or to soothe emotional distress. We also learn that refusing food can be very upsetting for people around us. Eating (or refusing to eat) particular types of food can become part of your religious or moral identity.

Our eating patterns, the amount we eat, and our food choices change as we move from childhood into adolescence. In these years we require far more energy to fuel the changes our bodies will make, and around this time we also tend to become more physically active. These rapid growth spurts can leave us feeling very hungry a lot of the time; ask anyone with a teenager how often the refrigerator needs refilling! In our teens we tend to "graze," snacking lightly but often. If we are left to grow through this normal stage, we will gradually learn to eat more regularly again, and are unlikely to overeat in the long run. Yet there are many social pressures, particularly on teenagers, to moderate or even limit their eating, so many start forcing their eating into restrictive patterns or into patterns that are fine for younger children and adults (who need less food)—for example, leaving longer gaps between meals, perhaps eating breakfast and having only a small lunch—and are discouraged from snacking. As a consequence they are actually more likely to end·up overeating!

This period of growth is particularly important when we are trying to understand the link between our emotions and eating. As children faced with the physical changes that come just before and during puberty, we naturally become preoccupied with our own sizes and shapes, and those of others. We are also learning to deal with a rapid surge in hormones that can make us very emotional and play havoc with our sleep, and are very aware of our developing sexuality and social relationships. No wonder our teenage years can be such a difficult time to manage. Perhaps it would have been easier if we had evolved like butterflies, whose caterpillars disappear into a chrysalis to mature and emerge a couple of months later as fully grown adults! Sadly, this isn't the case; in fact, the transition is getting longer. In Western cultures at least, puberty is beginning at a younger age, but we don't grow into our final physical state of development for at least ten years from then. This is a pretty long time, and given the various factors that can affect our eating, it's not surprising that many of us struggle with our relationship with eating during and after adolescence.

UNDERSTANDING OUR EMOTIONS

All organisms have motivations to survive and reproduce. One way of thinking about emotions is that they are a way to give us signals that we are succeeding or failing in these basic tasks of life. They help us to attach meaning to events and relationships, and to recognize the things we need. In his book *The Compassionate Mind*, Paul Gilbert (2009) outlines how we have evolved at least three types of emotional system. Each of these systems involves specific types of emotion, attention, thoughts, and behavior that can be very helpful in guiding us to meet the challenges of life.

- **Threat/Protection System:** The first system is linked to detecting and dealing with threats, so it involves emotions like anger, anxiety, and disgust.

- **Drive System:** The second system is linked to detecting and responding to good things, such as food, friendships, and sexual opportunities, and is linked to our drive to achieve and feelings of pleasure.

- **Affiliative Soothing System:** The third system is associated with calm and contentment, and is linked with feelings of soothing, safety, and peace, and also compassion and connection with others (affiliation).

These three systems and their key characteristics are shown in figure 3.1.

Source: Adapted with permission from Gilbert, P. 2009. *The Compassionate Mind*. London: Constable and Robinson.

Figure 3.1   Three Emotional Regulation Systems

The Threat/Protection System: Emotions of Danger and Protection

We are far better at detecting and responding to unpleasant emotions than pleasant ones (Baumeister et al. 2001). This makes a lot of sense, because when we were evolving, like all animals, we often needed to detect threats from other animals (or humans) or from our environments (such as poisonous foods). The threat/protection system is set up to work on the "better safe than sorry" principle. Imagine that an animal is eating in a field and suddenly hears a noise behind it. The best thing for it to do would be to run away, to assume that the noise came from a predator or some other threat. Nine times out of ten, there will probably turn out to be no threat at all, but if this risk-averse strategy makes the animal run away the one time it needs to, it will save its life.

So, strange as it may seem, our brains are designed to make mistakes. They are designed to rapidly attach meaning to events and to make us act quickly, because we go for "better safe than sorry" thinking. This design also affects your memory and the things you brood on. Imagine going shopping and finding nine retail clerks to be very helpful but one to be rude. Which one would you brood on and talk to your friends or partner about? Most likely the rude one! And we will forget the 90 percent of clerks we encountered who were actually kind to us.

Another difficulty with the threat/protection system is that it is designed to overrule positive emotions. So, for example, imagine you're having a good time at a party, when you find a text message on your cell phone indicating your friend or child has had an accident. Or imagine that you're having a nice picnic on a sunny day in the park, when you suddenly notice a swarm of bees approaching. In these situations positive emotions are quickly turned off, and you turn your attention to dealing with the threat. This is why sometimes when we are stressed, it's difficult to engage positive feelings; when the threat/protection system is activated, positive emotions can be suppressed. This doesn't always happen, of course, because some kinds of threats or risks are felt to be exciting—skydiving, for example—but the key consideration here is that we feel in control of the risk or threat so that we notice the drive (excitement) emotions more than the threat emotions.

What's very interesting and relevant to us here is that some people, when they are under stress and the threat/protection system is activated, can actually try to turn off threat emotions by activating the drive system, or with comfort eating. So we can use eating to regulate the threat/protection system! We will explore this in more detail in a moment.

This threat/protection system is associated with rapidly activated emotions, such as anxiety, anger, and disgust, and defensive behavior, such as the fight-or-flight response, avoidance, and submissiveness. It is very easy to turn on, comes with powerful emotions that are difficult to ignore, and can be hard to turn down; after all, we would not want a fire bell that's hard to hear! It tends to grab your attention with both hands, and can be switched on by real events, memories, and even your imagination. For example, I have a bit of a fear of heights. Even if I just close my eyes and imagine standing at the edge of a cliff and peering over, I will get feelings of vertigo and anxiety, and a strong desire to think about something else!

This threat/protection system has evolved over millions of years and operates on many levels, some of which we may not even be aware of (such as looking around the room for spiders if we are afraid of them). It is strongly influenced by our experiences, as we learn what a threat is and what is safe in the world. It is useful in helping us detect both physical and social dangers.

Although the threat/protection system can give us a hard time, it's important to always keep in mind that it was designed as a protection system; it is not our enemy. Once we understand it and begin to work with feelings of anxiety, anger, or loneliness (or whatever feelings the threat/protection system is feeding us), we can learn to respond to it in ways that have fewer unwanted side effects and that help us to manage life's challenges. Sadly, many of us learn quite early in life to be afraid of the threat/protection system and the emotions it arouses, for example, to be afraid of being upset, anxious, or angry. This often happens if others have responded to these emotions in a threatening way (for example, if someone told us off for crying or hit us when we were angry). Even worse, we learn to experience the bodily sensations that are activated when we feel threatened (the thumping heart, the sweaty palms) as a threat in themselves if we don't understand them. We can also learn to associate other sensations (for example, hunger) or even our own bodies with the threat, particularly if we are worried about our eating or weight. So, as you can see, the threat/protection system is a pretty tricky emotional system for us to manage.

The Drive System: Emotions of Achievement and Excitement

The second important emotional system concerns emotions that give us a sense of drive, vitality, and achievement. This is associated with emotions of (anticipated) pleasure and excitement. It has evolved to motivate us to do things and to actively engage in the world. We get positive feelings for doing and achieving things, such as passing an exam, going on a new date, going to a party, or winning the lottery. When these things happen, we become emotionally and physically activated, and often we have a desire to celebrate. When this positive feeling is interrupted or taken away—for example, when we experience setbacks or failures—we can experience this as a threat, which in turn can motivate us to try even harder.

Let's think how this might work if we're trying to lose weight. We can often be excited by new diets and feel a great sense of achievement, even pride, when we lose a few pounds. However, after several weeks, most of us will break our diets or not lose as much weight as we did at first. This can lead to our feeling disappointed, even angry with ourselves. We can become afraid of failing, which may make us try even harder to diet or lead us to give up. That, in turn, as we saw with Jane in chapter 2, can have the unintended consequence of leaving us feeling anxious, angry, or even disgusted with ourselves. Clearly, no one would want to feel this way, so our fear of losing this sense of achievement can be a great motivator. Indeed, many diet programs rely on this system and use rituals such as group weighing, with applause and congratulations to mark individual success, which are meant to give members a sense of achievement. Of course, they do not intend for those who don't lose weight to feel bad, but this tends to happen anyway! This is not to say that these groups are not helpful, but they may be helpful for different reasons, for example, because they offer affiliation with others, compassionate encouragement, and support from a group. These are benefits that belong to a different emotional system, as we will now see.

The Affiliative Soothing System: Emotions of Connection, Comfort, and Contentment

Our third emotional system is related to soothing and contentment through our connection to others (affiliation). It is linked to the experience of peaceful well-being and feeling safe. It is also linked to being soothed. For example, imagine a parent who, seeing that his child is distressed, responds lovingly and affectionately, hugging the child until she calms down. This very common event is actually extremely important because it tells us that humans, like other animals, can regulate their threat/protection systems and the feelings of distress and anxiety they generate by experiencing kindness, affection, and compassion from others (and from ourselves). Indeed, we now know that affection and kindness are so important to humans that they actually affect how our brains develop. There are special areas of the brain and particular hormones that respond to the kindness of others, and (as recent work has shown) to self-compassion and self-kindness. So there's no doubt that kindness does help to defuse a sense of threat. Indeed, perhaps one of the greatest sources of contentment is being with people you feel loved by and under no particular pressure to achieve anything.

This type of positive emotion, that of feeling content, safe, and affectionately connected to others, is a very different type of positive emotion from that gained by achievement. It can help calm down our threat detection and protection emotions, and manage the unpleasant feelings we can experience if our positive feelings associated with achievement are interrupted. This system develops in childhood in response to being emotionally and physically cared for, particularly when we are upset.

SOOTHING AND FOOD

As we have seen, food can be a way of giving us reward or excitement, and these positive feelings can temporarily make us feel better. We can also learn to use food to soothe ourselves. Indeed, the affiliative soothing system can become very easily associated with food, particularly sweet foods, and we can learn to turn this system on by eating. This isn't surprising, given that our earliest experiences of feeding are often associated with experiences of care and affection. You can probably imagine that one of the reasons why we soothe ourselves in this way is that we can find it difficult to reach out to others and deal with our emotions in an open way (perhaps because we're ashamed of or confused by them). We might even find that we're reaching for the food before we've even realized that there is emotional distress in us. Also, if we tend to be self-critical and find it hard to be compassionate toward ourselves, then one way to tone down these negative feelings about ourselves is to turn to food.

HOW ARE FOOD AND EMOTIONS LINKED?

Researchers have found that foods high in fat and sugar, the kinds of food we humans often resort to as comfort food, do in fact help to reduce stress in rats. Well, of course, we are not rats, but I do know that chocolate and cake have a distinctly soothing effect on me after a hard week at work! Further research is needed to look into these effects in more detail for humans. However, it's likely that these types of food do actually operate in a way that helps us to feel soothed; they really are comfort food. So part of the link between emotions and overeating may be that some foods directly help us to feel less anxious, angry, or upset.

Leaving aside the possibility of a direct chemical effect of comfort foods, there are several other ways we can learn to associate food and eating with our emotions. Positive emotions can become linked to food and eating via a process psychologists call *conditioning*, a learning process that connects one experience with another. We all have foods that we associate with positive memories. For me it is the smell of baking and the taste of uncooked cake mix direct from the bowl before it gets washed up. This is associated with memories of cooking with my mom and grandmother as a child. Even thinking about the smell and taste of these foods while I am writing brings back a feeling of warmth, happiness, and comfort; I start to salivate and feel the urge to bake a cake!

We can also be taught by others that certain foods or tastes are associated with having a good time or even with a certain social standing (for example, caviar), while other foods (such as chocolate) may have a more direct impact on our moods by increasing the production of chemicals in our brains that stimulate positive feelings.

We do not even have to eat the food to experience its mood-enhancing effects; for example, just imagining a nice meal or even the smell of cooking can lead us to feel full. We can learn to associate food as a treat, a comforter, or even our friend. If it is taken away or even if we feel we won't have it for a while, we can experience cravings.

Let's just imagine that I tell you that you must finish reading this chapter before you can go to the toilet. Do you need to go yet? Many people tell me that just imagining this makes them want to go to the bathroom, even if they had no inclination before. (Don't worry; you can go to the bathroom now if you want to!) So thinking or being told that we are not allowed to do something can produce the urge in us to do it even if we weren't thinking about it before. My clients tell me they find this happens to them all the time around food. When they tell themselves they are not going to have a cake, they find that the urge to eat one becomes overwhelming and they can't wait to have one. Indeed, we can take a great deal of pleasure in the craving for and anticipation of eating our forbidden foods.

If we are made to do without these forbidden foods, particularly if we use them to soothe ourselves, we can become angry, upset, and even anxious, and can end up feeling rebellious and resentful. I was watching a TV program on healthy eating recently and heard that a man of my age should eat a lot less sugar, and—yes, you guessed it—then I really wanted gummi bears and to tell the well-intentioned presenter to get lost! If we set these rules ourselves, we can get into a real pickle, wanting to rebel against the rules, but also beating ourselves up for being so weak as to give in to our cravings; we can't really win sometimes, can we?

There is also a darker side to the emotional associations we can make with food. We can also learn to link certain foods to being rewards we have to earn or even punishments we have to endure (like eating our greens). We can also teach ourselves or learn from others that certain foods are bad for us, even disgusting, and become very fearful of eating them, particularly if we are told (as the media often do tell us) that they will make us fat, unhealthy, or even just out of step with current fashions.

The Emotions Dieting Affects

Many people begin to diet just because they feel they've put on a bit of weight and want to lose it. But many others begin to diet as a way of managing difficult experiences in the past or current events, possibly including losses or major disappointments, bullying, rejection, and difficult relationships, which in turn may fuel a desire to be more attractive, or anxiety about health. And as we saw in chapter 2, restricting or even planning to restrict our eating can have a profound effect on our emotions.

In the early stages of a diet, we can experience a significant lift in mood and energy, which can help us feel better if we are feeling low and even help us feel more confident. Achieving the aim of losing weight or even just achieving the planned limits on our eating can also help give us the positive feelings associated with the drive system. Many people who diet are also concerned about the negative feelings they have about themselves because of their weight or shape, or are fearful of the judgments of others. Setting out to change your weight or shape, particularly if the way you diet is seen by others, can help you to feel in control of these concerns; it can also help to show others that you can control your desire for food so that you are successful in managing your eating. Diet programs, TV shows, and magazines are full of pictures, stories, and tips from "successful dieters." Planning to eat less can have a positive effect on your mood, as you anticipate the benefits this will bring you. It can also help to block out more difficult worries or concerns, by giving you something else to focus on that's more in your control.

So there are many reasons why dieting can make us feel good. However, as we also found in chapter 2, dieting tends to fail after a period of time, in part because of the body's need to eat, but also because dieting tends to create problems of its own, not least of which is the distress caused by having to be constantly vigilant about what we eat.

Of course, many people who overeat do not diet, but even thinking about restricting eating leads to these effects on our moods.

The Social and Emotional Influences on Overeating

As we have seen, eating plays a big part in our social lives. Depending on the situation, sometimes we will eat less in the company of others, but at other times we eat more (especially if the occasion involves alcohol as well as food). So social pressure can go either way: to help us moderate our eating or to encourage us to have another helping. We can find it more difficult not to overeat when we are in bigger social groups, particularly if we eat as a way of celebrating or belonging to a group (note that drive system). Indeed, as I've already noted, overeating is often encouraged, and we can find ourselves eating more than we need to in order to go along with others and fit in.

Many of us know people who encourage us to overeat. They may do this for any or all in a range of reasons, including using food to show their love and affection, because they feel we are undernourished, or because they see making us eat as some sort of competition or battle, even as a way of keeping us dependent on them. Supermarkets and television advertising put a great deal of pressure on us to eat more. Many food manufacturers have increased their portion sizes over the years and increased the amount of sugar and fat in our foods, and two-for-one and all-you-can-eat promotions are increasingly common. In fact, everywhere you look, you can see encouragement to overeat.

People who overeat also tend to be less aware of the messages their bodies give them about when to eat and when to stop. Again, our changing social lives can make it even more difficult to notice these messages. In today's Western culture, food tends to be eaten on the go or in front of the TV, and for many of us, eating has become a mindless activity. Drinking alcohol while eating, which is also very common in our society, can also distract us from the signals our bodies are trying to give us that we have eaten enough.

We have also become a less active society. Many of our jobs do not require much physical activity nowadays, but we are neither eating less nor doing more physical activity in our leisure time to take account for this. If anything, we tend to consume more calories as a society than we used to. We now live in a "supersize" culture, less in touch with our bodies' signals and having been taught that we should want more than we actually need. All of these social factors can play a role in patterns of overeating.

Attempts to solve this problem have centred on the rise of the diet industry, coupled with the belief that being overweight is both a moral and a medical problem. People who are even a little overweight are often demonized. The weight fluctuations and dietary habits of celebrities can be a source of national gossip and often scorn. Jokes about people's weight are socially acceptable, as is the very real discrimination that overweight people can experience. It's not surprising that many of us diet to lose weight or just feel so bad about our bodies that we can't see the point in doing anything to improve our health or eating. Sometimes we can even overeat to punish ourselves for being in some way morally inadequate because we can't meet society's expectations about what our bodies should look like. It's very sad that our children are not immune to these pressures. Their problems with eating can often begin very early in life. Children as young as eight can feel bad about their bodies and eating, even if they are perfectly healthy, at a normal weight, and eat what they need.

Sometimes overeating can be a form of rebellion against these social pressures. We've already noted that many people diet as a way of managing difficult experiences, either past or present; for a smaller number of people, overeating may be a way of trying to deal with painful events in their pasts, such as physical, sexual, or emotional abuse, or bullying or bereavement. A research study I was involved in suggested that at least half the people who come to National Health Service (UK) weight loss clinics are experiencing a degree of psychological distress that would warrant professional treatment. These problems included depression and anxiety, and also worries about size and shape at levels similar to those found in clients with a diagnosis of an eating disorder.

Being distressed, for any reason, can make it more difficult for us to control our eating, even if we are not limiting our food intake. Overeating or even anticipating overeating can actually help us to cut ourselves off from some of our emotions, and may even give us a sense of pleasure we may not be experiencing elsewhere in our lives.

OVEREATING, RULES, AND SELF-CRITICISM

Many people who overeat have a lot of rules about eating. These rules tend to develop over time and are personal to them, relating to their own personal histories and hopes and fears around eating. Some of these rules are driven by fear that something bad will happen when you eat; others are based on the hope that eating will help you in some way. Other rules we learn directly from the messages with which the media bombard us every day.

On their own, these rules are unlikely to motivate us to comply with them, so we tend to associate them with either a good or bad outcome (such as *If I overeat, people will think I'm greedy* or *If eat less, I'll be healthier*) and high levels of emotion (such as fear of failure or anticipated pleasure from achievement). These rules can also conflict with each other, leaving us very confused about how to behave!

Often we are not aware of these rules until we break them. When this happens, we can find ourselves overwhelmed with a rush of emotion, often accompanied by anxiety-provoking thoughts, images, or memories. Our rules tend to be plausible, even if we often exaggerate the consequences of breaking them. They will make sense to us, because they are based on our personal histories and our hopes for the future, and it can be very hard for any of us to be rational about our rules when we are caught up in the strong feelings they are linked with. It takes a very brave person to ignore his rules to test whether his predictions of what will happen really come true.

We will explore your own rules about eating and how you respond if you break an eating rule in chapter 7. For now we will explore how these kinds of rules can affect various individuals' eating and emotions by looking at the stories of David, Ann, and Alan.

Eating Rules in Action

David is typical of many people caught up in rules about eating. When he ate a reasonable diet and led a very active life, his weight was stable. Then, sadly, he became quite ill. Over the course of the next year, while unwell, he gradually put on more than fifty pounds. He became very concerned about this and, while recovering from his illness, decided he was going to eat less. David set up many rules about eating, such as *I must not overeat, or I'll get fat and have a heart attack or get cancer again.* His key message to himself was that if he did not keep to a very strict diet, his illness would come back. David became very afraid that if he did not lose weight quickly, he would become so ill that he would never be able to work again and might even die. Of course, these thoughts were frightening enough to motivate David to limit his eating, and he very rapidly lost weight. As time passed, though, he had strong urges to overeat, and after a couple of months, he lapsed and broke his diet. Full of self-recriminations, he forced himself back onto his diet until the same thing happened again. David followed this pattern of yo-yo dieting, driven by fear and self-recrimination, for the next ten years.

Sadly, Ann had a difficult upbringing. She lost her father at an early age and found it hard to make friends. She found that eating could be a real comfort to her and gradually came to believe that only food could make her feel better. She had a lot of rules about when she should eat, such as *I must eat when I want to or I'll go crazy,* and would often hoard food to make sure she never ran out. She feared that if she couldn't eat when she was upset, her feelings would become so overwhelming that she would end up in a psychiatric hospital.

Alan told me that food was always used as a treat in his family. An only child, he remembered with a great deal of affection how his parents and grandparents always gave in to his demands for sweets. There were very few boundaries for him, particularly around eating at mealtimes. He couldn't recall ever having been told that he was not allowed to eat something the moment he wanted it. He had never learned to use his appetite to regulate his desire for food; instead he believed that not eating whenever he wanted meant he was being deprived or hurt in some way. Alan often got into a battle with himself when he tried not to overeat. He had two sets of rules: one was organized around the belief that he should limit his eating because of his health, the other around the belief that he should eat whatever and whenever he wanted, and if he couldn't do this, it meant he wasn't caring for himself. The tension between these two sets of rules often led him to be very distressed when he ate anything, and he became very self-critical because of his difficulties with eating.

The idea of rules sounds very formal, but all these rules are tied up with important emotions. For example, because Alan had never been limited in his eating, the emotions he associated with limiting his food were ones of deprivation, not compassionate helpfulness. This sense of deprivation was associated with a range of other painful feelings, including anger, frustration, and helplessness, making it very difficult for him to see and experience taking control of his diet as being kind and helpful to himself.

Rules and Self-Criticism

You can see that David, Ann, and Alan didn't create the difficulties they experienced around eating; their challenges arose as a consequence of their personal experiences and attempts to manage their lives in the best ways they could, and were certainly not their fault! Their stories show how social and emotional factors can affect our relationship with food, and how we can develop a lot of rules to help us manage this relationship.

Rules can be a helpful guide for how we should manage our lives and relationships; indeed, without rules life would become very chaotic and unpredictable. The problem with rules is that if they are too rigid, we are likely to break them. This can cause us a great deal of distress, because when we break our own rules, we can often be very self-critical of our inability to keep to them. This is often because we are trying to encourage ourselves to do something that we believe will help us to feel better, so we can tend to see our inability to keep to our eating rules as a sign that we are weak, bad, or inadequate.

Marie was typical of many people who overeat. Although she was not actually dieting, she had two competing rules about eating. The first was that she should keep strict control over eating sweets or other junk food and that if she could not do this, she would become fat and be bullied, as her sister was. However, she also believed that chocolate helped her to feel better if she was upset. So she spent her time oscillating between avoiding and craving sweet foods. She allowed herself to eat sweet foods to fit in with people (for example, if someone brought a birthday cake to work) or if she felt low, but if she did partake, her initial experience of pleasure from eating was rapidly washed out by the shame and guilt associated with breaking her rule. She tended to call herself names after eating sweet foods and feel disappointed, angry, and even contemptuous of herself. She would then become self-critical, harshly ordering herself to *Get back on the straight and narrow*. She often became angry with others for tempting her, and very angry with herself for being so weak in the face of temptation. Occasionally she got sick of her rules and had a "screw it" day, when she ate as much chocolate and sweets as she wanted to help her deal with the misery of daily resisting temptation.

Marie was caught between two parts of herself: one that was condemning and critical, and one that was angry and rebellious. These two parts of her would battle it out, and neither was particularly helpful to Marie as a whole. Happily, she found a more helpful way of dealing with this conflict, by learning to pay attention to a third aspect of herself, which was compassionate, understanding, and kind. In this way she could escape the constant seesaw between being forced into change by self-criticism and self-dislike, and being pushed into breaking out of her restrictions by feelings of anger and rebelliousness.

SUMMARY

As we have seen, the relationship between our emotions and food can be very complex. We can learn to experience positive emotions because of the foods we eat, or the associations we have with eating or not eating, and our culture and social environment can also prompt us into overeating. We can also learn to attack ourselves for the relationships we have developed with food, particularly for overeating, and this self-criticism can in turn make us overeat even more.

In the next chapter we will explore how compassion for these dilemmas and for ourselves can help us to develop a healthier and less distressing relationship with food and eating. We will look at how to manage feelings of distress, how to deal with our desires, and particularly how to manage the self-critical spirals that many people who overeat find themselves in. We will also see how compassion can also help us learn to resist the social pressures we all experience that affect our eating, and help us with the struggle with food that many of us face.

CHAPTER 4

The Compassionate Mind

In the previous chapter we explored how our relationships with food and eating can be very tricky to manage in today's Western culture. In the following chapters we will explore your personal relationship with food and eating in more depth, and suggest practical ways to develop eating patterns that will help you to manage overeating. Now, at this point you may have the urge to skip straight to chapter 12 in an understandable rush to "do something." However, please do bear with me for just a while longer. We have already seen that people who have any kind of difficulties with food and eating are often very self-critical, which can make the problems worse. What we are working toward is a compassion-focused approach, which helps us recognize our self-criticism and disengage from it. When we can do this, we are on our way to taking long-term responsibility for our bodies, rather than just criticizing ourselves into short-term compliance with yet another eating plan!

To do this, obviously, we need to be clear about what we mean by compassion and the compassion-focused approach. So in this chapter we will explore the nature of compassion itself. The chapters that follow will guide you through some exercises to introduce you to the skills and practice of self-compassion, before we move on to considering how you can apply this compassion-focused approach to your relationship with food and, specifically, to overeating.

WHAT IS COMPASSION, AND WHY IS IT IMPORTANT?

Many spiritual traditions have suggested that compassion plays a key role in being able to develop happy relationships with other people and happiness within ourselves. According to Buddhist beliefs, over twenty-five hundred years ago in India, the Buddha came to realize that our minds are often chaotic, under the push and pull of various desires and wants that are a source of deep unhappiness. This is because we can't always fulfill them, and even if we can, it doesn't always lead to good outcomes. As we have already seen, simply eating anything we want when we want (as is now possible in our modern environment) is a recipe for problems.

The Buddha's solution to such difficulties of wanting, craving, and attachment to things was the development of two key qualities of mind. The first is *mindfulness*: the development of a clearer, more observant awareness of how our minds work. This includes understanding how our minds create different thoughts, feelings, urges, and desires within us. By learning to pay attention, in this moment and without judgment, to stand back from and observe the changing climates of our minds (with the arising and passing of feelings and desires, fears and hopes), we can gradually learn to see these patterns of feelings and desires for what they are and, as a result, to make better choices about what we do, which feelings we will and won't act on. There are now many books on mindfulness and an increasing number of places where you can learn more about it and practice it on retreats or under supervision. We will touch on the basics of mindfulness a little later.

The second key quality of mind the Buddha identified, and the one that's central to my approach in this book, is *compassion*. Indeed, mindfulness is a way of helping us develop compassion by helping us to recognize that some of our motives, intentions, and feelings are not in our own or others' best interests.

At its simplest, Buddhism defines compassion as openness to the suffering of ourselves and others, linked to a commitment and motivation to try to reduce and alleviate that suffering. To alleviate suffering, we need to understand its nature. The compassion-focused approach of this book acknowledges a debt to Buddhist thinking, and places these aspects centrally in its view of compassion. However, it also turns to new scientific thinking about our minds: how they work and are influenced by different processes that are linked to the way our brains have evolved.

The Buddha outlined a whole program of living, which he called the *eightfold path*, geared to being compassion focused in the way we think, behave, and act toward others. Now, the approach to compassion we will take here overlaps quite a lot with the Buddha's notion of the eightfold path, but with a very important additional aspect. This is rooted in the fact that we are all evolved beings, products of the flow of life on this planet. As such, you have evolved to need to be cared for from the day you were born to the day you die. Feeling cared for by others—your parents, friends, lover, partner, and even your doctor—has a huge impact on how your brain, body, and mind works. So does feeling cared for by yourself: self-compassion. Very good research evidence now shows that developing compassion for ourselves and others is of great benefit to our mental performance, our emotions, the quality of our relationships, and our abilities to understand and cope with difficult feelings and desires.

DIFFERENT STATES OF MIND

We've all had the experience of being in different states of mind: being angry or calm, excited or low. We can call an overall state of mind a "mind-set"; for example, we can be in a compassionate mind-set or a threatened mind-set. The type of mind-set we are in affects a whole range of ways in which our minds work. It will direct our attention, focus how we think, urge us to behave in certain ways, texture the emotions that flash through us, influence what we're motivated to do, and even affect the things we fantasize, dream, or ruminate about. To show how this works, figure 4.1 sets the threatened mind alongside the compassionate mind. As you can see, the six bubbles surrounding the central bubble are the same in both cases; only the core is different. So, for example, the threatened mind will generate one kind of emotions, while the compassionate mind will generate another kind.

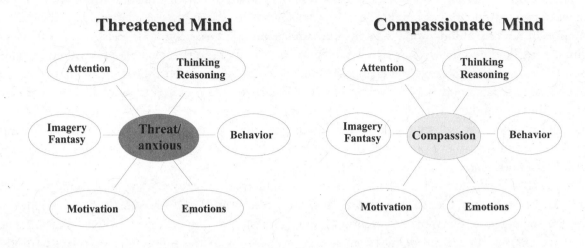

Source: Adapted with permission from Gilbert, P. 2009. *The Compassionate Mind.* London: Constable and Robinson.

Figure 4.1   Two Types of Mind

Let's explore the concept of different types of mind-set, because it's a key idea in learning to develop a compassionate mind. Imagine that you are going for a job interview. This kind of event is naturally likely to get your threat/protection system activated. Remember, your threat/protection system is easy to activate, because it's there to detect threats and help you respond quickly to them or avoid them. So even before the interview, your threatened mind is working for you, and it may well start to switch on an anxious pattern. Let's look at this pattern by going around the circle in figure 4.1, starting at the top left-hand bubble.

In an anxious pattern, what are the things you attend to and focus on? You may well focus on what the other people will be like: *How will the interviewers be with me, friendly or challenging?* You might have intrusive images or thoughts about previous occasions, perhaps when things didn't go so well.

How are you thinking and reasoning? Do you remind yourself that you've prepared a really good presentation and think how impressive it might be? If you're anxious, that's unlikely; it's more likely that you are thinking you might not come across very well, reasoning that because you're anxious, you might not present yourself at your best and that the interviewers might take a rather dim view of you, or that someone else is bound to do better than you and get the job. So your thinking and reasoning are focused on the possible threats in the situation.

What about what your body wants to do? How does it want you to behave? Now, you may want to go to that job interview because you need the job, because it would be a step up, because it means a move to somewhere you want to go, any of the potential payoffs. However, another part of you would rather not have to face it and wants to avoid going. Indeed, if you suffer from a lot of shyness and anxiety, you might even have not applied for the job in the first place, despite any or all of these reasons for wanting it! So when your threatened/anxious mind-set is running the show, it can fill you with strong urges to run away or avoid things.

The emotions of our anxious mind-set can be simple or complex. If it's only anxiety we feel, then that's reasonably straightforward, but sometimes it's mixed with wanting to engage, so that our positive desires pull against the protective ones of avoidance. Indeed, the more badly we want something, the more anxious we often are! Sometimes, when we get anxious about things we would like to do, we can be angry with ourselves for getting anxious, for example, getting annoyed or disappointed with ourselves for feeling shy in certain situations. We can become angry with our anxiety because we feel that it's holding us back, or as if we are somehow different from others. You can imagine how getting angry with ourselves gives an extra stimulus to our threat/protection system. We now have two threat emotions to cope with: anxiety and (self-directed) anger—certainly not a soothing mixture!

The same potential for conflict applies to our motives: our basic desires, wants, and wishes. There can be two types of motive: one relating to our immediate feelings and circumstances (wanting to get away from this threatening situation), and another relating to the longer term (wanting a better future). Our immediate motivation under the pressure of anxiety may be to run away or avoid the threat; after all, our threat/protection system is set up to reduce anxiety by removing us from any possible threat as quickly as possible. It's simply the way our brains are built. Afterward, we may well feel sad because we've missed an opportunity, and that can, once again, lead us into self-recrimination and self-criticism.

Last but not least are the images, fantasies, and daydreams we create in our minds. These complete the circle, for they are linked to attention. When we become anxious, we may have fleeting images of anxious memories or future possibilities. For example, if you are anxious, you might create a picture in your mind of sitting in a chair in front of the interview panel, feeling anxious and a bit dumbstruck and looking awkward, while the interviewers look at you with stern faces.

So our threatened/anxious mind-set pulls on different aspects of our minds to create a pattern, and the different elements of this pattern feed each other. For example, the images that we create in our minds will affect our attention, thinking, and feelings, and how our bodies work. The way we think and reason about what's making us anxious will affect our attention, feelings, motivation, and behavior. This is why we can call the whole thing an anxious mind-set, because it's about many aspects of the mind working together, with a common, single focus on trying to deal with what we perceive to be a threat. The fact that these elements can feed off one another is important: your thinking can drive your anxious feelings and your anxious feelings can in turn drive more anxious thoughts, all of which pushes you along the road to more overall anxiety. And all of this happens, remember, because of the way our brains have evolved to live in conditions very different from the present ones. Thanks to evolution, we have brains that are very tricky to live with today!

Fortunately, there is an antidote to the anxious mind-set that we can work on developing: the compassionate mind. Because this mind-set is based on understanding and caring, it will be more likely to activate the third of our emotional systems, the affiliative soothing system, which, as we saw in the last chapter, is a natural counter to the threat/protection system. The kinder and more understanding we are, the easier it is to tone down the sense of threat that drives this spiral of increasing anxiety.

As well as the more general types of mind-set, such as the threatened mind and the compassionate mind, we develop more particular types of mind-set in responding to particular types of problem. Let's take a look now at some of the most common mind-sets that develop around food and eating.

FOOD AND OUR STATES OF MIND

The Dieting Mind-Set

If you have struggled with your eating for a while, it's likely that you have tried to change your see-food-and-eat-it mind into a dieting one. The dieting mind has two elements: it tends to see certain foods both as desired and also as potential threats, and it also tends to focus on the achievements that dieting will bring us. Thus it tends to activate both our threat/protection and drive systems.

FOOD AS THREAT

For most people who diet, the threat will be one of weight gain. This means that, for many people, food itself becomes a threat because overeating interferes with the real or imagined positive consequences of controlling their weight. Of course, if this is the case, your mind will organize itself in ways to help you avoid the threat that eating poses.

In this mind-set, certain foods in particular tend to be seen as threatening, because they have become associated with weight gain or triggering overeating. The threat they pose may be related to their calorie content or to other nutritional qualities (such as carbohydrate, fat, or sugar content). However, the allocation of "threat" is not always a purely logical decision: sometimes we see a food as a threat because it makes us feel full or we enjoy its taste, and we associate these feelings with weight gain or the risk of overeating, even if it's less likely to lead to weight gain than other foods we have eaten that day.

If you are in this mind-set and certain foods have become a threat, you will learn to pay attention to food in ways that people who don't diet are not really aware of. You may know the fat, calorie, carbohydrate, sugar, or fiber content, or the glycemic index of the foods you eat or drink. You may also be very aware of the calories you use when you are active or exercising. You are likely to spend lots of time thinking about eating and to have many rules about what and when you can eat. You are also likely to invest a lot of time and energy in finding ways to avoid overeating, possibly including planning and being on a diet, joining diet clubs or programs to help you manage your eating, and deliberately finding ways to avoid eating (such as not going out for meals with others). You may become acutely aware of your feelings of hunger in your battle to avoid eating, but you are also more likely to be preoccupied with the smells, tastes, and textures of food. You may even dream about eating!

Your dieting mind will also make it easy to remember and think about the problems that overeating may cause you. For example, it may call up painful images of being bullied about your eating or weight, or concerns about your health. You may think other people will notice and disapprove of your eating and weight; you may imagine they think you are greedy or out of control of your eating; you may even spend a lot of time comparing how and what you eat to what others eat, constantly compare your body size with those of others, or be particularly attentive to how people look in real life or in magazines and the media.

ACHIEVEMENT THROUGH WEIGHT LOSS

Most people in the dieting mind-set will also become very engaged with the drive system. As we saw in chapter 2, the drive system gives us good feelings when we pursue things we want or succeed in getting them. This can be true for dieting. The problem here is that the drive system is a double-edged sword. On the upside, when you manage to keep to your diet, you get a buzz of pleasure and feel good about yourself; you feel that you are in control and succeeding. Indeed, our biological responses to restricting our eating have actually evolved to give you this boost to your drive system to help you deal with famine, particularly in the early weeks of eating less. So at first you get a double whammy: success in doing something you hope will improve your life, and the biological buzz from dieting. This can make you feel great!

To boost these positive feelings, we may provide ourselves with many opportunities to check on and experience this success, such as frequently weighing ourselves, sharing our dieting success with others, planning for the good things we imagine will happen when we lose weight (for example, buying new clothes), even comparing our own successes with the failed diets of others.

Of course, it's understandable that you want these positive feelings, and for a while they can even calm down your threatened dieting mind. However, if you start to struggle to keep to your diet, if you feel low for some reason and resort to comfort eating, if you start going out more often and having a good time and eating more, or if you just get fed up and decide to rebel, then these positive feelings can quickly dry up. When we have tried for something and then fail or suffer a setback, the balked drive system can switch on the threat/protection system, and in come all those familiar sinking feelings: disappointment, frustration, even anxiety.

So then you criticize yourself and try to force yourself back onto your diet. And lo and behold, if you have a few successes, you start to feel better again, get that initial buzz again, and the self-criticism and self-dislike die down. But of course, it probably won't be any easier to sustain this time around, so you experience setbacks; the weight creeps on again, as does the disappointment and frustration; and you're back on the merry-go-round.

You can see how these two aspects of the dieting mind-set can work together in figure 4.2.

So, although on the one hand, feeling good about achievements can be helpful, on the other hand, we need to be very careful about relying on it. This can be one of the problems with weight-loss groups, which may overstimulate the drive system by being very positive about success and, in so doing, increase the chances of overeating or having mood problems when people fail. It would be interesting to know, for example, how many people leave these potentially supportive groups because they feel ashamed that they can't maintain their weight-loss targets.

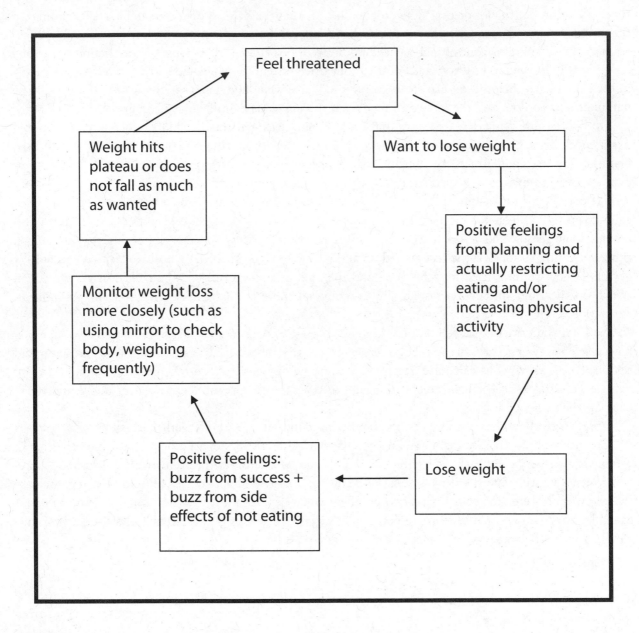

Figure 4.2   The Dieting Mind-Set

The Comfort-Food Mind-Set

Another state of mind associated with overeating is what we can call the "comfort-food mind-set." This kind of mind-set aims to help us with painful events, memories, and feelings. You may remember from chapters 1 and 3 that we learn from a very early age that food is comforting, because it is often associated with the warmth and security that being fed by an adult can bring. The comfort-food mind-set also relies on the mood changes, whether learned or innate, that we associate with certain foods. In trying to ease our distress, this mind-set draws us to the types of food and ways of eating that can either soothe present pain or block out memories of painful feelings. We can be preoccupied with over the shortest period of time, eating as much as possible of the foods that will help manage our moods. This mind-set can also involve a lot of planning, food shopping, and arranging time and space (uninterrupted by others) for overeating. It will remind us of the painful experiences or memories that cause us distress, and often of our previous failed attempts to manage these problems without food. This kind of mind-set will help you to override your sensory feelings of fullness and instead to focus on the emotional benefits of overeating.

As we saw in chapter 3, our earliest experiences of eating (that is, suckling) are entwined and infused with feelings of emotional closeness, safety, and comfort, as well as the physical alleviation of hunger. We can also draw comfort from what is called *oral gratification*: the sheer taste and feel of those lovely foods in our mouths. What we want in this mind-set is the comfort that comes from the process of eating itself, from the textures and tastes and the act of swallowing, rather than the feeling of fullness from having eaten enough. Comfort eating can help us to deal with a sense of threat, too, because if we're focusing entirely on the sensory experiences of eating, our minds are totally occupied, and we can't focus on other feelings as well.

This kind of mind-set is focused on the short-term alleviation of our pain and distress. Of course, in the long term, it is likely to lead to weight gain and may not help us find other ways to manage the challenges we face in life. But when we are in pain, we tend to be less aware of these unintended consequences, or if we are aware of them, we are so desperate to ease our distress that comfort eating feels like our best option.

It's very common for the comfort-food mind-set to be linked to loneliness. When Carol began to monitor her eating behavior, she noted that she tended to overeat in the evenings, when her husband worked late and she was home alone watching television. It took her a while to recognize that actually she was eating because she was lonely and trying to "while away the time." A deeper exploration revealed that, although she loved her husband, she felt somewhat dependent on him and had become rudderless in her own life, feeling that she was "just drifting." So she thought carefully about this problem and decided that, rather than just focus on her eating and wait for her husband to come home, she would go and do some volunteer work on those evenings when he worked late. She found a group of people to join, which improved her social network and lessened her sense of isolation, giving her a sense of purpose and raising her self-esteem. This is an example of where understanding what emotions are behind our comfort-eating minds can generate some very interesting solutions that actually have nothing to do with food! As you will see throughout this book, understanding our relationships with food often requires us to understand our relationships with ourselves and how the many facets of our lives interact.

For the moment, though, you can see that the dieting mind-set and the comfort-food mind-set are both frameworks that our brains create to manage problems in our lives. It's really helpful to see that the way our brains do this—setting up patterns in response to challenges, whether these have to do with eating or managing your emotions—is something they have evolved to do over many thousands of years, in order to help us survive and thrive. It's not your fault that sometimes, in the modern world, they actually make things more difficult for us! One of the difficult problems in managing these types of mind is that they can exist in us at the same time, although we may pay more attention to one or the other at different times. This can lead us into all sorts of tangles as we try to work out whether to diet or comfort-eat, whether to diet to deal with the unintended weight gain that results from comfort eating, or whether to comfort-eat to deal with the distress of blowing our diets!

The Food as Fun Mind-Set

Of course, we don't only see food as either threat or comfort. As you have seen, eating is often associated with sharing, closeness, and having a good time.

Being a good host often means providing food for people. There are literally hundreds of books and television programs dedicated to cooking and presenting aesthetically pleasing and delicious-tasting foods. There's no doubt that food can play an important role in a whole range of enjoyable social activities. So we can get into problems with eating because we're just having a good time. You go to the restaurant without intending to have that apple pie just after steak and fries, but everybody's enjoying themselves and you're one glass of wine the better, so what the hell—why not have a good time!

We often feel that our lives are so busy, hurried, and stressful that we deserve a good time; we don't want to constantly think about limiting or denying ourselves. We want to go with the flow and to hell with tomorrow. So the food as fun mind-set is rather childlike, wanting to do as it pleases and have a good time.

Now, this type of mind-set can actually be a source of pleasure and enjoyment; it's the one that starts looking forward to (say) the weekend, to going out, to what you're going to eat and drink—to what you can have that would be pleasurable. This is not about comfort eating; it's more about the drive system taking over the show. You might also have noticed that this mind-set can get quite irritable if it's told to set limits; it can take quite a firm grip on the controls and be quite resistant to any thought of constraint.

However, the self-critical mind that's so strong a part of many of us who diet, overeat, or both can be especially down on this food as fun mind-set the day after. We wake up feeling fat and bloated, maybe with a hangover to boot, and think to ourselves, *Oh, why did I do that? Why don't I just have a little more control?* So the self-criticism kicks in, until the next weekend, when maybe the rebellious, childlike mind-set says, *To hell with it! Let's have fun!* And so the merry-go-round goes on.

The Eat to Fit In, or Affiliative Eating, Mind-Set

This type of mind-set centers on the positive feelings we get from our natural inclination to be part of a group. Sharing eating can help to bring our affiliative soothing system (which we explored in chapter 3) into play. The combination of these feelings of belonging and safety with the physical pleasures of eating can be a really powerful factor in leading us to overeat.

This mind-set can be associated with the food as fun mind-set, but this is not always the case. As we saw in chapter 2, we can often eat to fit in with others. Now, if people around us are eating a little less than we usually do, we will, unconsciously or deliberately, adapt our eating to fit in with them. The reverse can also be true.

In this mind-set, we want to fit in with others so that we are seen as part of the social group, just to go along with the flow, or to make us appear desirable in some way. A good example of this mind-set in action is the business lunch or dinner. Often I have been out for a meal after a conference or meeting. Usually this is at the end of the day, when I have already eaten most of what my body needs. What I really want to do is have a light snack and go to bed! But out of my desire to be with people I like, or because I feel they will see me as impolite if I just slip away, I can all too easily end up eating a big meal that my body doesn't really want or need. And of course, if I have a drink or two as well, my resistance just drops like a stone.

Sometimes we eat like this to please the people we love; for example, if a partner has cooked a meal for us, even if we already feel full, we may eat it to make this person feel appreciated.

This desire to use food to cement social bonds goes back millions of years, but of course, our ancestors didn't find it so easy to feast as often as we do! Like the food as fun mind-set, this can lead to self-recrimination in the morning and activate the dieting mind-set.

The Food as Punishment Mind-Set

This type of mind-set may be a little less common, but it will be familiar to some people who overeat. They know that the food or the way they are eating is not good for them, but believe they don't deserve to be treated any better; they may even use the food or feelings of discomfort from overeating to hurt themselves for some reason. Often people who experience this mind-set have traumatic or abusive histories and may need professional support to change their relationships with themselves.

An Overview of Our Mind-Sets

So we can see that there are different mind-sets, different parts of us, if you like—the dieting part, the comfort-seeking part, the "let's have fun" part, the one-of-the-gang part—all of which (and you may well be able to think of others) have the potential to fuel problems with our relationship to food. Looking back to figure 4.1, we can see how our different mind-sets affect the way we attend to things, the way we think about things, the way we behave, how we feel, our motivations, and the kinds of images and fantasies we create. This is why, in compassion-focused work, we talk about these parts of us as mind-sets, because they integrate different aspects of our minds. So we use the concept of a compassionate mind-set, or, for brevity, compassionate mind, because it helps us to recognize that we're dealing with an integrated style of thoughts, feelings, how we pay attention to things, what we want to do, and so on.

The other central point to remember all the time is that these mind-sets, or parts of ourselves, that cause us difficulties with our eating behaviors arise mostly because of the kinds of lives we lead in the modern Western world—and I want to keep stressing this: for it is only in the modern Western world that it has become so easy to obtain foods that have been artificially enhanced in color, taste, and texture specifically to stimulate our appetites and to act as a source of comfort.

As we begin to understand in detail the key issues that lie behind our eating difficulties, we will come to see more and more clearly why we need to develop a compassionate mind so that, working with these other mind-sets and using wisdom and understanding, we can take responsibility for our own bodies and learn to live contentedly and healthily with our see-food-and-eat-it brains in our modern world.

SHIFTING TOWARD A COMPASSIONATE MIND

It can be very helpful to learn to become more aware of how the threatened mind works and, if we are overeating, to understand in particular our dieting and comfort-food mind-sets. As we become mindful of these patterns and come to recognize how the threat/protection or drive system drives them, we can also learn to take steps to activate a different type of mind, one driven by the affiliative soothing system. This in turn can help us to learn to manage our see-food-and-eat-it brains, and to deal with the painful challenges of life and the pressure to just enjoy ourselves regardless or eat to fit in.

As we will see, the compassionate mind is never critical but always understanding of the difficulties of modern living and of the complexities and hardships we face. However, it is by no means passive. It is focused on and develops our inner wisdom. It is motivated to work in our best interests, to do things that are genuinely caring, and to help us to develop a sense of well-being in the long term. Compassion takes the long view about our health and happiness, looking over and beyond just having a good time on a particular day or just eating to get rid of feelings on that day. Compassion always seeks the middle way and avoids rigidity and black-and-white decisions or behaviors—such as those inflexible dieting rules.

There is another reason why cultivating compassion is helpful, and this is related to how our three emotional systems interact. Although, as we saw in chapter 3, different types of feelings can sometimes coexist (we can be anxious and excited at the same time, or angry with people we love), harnessing one type of feeling tends to reduce other types of feelings—at least for a time. In the West a group of psychotherapists called *behavioral therapists* (who focus on changing our behavior) came to realize that we can learn to generate one emotion to dissipate another. They first focused on anxiety and suggested that the state of relaxation could not coexist with the state of high anxiety. This led to the development of relaxation training. So now many therapists teach anxious people ways to relax—and indeed, help people to develop different feelings by creating certain states of mind—through imagery, relaxation, bodywork, or even dance. The point here is that learning to develop the compassionate mind-set can reduce the power of our threatened, dieting, and comfort-food mind-sets and help us to find other ways to deal with the challenges of life. Equipped with a compassionate mind, we are better able to make responsible and wise decisions that genuinely are in our best interests and support our well-being in the long term.

OUR COMPASSIONATE MIND: AN OVERVIEW

Now, before you read this section, you might like to stop and look again at the outline of the compassionate mind in figure 4.1. We will now take a quick tour around the circle to see what each of the six aspects means in the context of the compassionate mind.

Compassionate attention will turn to helpful, supportive memories and a positive focus. Let's imagine that sometimes you overeat to comfort yourself for a lack of confidence; perhaps you feel uncertain how other people see you or whether they like you. Your threatened mind will focus on the times when things didn't seem to go well—that's its job, of course, to bring the threat to your attention—further encouraging your comfort-eating mind-set. Your compassionate mind, on the other hand, will direct attention to times when you have been successful, times when you got along well with others, and will prompt you to remember the times when people have been kind.

Compassionate thinking and reasoning focus on understanding that overeating is a very common problem, and we all suffer from it to greater or lesser degrees, because evolution has given us very tricky brains and bodies to deal with, *not* because of some moral failure on our part; this is an important compassionate insight. It's also important to recognize how we can overeat either accidentally or deliberately, and how our biological impulses and responses around eating developed because they gave us an evolutionary advantage.

Compassionate behavior is working out and taking actions that are in our best interests and, of course, the best interests of others. Sometimes this is fairly straightforward, but sometimes it may require us to develop courage and learn how to engage with things even when we are frightened of doing so or they are difficult. Compassionate behavior might also involve learning more about our eating and practicing different ways of coping with our feelings and nurturing ourselves. Thus we can learn ways to manage our emotions and our see-food-and-eat-it brains, which will help us develop a healthier and happier relationship with food. It's very likely that we will need to develop compassionate behavior one step at a time. It's usually best to practice slowly and to get skills in place before we need them. This means practicing certain things when it's easy to do so. For example, if you're learning to swim, it's not helpful to learn in the open sea in a storm; it's far better to start off in the shallow end of a warm swimming pool! Sometimes it's hard to face up to things, and if we don't want to think about them, we don't practice and prepare ourselves. Compassionate behavior is about kindly encouraging ourselves to do those things that are in our long-term best interests, even if it's uncomfortable in the short term.

Compassionate emotions are linked to feelings of warmth, support, kindness, and belonging. If you try to give yourself encouraging thoughts, are you able to hear those in your mind with kindness and warmth? For example, if you're going to an interview and think to yourself, *I've done this before, and if I don't get the job, I'll be disappointed, but I can cope*, do you hear that in a genuinely kind and concerned tone or in a kind of *Pull yourself together, and stop being silly and working yourself up* tone? The emotions that we generate by talking to ourselves can affect how helpful our thoughts are. So it's helpful to create compassionate tones and feelings in our minds when we are being supportive. The next chapter will introduce some exercises that, with the help of compassionate images, will enable you to practice this, and there are more exercises along these lines throughout the book.

Compassionate motives are at the core of our idea of compassion. They are the desire and intention to relieve suffering, in both yourself and others, and to behave in ways that genuinely enable you to flourish in the long term and support your own and others' well-being. Now, you might think the best way to relieve suffering if you're anxious is simply to avoid the things that make you anxious—no more anxiety then! The problem is that this sets up another source of suffering, for if you have been anxious about going for something you wanted, then you haven't been able to achieve your goal. Also, avoidance cuts down your options and increases the chances that you will feel anxious again. So, rather than learn how to deal with the anxiety, you get stuck with it. To make progress here, you have to be honest with yourself: to really think about your values and the kind of person you want to be (or become), and how to bring that about. In relation to overeating, compassionate motivation involves harnessing the inner desire to reduce our suffering and act in ways that generally support our well-being, whether this be tackling overeating itself or its consequences, such as weight gain.

Compassionate images are supportive, understanding, kind, and encouraging. When we are anxious, it's very easy to generate frightening images or even self-critical ones. But we can train ourselves to deliberately create different types of images in our minds and in this way stimulate different brain systems, especially the affiliative soothing system. Again, the exercises introduced in the next chapter will help you learn to create this supportive kind of image and to practice calling these images up when you need them.

OUR COMPASSIONATE MIND: THE BIGGER PICTURE

We are now ready to explore in a little more detail what we mean by a compassionate mind. Why would we want to be compassionate, and where do our desires and abilities to be compassionate come from? These are interesting questions. The short answer is that they come from our motives and capacities to be caring. For example, as a species of mammal, we give birth to live babies whom we look after and nurture. Evolution has given us protective and caring feelings toward our children. We enjoy seeing them grow, and we become unhappy if they are unhappy, distressed, or hurt. Later in life we begin to recognize that we can have caring feelings for other people, especially people we like and our friends. We enjoy seeing them be happy and are distressed if they are hurt or upset.

The reason why evolution gave us these motivations and feelings is complex, but basically it boils down to the fact that humans and other animals are motivated to help each other survive and reproduce better than those who are not. This doesn't mean that at times we are not very selfish, critical, and cruel; clearly we have those potential mind-sets in us too. It's important to recognize that our brains have programmed into them a host of different potential states of feeling and thought. It is our responsibility to understand them and equip ourselves to choose which ones we want to activate.

Interestingly, it is usually when the threat/protection system raises its head that we are likely to turn away from caring. We are less likely to have caring feelings for people whom we're frightened of, who seem more powerful than us, or whom we don't like. Our attitudes toward these people are often wary and defensive, and that, of course, turns off our interest in compassionate caring. We fight our enemies rather than care for or about them.

As we will see later, the same is true when it comes to relating to and thinking about ourselves. If we are angry with and critical of ourselves, that tends to turn off our caring and soothing motivation and feelings toward ourselves, the very systems that could help to combat the threat/protection system.

As I said, the reasons why these motives and feelings arose are complex; fortunately we don't need to worry too much about their origins, apart from understanding that they evolved over many thousands of years. What we do need to do is understand them and then learn to harness them. So now I'll introduce you to the compassion circle developed by Paul Gilbert, who derived it from the research and ideas of many other people, including, of course, those from various spiritual traditions.

Figure 4.3   The Compassion Circle

The full circle is given in figure 4.3. Okay, it may look a bit daunting, but in fact we've already gone through a lot of it. You see that the figure separates compassionate attributes (in the inner ellipse) from compassionate skills (in the outer ellipse). The attributes are the qualities that power compassion along, while the skills are the capacities that harness those attributes and through which they are translated into action. We have covered the skills in the previous section, so here we will focus on the attributes.

Compassionate Attributes

CARE FOR WELL-BEING

Let's begin outside the right-hand side of the innermost ellipse, where you can see "care for well-being." This attribute captures the motivation to be caring, the decision and commitment to relieve suffering (in yourself and others). This might be a place to begin to look at the advantages and disadvantages of becoming compassionate: to think about what you have to lose in trying; to see if perhaps you feel you couldn't do it, so you've decided against it already—"What's the point?" you say. Or maybe you feel that you have so many angry or other unpleasant thoughts and fantasies you can't imagine being caring. Well, all humans have difficult feelings and fantasies, and this does not make you in any way less able to be caring, though it might mean you will need to focus on developing this attribute.

SENSITIVITY

Moving one place clockwise around the inner circle, we come to "sensitivity," which means being open to what's going on in and around you, learning to pay attention and notice when you or others are in distress or are experiencing certain emotions. Sometimes when we feel distressed, we try not to notice it; we try to avoid our feelings because we "don't want to go there." Sometimes when we overeat, we don't want to think about the feelings that might be associated with what we're doing, or we might become angry with ourselves (*Oh gosh, here I go again! Why do I eat so much? What's the matter with me? Why can't I be like other people?!*), rather than be sensitive, gentle, and understanding. Many of us say unpleasant things to ourselves that we wouldn't dream of saying to another person who struggles with her eating. If we're honest, we lack sensitivity to our see-food-and-eat-it brains.

SYMPATHY

Next around the circle is "sympathy." Some people think that sympathy is a bad thing, that it's like indulging yourself, feeling sorry for yourself, or, even worse, pitying yourself or others. That's a big misunderstanding of sympathy. Sympathy is simply the ability to be emotionally moved. Suppose you see a three-year-old child happily walking down the street. You may smile at her happiness, but then she trips over a curb, bangs her head heavily, and is hurt. Her laughter turns to tears of real pain. You are likely to feel a flash of sadness and anxiety, and to want to rush out and make it better. Sympathy is that emotional connection to pain; it arises without thinking, moving us immediately. Developing sympathy for ourselves can sound more difficult, but it's the same principle. So, with wisdom, we can learn to be sensitive and open to our difficulties and also moved by them.

DISTRESS TOLERANCE

If we are aiming to cultivate sympathy and the ability to be moved by suffering, it may seem strange that we should "tolerate" distress. In fact, this is a very important attribute. Here's why: When the threat/protection system is in control, it pushes us into avoidance, away from unpleasant feelings that are threatening us. This is what it is designed to do, but the trouble is, if we always shy away from painful or frightening emotions and situations that ignite them, we never learn that those difficult feelings are in fact bearable and that we can learn how to cope with them and the situations that provoke them. And the more we avoid the unpleasant feelings or situations, the more we feel that we could never cope with them, so the more anxious we become about them. On the other hand, if we learn to accept the difficult feelings—kindly, gently, uncritically—we learn both that they are not in fact unbearable and that there are ways to cope with them. So learning how to tolerate our urges to overeat and our desires for food without acting them out (even postponing them for just a short time), and noticing how we can stay with our feelings without taking action, can be very important in helping us cope with them. We are learning to tolerate, as opposed to act on, our feelings. Learning to be mindful and observant, having sensitivity, can help us tolerate distress. Learning to be more empathic and less judgmental (the next two attributes) will also help us.

You can see how this works in practice if you think of a child who is anxious about going out with other children. Researchers have found that many anxious children have anxious parents. So if the child becomes anxious about going to a party with other children he doesn't know very well, the parents might let him stay at home so he won't be anxious anymore. Unintentionally these parents are teaching their child a number of things. One is that painful emotions are not to be faced and dealt with, but are best avoided; another is that painful emotions can be overwhelming. Because the child did not go to the party, he won't become familiar with the children he didn't know, so next time there's a party with those children, what is he likely to do? Yes, feel even more anxious and want to avoid it again. Sadly, while only wanting to protect their child, these parents are not helping the child to understand how his mind works, or how to face and cope with difficult feelings and situations, which is a skill the child will need in the future. It's tough to tolerate distress, but as you can see, compassion is not about avoidance; it's about doing those things that are genuinely helpful in the long term, and doing them kindly, gently, and without harsh criticism.

Another reason distress tolerance is very important is that sometimes people think compassion is about soothing painful feelings away, getting rid of them. Now, of course, sometimes we can soothe painful feelings away, but that's not always possible or even desirable. If we are very angry about something, we may need to learn how to deal with the anger: to be honest about our feelings and learn to be assertive. Compassion is not about avoiding addressing issues. Sometimes we have to learn how to tolerate powerful feelings and fantasies we don't like, even thoughts of hate. One of the biggest confusions and misunderstandings of compassion is the idea that it's just about being nice and hiding your feelings or suppressing them. That's neither helpful nor compassionate, and while brutal honesty all the time isn't helpful, neither are suppression and avoidance. Of course, this is not an excuse to be rude or unpleasant, either. There are respectful ways to be assertive and powerful.

EMPATHY

Empathy is the uniquely human ability to think about and understand the nature of our minds and those of others. Unlike other animals, we recognize that people do things for reasons: because they are motivated, because they want things and have desires, because they're anxious or angry, because they might not know the full picture, or because of impulses they're not even aware of. We recognize that people can be mistaken in their views and have false beliefs. Just as we can understand the minds of others, we can also come to understand our own minds. We can reflect on and think about how our minds work. When we have empathy for our struggles with food and eating, we're able to understand the nature of these problems, how they are rooted in the way our bodies and brains have evolved, how our own personal difficulties with overeating may have developed, what situations can make the problem worse, and the kinds of things we do when we feel the urge to overeat, eat unhealthy foods, or restrict our eating too much. Empathy is a very important attribute in compassion, because it is based on a deep understanding and acceptance of how our minds and bodies work.

NONJUDGMENT

Last but not least is the attribute of nonjudgment. Now, not judging doesn't mean having no preferences or desires. Indeed, we know that some of our desires and preferences for food are inbuilt. Nonjudgment really means noncondemnation; it means letting go of that angry desire to attack and be critical. It's also an essential part of that other key quality of mind that goes along with compassion, as we saw at the beginning of this chapter: mindfulness. The more we ease back from charging in and criticizing, which can sometimes be our immediate reaction to a problem or perceived failing, the greater our chances for reflecting and thinking about how best to deal with it.

How It All Fits Together

You can probably see from this brief tour of the compassionate attributes that they all build on and support one another. So, the more compassionate motivation you build up, the easier it may be to develop the other attributes. Equally the more sensitive and the more empathic you become to your eating difficulties, whatever they may be, the more strongly motivated you will be to deal compassionately with them. In the chapters to come, we will be working with this family of attributes to build on the compassion-focused approach.

We will also be working on the skills located in the outer ring of figure 4.3. As with all skills, these are learned with practice, so we can train ourselves in (for example) creating and building images that are helpful and compassionate, aimed at stimulating the soothing emotional system; we can train our reasoning and thinking to focus compassionately; we can train ourselves to behave in compassionate ways that are in our long-term interests. We can train our bodies to create compassionate sensations (for example, by using imagery), and we can use our images and other ideas to generate compassionate feelings. Last but not least, we can practice compassionate attention, looking for what's helpful and supportive in and around us, rather than letting the threat/protection system always direct us toward the things we are frightened of or angry about.

SUMMARY

By now you will have seen how our three inbuilt systems of emotions become involved with eating, and how complex these links and effects can be. Certain foods can be threats; losing weight can become an achievement that gives us good feelings when we feel in control, but then we can get into trouble if we lose control. Eating can be a source of comfort or a way of rebelling against constraints and rules, a way of belonging to a group and even a way of punishing ourselves.

In the chapters ahead we will see how developing a compassion-focused approach can help us to deal with all of these mind-sets that can get us into problematic relationships with food. By way of preparing the ground, this chapter has provided an overview of how we see compassion within this compassion-focused approach and of the various elements that make up the compassionate mind. In the following chapters we will explore all of these elements and how you can apply them to help you manage overeating.

CHAPTER 5

Preparing Your Mind for Compassion

The last chapter outlined the various aspects of the compassionate mind, a mind that's open to our suffering and that of others, and committed to trying to reduce that suffering. A focus on compassion influences our attention, the way we think and reason, the way we behave, and our emotions and feelings. In the coming chapters we will explore compassionate ways of helping us change our relationships with food, eating, and our bodies toward a healthier balance.

This chapter begins by introducing work with imagery and then sets out some initial exercises that will help you to prepare your mind for a compassionate focus. It then moves on to additional exercises that explore ways to develop different specific facets of your compassionate mind. Some of these exercises are like physiotherapy for your brain, stimulating your brain in various ways. Just as our bodies respond to physical exercise by getting fitter and better toned, so research shows that practicing self-compassion can affect our brains, increasing positive moods and feelings of self-confidence, and thereby benefiting our social relationships. In later chapters we will see how we can use these exercises and basic ideas to help us reexamine our beliefs and change our relationships with food and eating.

As someone who has played a lot of sports and had a lot of sports injuries, I know that physiotherapy and exercises to get fit or develop athletic skills take time and practice to show their effects. I also know that progress is often best achieved by taking small steps rather than trying to do too much at once, and that sometimes we need to strengthen certain parts of ourselves before we tackle some of the more demanding exercises. It's just the same with the exercises in this book aimed at developing your compassionate mind: the more you practice, the better you'll get, but it's a good idea to take it slowly and not to ask too much of yourself all at once.

Also, as with any new skill, we don't want to try to practice under pressure. Ideally, try to practice the skills described in this chapter when you feel relatively okay or at least not when you are really cross, miserable, or frustrated with your eating habits. As you get better at using each skill, you will gradually be able to incorporate it into your alternative ways of managing discomfort or distress.

WORKING WITH IMAGERY

Images can be very powerful and rapidly activate various systems in our brains. Certain images can stimulate the parts of our brains that help us to feel soothed and safe, and at the same time tone down other emotional systems (especially the threat/protection system) that may be associated with eating difficulties. In this way they can help us to break the association between food and emotional comfort.

Now, people sometimes think that when we try to create images in our minds, they should be like photos: clear and sharp. In fact they don't have to be anything like that. Sometimes imagery only gives us a sense of something, and we never see anything clearly. So imagery doesn't have to mean fully formed pictures; very often it consists of just fleeting impressions.

People often say they're not particularly visual or good with fantasy. But suppose I say the word "bicycle." What popped into your head? Now suppose I ask you, "Where are the brakes on a bicycle?" What pops into your mind now? How does your mind provide you with this information so that you can answer the question? Basically, you're running images in your head, without even trying to.

Now, in working with imagery to develop the compassionate mind, we're interested in the way certain images are related to certain feelings and mental states. So, for example, if you have an interview coming up tomorrow and are a bit anxious about it, you might have images and thoughts popping into your head that make you anxious. However, you might take your children to the park, and find that playing with them distracts you from your anxious thoughts and images so that, after a while, you feel less anxious. Eventually you forget all about tomorrow. But then, after the children have had dinner and are in bed, you're lying in the bath and all of a sudden remember that tomorrow, you've got that interview. In a flash the anxious images pop into your mind again (a stern figure behind a desk, a dark room, the feeling of nervous perspiration on your hands), and up comes the anxiety again. Now, if we imagine that the interviewers will be very supportive, kind, and interested in us, that the room will be comfortable and pleasant, we might have a different emotional experience. We are likely to feel far less anxiety than if we imagine they're going to be very tough, aggressive, and critical. So the nature of the image will have a major impact on how anxious you feel.

Images that set off our anxiety typically come to us at the end of a hard day, in our dreams, or while we are between sleeping and waking. They can even wake us up! But, rather than let those images, which will influence our feelings, come and go as they please, according to what's going on inside and around us, we can actually turn this ability to fantasize and imagine to our advantage by deliberately choosing images that will stimulate the affiliative soothing system rather than (say) the threat/protection system. One way to do this might be to begin by focusing on the feelings of contentment and safeness in a particular place. We call this "safe place" imagery and will explore how to help you do this a little later in this chapter.

CHOOSING WHAT WE PAY ATTENTION TO

You may have already noticed that our minds can be quite unruly things: *I am doing my best to concentrate on writing the next sections of this book, but I have at least three other things buzzing around in my head, including planning for the weekend, wondering what to cook for dinner, and the tax return I need to complete tonight!* The good news is that this is perfectly normal; our brains have the ability to multitask. However, we can find it especially difficult to concentrate on one thing if the threat/protection system is very active. In evolutionary terms this makes sense, because we need to pay attention to any threats, so the threat/ protection system has evolved to be very good at distracting us from anything else! These days, though, our feelings of threat are quite likely to relate to things that are not a danger to our survival, and we need to learn alternative ways to manage them, including being able to focus our attention where we want it. This can be especially useful in dealing with impulses to restrict our eating, overeat for comfort, or criticize ourselves for how we are eating.

We'll now explore two ways of working with your attention. The first is to develop your capacity to be *mindful* of the thoughts and feelings you experience. The second is to develop your ability to deliberately refocus your attention.

Mindful Attention

There's a very long tradition in Eastern religions, particularly Buddhism, of training attention. The practice of doing this is known as mindfulness. In recent years, Western therapists have discovered that learning to be mindful is extremely beneficial for a range of psychological difficulties and for dealing with the stresses that all of us face to some degree in our lives. Mindfulness is a way of paying attention to the things going on around us and in our own minds. The aim of mindfulness is to be fully in the present in each moment, rather than constantly being pulled away from the present moment with worries, plans, and ruminations. Learning to recognize this shifting away from the present moment is key to mindfulness. So the key skill we need to practice in developing it is the act of noticing the shift and then returning the attention to our desired focus. Mindfulness is *not* "making" your mind pay attention or emptying your mind of thoughts. It is noticing the shifting of your mind and then returning it to its focus. As we will see later, this can be very helpful when doing compassion exercises.

A second aspect of mindfulness is noticing how our thoughts and emotions emerge, for example, learning to pay attention to the bodily experiences of wanting to eat and to label them. So we might say to ourselves, *I'm having the feeling in my body of wanting to eat; I'm having fantasies of cookies and chocolate cakes; I'm feeling the urge to put those in my mouth.* In this way the feelings are no longer just semiconscious impulses guiding your behavior; by bringing them into the forefront of your consciousness and paying them attention, you learn to observe them and really know what they feel like. Learning to speak the feelings out like this, putting words to your thoughts, feelings, and fantasies, helps us to slow down and become more observant and more aware of things emerging in our minds and bodies, rather than just follow our impulses without stopping to consider them.

You might also become aware that when you try to resist the urge to eat, another set of feelings, urges, and thoughts will appear in your mind that tries to nudge you toward overriding any resistance to eat, including the "screw it" thoughts, such as *Oh, screw it, I want to eat and I'm going to!* or *To hell with it!*

I don't want to think about this, so I'm just going to eat! You might then follow that thought curiously and wonder where it came from, what it's about, and what happens if you challenge it. Or, if you have feelings of anxiety about eating, when you become mindful, you will pay attention to the anxiety *as an observer* and again be curious about the thoughts that pop into your mind as a result of the anxiety.

So, to be mindful is to become more observant of the ever-changing flow of emotions and thoughts that ripple through our bodies and pop in and out of our minds. Once we have learned to observe these thoughts and feelings, we can begin to make choices about whether to act on them or not. So the key to mindfulness is this slowing down, paying more attention to the present moment, and becoming more observant of the contents of our minds and the feelings in our bodies. We will explore this approach in the first exercise shortly; but first we'll take a brief look at another way of training our attention.

Refocusing Our Attention

This is somewhat different from mindfulness. It involves learning to use imagery or physical activity deliberately to shift your attention away from the present to a mind-set you would prefer to be in. Like summoning up fleeting images, this is something we do naturally and voluntarily; for example, all of us have probably chosen to daydream about an upcoming vacation to take our minds off some rather humdrum or unpleasant task, or to do something we know will distract us from thinking about something difficult. Later in this chapter we will look at how you can learn to refocus your attention to get yourself into a specific mind-set when we explore the idea of a "safe place" and compassionate imagery. In the next chapter we will also look at more practical ways you can use this skill to help you manage the emotions that may arise when you change your eating habits.

Exercise 5.1 Mindful Attention

Sit quietly for a moment and focus on your breathing. Allow the breath to come right down into your lungs slowly and evenly before it leaves your body slowly and evenly. If you find this difficult, you may simply want to try to focus on the sensation of your breath coming in and leaving through your nose. Try spending two minutes simply holding your attention on the experience. If you don't like focusing on your breathing, you could use a pebble or a shell and try to focus your attention on the experience of looking at it and feeling it.

You may notice that within just a few moments, your mind will have wandered off to something else. This happens to all of us; we all have things in our minds, and our attention easily gets pulled toward them and away from the present moment: It happens whether the things in our minds are worrisome (such as an upcoming interview), something to look forward to (like a party), or something we need to do (pay a bill or remember to call a friend); whatever's in our minds, our attention will skip from one to another. This is absolutely typical of how our minds work; indeed, recent research evidence suggests that this is our natural state.

One aspect of practicing mindfulness is just learning to notice when your mind wanders and to bring your attention *gently* and *warmly* back to what you want to focus on, that is, not beating yourself up for having a grasshopper brain but kindly and uncritically pointing your attention back to the moment. Again, mindfulness is not *making* our minds pay attention or *emptying* our minds of thoughts; and telling ourselves off for being unable to pay attention isn't being mindful either! Indeed, this forceful approach is counterproductive, because it's actually very useful to notice where your mind wanders off to; this will often help you to identify issues that are bothering you. When your mind wanders, it's not a sign that you have failed to be mindful; it's just a normal part of the process. It is the act of noticing the wandering and then returning the attention to the desired focus that is central to mindfulness. The very fact that you find this difficult is itself evidence that you are engaging in mindful practice!

You might try to practice this mindful attention exercise for a couple of minutes, three times a day. In the early stages you may only be able to focus your attention for ten to twenty seconds at a time. That's fine; remember, the key to mindfulness is to notice where your mind wanders to and gently bring it back to the present moment, focusing on your breathing, or your shell or pebble.

Developing your mindful-attention skills can provide you with a useful way to slow down the rush to follow your impulses to eat and help you to notice what drives these impulses. However, I have found that it can be helpful to have a structure in place for eating before applying mindfulness to the experience of eating, so we will postpone exploration of eating mindfully until chapter 13.

ACTIVATING YOUR AFFILIATIVE SOOTHING SYSTEM

One of the keys to developing self-compassion is learning to turn off, or at least tone down, the threat/protection and drive systems of emotional regulation. If either of these systems is in full flow, it can be very difficult for your compassionate mind to get through. So, the first thing you need to do is to learn how to bring to the fore the third of those emotional regulation systems: the affiliative soothing system.

Soothing Rhythmic Breathing

As we saw in chapter 3, our threat/protection and drive systems are associated with particular types of physical and emotional responses. The affiliative soothing system is also associated with a set of physical and emotional responses: feeling calm, contented, connected, and safe. Soothing rhythmic breathing is an exercise specifically developed to activate this system. Unlike some relaxation training exercises, it is designed to help you find your own soothing rhythm for breathing, rather than asking you to follow a specific rate or pace. It also includes an element of mindfulness that can begin to develop the skills outlined in the previous section.

Exercise 5.2 Soothing
Rhythmic Breathing

Begin by finding a quiet place where you know you can sit without being disturbed for at least ten minutes. Sit in a chair, maintaining an upright posture (don't let your head fall forward), and place both feet on the floor about shoulder-width apart. Rest your hands on your thighs.

Begin by gently focusing on your breathing. Initially, just notice the breath going in and out though your nose. As you breathe, notice the air coming down into the bottom of your rib cage. Feel your diaphragm, the area underneath your ribs, move as you breathe in and out. Just notice your breathing and experiment with the pace: breathe a little faster or a little more slowly, and notice the difference in how your body feels. Generally, soothing rhythmic breathing is slightly slower and slightly deeper than your normal breathing rhythm. You might start by trying a count of about three seconds while breathing in, pausing slightly, and then three seconds while breathing out, but this is just a guideline to get you going; the point is to find a breathing pattern that seems to you to be *your own* soothing, comforting rhythm. It's as if you were checking in, or linking up, with the particular rhythm within your body that is soothing and calming to you. Whatever comfortable, soothing pace you settle on, try to ensure that your breaths in and out are smooth and even. For example, notice if you're breathing a bit too quickly, snatching a bit tensely at the inbreath, or rushing the outbreath.

Now spend thirty seconds or so just focusing on your breathing. Just notice the breath coming down into your lungs toward the diaphragm, the diaphragm expanding, and then the air moving out through your nose. Sometimes it's useful to focus your attention on the point just inside your nose where the air enters.

Even in those thirty seconds, you may have noticed that your wandering mind crept in with other thoughts, or that you became distracted by other noises in or outside the room. When you first do this exercise, you might be quite surprised at just how much your mind does shift from one thing to another. This is all very normal, natural, and to be expected. When it happens, just notice that your mind has wandered, and gently and kindly bring it back to its focus. At all times remember that you're not trying to force yourself to do anything, to clear your mind of thoughts, or to make yourself concentrate. You are simply noticing and gently refocusing, noticing and gently refocusing. In this case you are gently refocusing on the feelings of your breathing and your body slowing down. You might notice, for example, that you feel your body becoming heavier in the chair.

Remember, we are not aiming to achieve any specific emotional or physical state in this exercise. It is designed simply to help you link to your affiliative soothing system and see what happens. Some people report that finding their own soothing breathing rhythm helps them to feel calmer, slows down their thoughts, and relaxes them. Some people even use this exercise to help them get ready for sleep. These effects can be very helpful, but the central purpose of the exercise is to begin to learn to train your attention by establishing a breathing rhythm that can activate your affiliative soothing system. You can use the motto "notice and return" to guide you: *notice* the distractions and *return* your attention to your breathing. If you have a hundred thoughts or even a thousand thoughts, it doesn't matter at all. All that matters is that you notice and then, to the best of your ability, gently and kindly bring your attention back to your breathing.

As you practice "notice and return," you may find that gradually your mind will bounce around less and you will have fewer distracting thoughts. It may become easier to focus your attention on your breathing, but some days it will be easier than others. If you worry that you are not doing it right or that it can't work for you, then just note these thoughts as typical intrusions and return your attention to your breathing. Remember, the wandering mind is normal, and indeed can provide us with very useful information to work with later on. So don't get angry with it or become self-critical; just kindly bring your attention back to the focus of your breathing. It is the act of noticing how our minds wander that is the beginning of mindfulness.

You can do these two exercises anytime and anyplace; you can even do them standing up (say, on a bus or subway train, or in line at the post office). All they require is that you allow yourself a few moments when you focus on your breathing and gently bring your mind back to that single focus when it wanders. The key thing is our mindful attention to the process rather than the result.

One of the key elements of mindfulness is to *remember* to become mindful. We can, of course, spend time deliberately practicing mindfulness by focusing on our breathing or some other activity, and indeed at the beginning, this is just what we need to do; but actually every moment of our lives could be lived more mindfully. This is an approach you can use in many aspects of life, and indeed you can practice becoming more mindful in all that you do.

Developing Your Safe Place

Some of us, when we are distressed, naturally conjure up images of being in a better place, maybe somewhere we remember from the past or somewhere we hope to be in the future. Now, of course, we may do this simply to escape or avoid difficult feelings or situations. However, we can also use this tactic to help us cope with difficult situations *without* avoiding them, because it can help us to learn ways of containing and creating soothing feelings within ourselves.

The safe place exercise builds on this natural way that people activate their affiliative soothing systems. The feelings of safeness and calmness it encourages are useful in activating the affiliative soothing system, and when this system is engaged, it becomes easier to think about our difficulties from a more compassionate perspective and also to experiment with new ways of coping. Developing a safe place does not mean either accepting or ignoring bad things that are happening to us, or not trying to change things in our lives. It's simply a step toward feeling calm enough to tackle these things without resorting to overeating as a way of coping with difficult feelings that may arise.

I have found that many people find it easier to develop their safe places when they have a little practice in using soothing rhythmic breathing. So we will begin the next exercise with this. If you find that you can get straight into your safe place without practicing soothing rhythmic breathing, that's absolutely fine. In a compassion-focused approach, we are always experimenting, trying out things to find what's *personally* helpful for us.

Some people have clear ideas about places they like or places where they feel safe, but others don't. If nowhere springs to mind for you, it's a good idea to try thinking about the sorts of places where you could feel safe before you do the exercise. So, when you have some space and time to fantasize, ask yourself what sort of place would make you feel safe. Would it be outside or inside? If outside, what would the weather be like? What colors would there be around you? Remember, you're aiming to think of a place where you will feel safe, calm, and contented. This can be a real place or somewhere you invent. The act of really thinking about what sort of place helps you feel safe can be an important part of preparing to bring the image to life in your imagination in the exercise we're about to do; maybe you've never really thought about this before. Try to engage in the exercise with curiosity and interest, as if you were an artist designing something for the first time, seeing if you like this here or prefer that there.

If you are using a real place, try not to use one that has other feelings attached. For example, someone I worked with initially wanted to use the bedroom she slept in at her grandparents' house when she was a child. On the face of it, this place held good memories of feeling safe and cared for. Sadly, her grandparents had recently passed away, so remembering this room brought back her grief. Instead we built an ideal bedroom as her image; this had some features of her real room, but others that were new enough to help her feel safe.

Some people like to have an actual picture of their safe places to focus on while they do the exercise. Other people like to have particular smells or sounds around them that they associate with their safe places. So, for example, one person I worked with liked to have a particular hand cream with her, because she associated the smell with her safe place. These kinds of associations can be helpful in activating your affiliative soothing system in day-to-day life, because you may be able to keep the sound on your MP3 player or the smell on a handkerchief and use them to rapidly activate your memory of safeness whenever you feel under threat.

Exercise 5.3 Imagining Your Safe Place

Begin by finding a comfortable place to sit, where you won't be disturbed for at least ten minutes. Establish your soothing rhythmic breathing.

Feeling Safe

When you feel ready, try to create a place in your mind that could give you the feeling of safeness and calmness. You can close your eyes if you feel okay with this. If you'd rather not, focus your attention on the image in your mind or on a reminder of your safe place (for example, a particular scent, a piece of fabric, or even a photograph). Alternatively you can focus your attention on your pebble or shell and imagine your safe place, again without closing your eyes.

When you feel you've got some kind of fleeting, impressionistic idea of a safe place, you can start trying to fill out the detail by going through your sensory impressions, starting with the visual ones. For example, what sorts of colors are around you? If you're outside, are you on a beach (is it sandy, rocky, pebbly?), in a garden (formal or wild? What kinds of flowers or other plants are around?), or perhaps in the country (are there trees around, animals in the fields? Is the sky blue or cloudy, or is the sun rising or setting?). Then think about any sound you can hear, because sometimes people find that sounds create a sense of safeness. One person liked to imagine the sound of a little waterfall. You might hear birdsong or the crackling of a log fire. Then think of any other sensations, such as a gentle, cooling breeze or the warmth of the sun on your face, perhaps the smell of hay or a salty breeze on the shore. Going through the sensory details of the image can be quite helpful to fix it and make it real.

Your wandering mind will take you away from this place. So just notice where it goes, and then gently return your attention to the elements of your image that feel safest. When you have the image back, gently expand it again to other parts of your safe place.

Some people find it helpful to imagine seeing themselves in their safe places: to imagine the look on their faces, and how they would sit or lie when they felt safe, relaxed, and contented. Other people don't want to see themselves there, and prefer just to imagine their safe places and their feelings of being in them. It's okay to do either.

There's no right or wrong about your safe place. It's just a place where *you* feel safe. You may find that different images work better at different times of the day, or when you are experiencing different levels or kinds of threat or distress.

After a little practice you may find an image that really works for you. Remember, it won't be in complete high definition in 3-D with surround sound and "smello-vision"; it's an internal image, not a high-tech film, so the more reminders you can develop to help you focus on your image, the better. When you have a safe place you find helpful, you can write your own script to help you recall and stay in your safe place. You might even want to record this to make your own CD that you can play back for yourself.

Feeling Wanted

In the compassion-focused approach, you add an extra important element to your safe place image, which again is designed to stimulate your affiliative soothing system and your compassion system. After you've been in your safe place for a few minutes and when you're ready, just dwell on the fact that this place is your creation, so it really welcomes you, wants you to be here, and wants to offer you safeness and rest. The feeling of being wanted by a place may seem strange, but try it and see how it goes. Just focus on feeling that you are in harmony with this place. You might find that allowing your face to relax into a gentle expression of contentment or compassion helps with the experience. At all times remember that nothing is being forced here. You're not trying to *make* yourself feel safe in this image; you are engaging in a gentle, curious practice to see how a sense of safeness might develop over time and how your image might change along with that sense of safeness.

Don't worry if you find yourself feeling quite sleepy when you do this exercise. This is quite common, and some people even use it to help them sleep. That's okay too. However, the main aim is to activate your affiliative soothing system, so that you can think about your difficulties a little more easily than when you are caught up in the drive or threat/protection system.

SWITCHING ON THE COMPASSIONATE MIND

In chapter 4 we explored how different mind-sets can affect our motivations, thoughts, feelings, and behavior. In chapter 7 we will build on this idea to help you develop a personal understanding of the different mind-sets you experience in relationship to food and eating. In this chapter and the next, we will work on developing your compassion mind-set. The idea is that you will be able to use the skills and attributes of this mind-set to help you deal with the experiences that in the past prompted you to turn to eating, and also to deal with any emotional consequences of giving up overeating.

So a little down the line, we'll look at how we can switch from, say, a dieting or a comfort-seeking mind-set to a compassionate mind-set. But first it's worth looking at how switching mind-sets occurs naturally. Imagine that you are walking down the street, planning your next diet. You are likely to be thinking about why you want to diet, the food you need to buy to help you diet, the activities you will start doing to help you lose weight, and all of the good things that will happen for you when you lose weight. You may even start to experience some of the positive feelings you associate with being successful at losing weight. At this point your attention is focused inward, toward your plans for the future and the positive experiences you expect to get from dieting.

Suddenly you see a small child run out into the road. A car skids to a halt, and the child is standing in the middle of the road, crying. At this point you will almost certainly find that your attention has instantly switched to the events going on around you. You are focused on the child's distress and rush to help him, perhaps putting an arm round him and helping him to the pavement. You may look around to see if the parent is nearby or, once you feel the child is safe, look after the shocked driver.

Without your making any conscious decision, the event has switched on your compassionate mind-set. Your response was automatic; you didn't decide not to think about your diet anymore; you just forgot about it when something more important claimed your attention.

This switch of attention is often associated with a rapid change in our thoughts, feelings, and bodily experiences. Witnessing this type of incident can be quite upsetting. Your sympathy for the child, parent, and driver may lead you to feel upset for them. You may find yourself dwelling on how things could have been far worse or on the things you wanted to do to help but couldn't do (for example, stopping the child before he ran into the road). You may feel a bit shaky, even tearful. A little later, once the incident is over, you may find that your compassionate mind focuses on other ways you could have helped or on wondering how the child, parent, and driver are. You may find it difficult to think about your diet for the rest of the day while your compassionate mind remains concerned about the people involved in the near miss. Or you may find that another mind-set takes over to help you with the feelings of distress the incident has called up in you. You may use your comfort-seeking mind-set to help you. Alternatively, you may use your dieting mind-set to take your thoughts away from the events you have witnessed.

If you could stay with your compassionate mind but redirect it toward yourself, you could help yourself to understand and sympathize with the distress that seeing this incident has caused you. This response is likely to help you manage your feelings better than either the dieting or the comfort-seeking mind-set, and to enable you to react in compassionate ways again if you are faced with a similar situation in the future. A compassionate response may congratulate you on your humanity and value your compassion for others, while helping you consider ways you can support yourself while still feeling upset about what you've seen, for example, talking it though with someone else. It may focus on the good you *have* done, rather than on all the things you *could have* done.

As you can see from the previous example, our minds are pretty flexible, with the ability to refocus our attention to help us to manage life's challenges. And as you can also see, our compassionate minds can switch on pretty automatically when directed toward other people. However, we can find it a lot harder when it comes to being compassionate toward ourselves.

EXERCISES TO DEVELOP THE COMPASSIONATE MIND

The compassion-focused exercises in this section use imagery and are designed to create the feelings that accompany the experience and practice of compassion, both toward others and ourselves. The exercises are adapted from those on the Compassionate Mind Foundation website (for details, see the "Useful Resources" section at the back of this book), with the kind permission of Paul Gilbert and the foundation. Many people I have worked with on eating problems find the structure these exercises offer to be very helpful. As always in the compassion-focused approach, it's important that you work through them at your pace and decide which ones work best for you.

The compassion-focused exercises that follow are focused in four main ways:

- *Developing the inner compassionate self:* In these exercises we will focus on creating a sense of a compassionate self, just as actors do when they are trying to get into a role.

- *Compassion flowing out from you to others:* These exercises focus on the feelings in your body when you fill your mind with compassionate feelings for other people.

- *Compassion flowing into you:* Here you will focus on opening up to compassion, to stimulate areas of your brain that are responsive to the kindness of others.

- *Self-compassion:* This set of exercises is focused on developing feelings, thoughts, and experiences that direct your capacity for compassion toward yourself. This is just as important as changing your eating patterns; working on the things that can make us overeat can be difficult, and learning how to generate self-compassion can be very helpful during these times, particularly in dealing with our emotions.

Developing the Inner Compassionate Self

As we have seen, we all have the capacity to experience different mind-sets and act accordingly. We have many parts to ourselves. In the next exercises you will work to develop the compassionate part of yourself. We'll begin by taking a look at the key qualities of the compassionate self.

WISDOM

Wisdom has two important aspects. The first is acknowledging that all of us just find ourselves here, with a particular set of genes inherited from our ancestors and a very complicated brain that evolved over many millions of years, neither of which we designed or chose. The second is acknowledging that our sense of self and our memories come from our own experiences of life, beginning with the relationships and situations into which we were born.

Your compassionate self knows you had no choice over the design of your body and brain, or over the life into which you were born. So you further acknowledge that while working with some of what goes on in your mind—powerful emotions, mood shifts, unwanted thoughts or images, and painful memories—can be difficult, there's no point in blaming yourself for things over which you've had no control. You just found yourself here and have to deal with what you found as best you can, using the brain and body you inherited and the experiences of life you gather.

STRENGTH

This kind of strength is also called fortitude and is related to courage. It's not an aggressive power, but a source of inner confidence and authority that comes from wisdom. Strength helps to maintain your commitment and determination to face and heal suffering.

WARMTH

The compassionate intention to relieve suffering is not cold or clinical but warm, friendly, and gentle. The warmth of compassion is not (just) about being nice—it can be firm and persistent—but ensures that all its efforts are made out of a real desire to be helpful and noncritical, soothing rather than harsh, and are expressed in a gentle, warm, friendly, and open voice and manner.

RESPONSIBILITY

Compassion is focused on facing rather than turning away from life's challenges. It involves recognizing that even though you didn't cause many of the problems you face, you can still make a commitment to yourself and others to do something about them, even if you work only in small steps. So assuming responsibility is not about blaming or criticizing, but about genuinely wanting to act in ways that are helpful and based on your wisdom, strength, warmth, and desire to improve things for the future.

It can be helpful to practice focusing on each of these key qualities in turn and imagine having each one, noting what it feels like and any effect this has on your body.

Exercise 5.4 Envisaging the Compassionate Self

This exercise is designed to help you focus on the feelings associated with creating compassion in yourself. It's hard to offer ourselves or others compassion if we don't have a good idea of what this feels like. As you do this exercise and the ones that follow, keep in mind that it doesn't matter whether or not you feel that you have these qualities. It is the act of imagining that you have them that is important. This is the kind of approach that "method" actors use to get into a role: they imagine themselves to have the characteristics of the character they're playing. In this way they are stimulating certain qualities in their minds and bodies, and as a result their acting is convincing, because during the short time they are "in character," they in effect "become" that character. Of course, when they come out of their roles, they may not want to be anything like their characters (particularly if they are playing someone like Hannibal Lecter!), whereas in compassion-focused work the idea is that over time you will want to retain the aspects of the role you've been practicing. But for the purposes of this exercise, it's just putting yourself into that mental state that's important. As with so many exercises, the more you practice this, the easier you'll probably find it.

What you will do in this exercise is take each of the qualities I've just described in turn—wisdom, strength, warmth, responsibility—hold each in your mind, and imagine yourself having it. Work through each quality steadily, playfully, and slowly. You may find some qualities easier to imagine yourself having than others, and this is perfectly normal. Try to notice how each quality can affect your body differently. Remember that you may get only glimmers of images and feelings, perhaps because your mind wanders or you can't really focus. This is very typical of what happens when we're trying something new; just as if we were trying to learn to play a piano, we'd be all fingers and thumbs to start with. Regular practice will help.

So, to begin the exercise, find a place where you can sit quietly and won't be disturbed for at least ten minutes. Establish your soothing rhythmic breathing. When you feel that your body has slowed down (even slightly), you are ready to practice imagining that you are a very deeply compassionate person. Think of all the qualities you would ideally have as that compassionate person. Try to spend at least one minute focusing on each quality, longer if you can.

Now focus on your desire to become a compassionate person and to be able to think, act, and feel compassionately. Imagine being a wise person, with a wisdom that comes from your understanding about the nature of our lives, minds, and bodies. You are wise enough to know that much of what goes on inside of us is not our fault but the result of our evolution and of experiences over which we had no control.

When you are ready and have a sense of your wisdom, you can switch to imagining having strength, maturity, and authority. Explore your body posture (sitting or standing confidently and assertively) and your facial expressions when you are in this mode. Keep your head upright rather than let it drop forward; your sitting or standing posture should be one of confidence. Remember, you are imagining yourself as a person who understands your own and others' difficulties in a nonjudgmental way, and has the confidence to be sensitive to suffering and to tolerate distress in order to gain a better understanding of how to alleviate it.

When you have a sense of your wisdom and strength, you can switch to focusing on qualities of warmth, a gentle friendliness. Imagine being warm and kind. Create a compassionate facial expression. Try to imagine yourself speaking to someone, and hear the warm tone of your voice.

Now reach out with that warmth to feel what it might be like to offer it to another.

Next, switch to imagining feelings of responsibility. Imagine that you have lost interest in condemning or blaming and just want to do the best you can to help yourself and others move forward. Hold on to your compassionate facial expression and warmth, but focus now on this experience of committing yourself to a compassionate path of self-development.

Finally, you can imagine yourself having all of these qualities and incorporating them into the way you are with yourself and others.

When you have finished, bring yourself gently back into the room. You might want to write down what it felt like to have these qualities and how it might affect the way you want to act in the future.

Exercise 5.5 You at Your Best

Another way you can explore and get close to the idea of your compassionate self is to remind yourself of a time when you felt compassion, acted in a compassionate way, or both; it doesn't matter to what degree. When we are struggling with difficult things in our lives, it can be easy to forget that we have the capacity for compassion at all, so actively bringing these memories to mind can help you to remember that you do have these qualities within you and to bring them to the fore again. You can think of your compassionate self as "you at your best."

It's a good idea to begin by establishing your soothing rhythmic breathing or your safe place image. Then bring to mind a time when you were kind and compassionate to somebody. Choose an occasion when you were satisfied with how helpful you were, and try not to focus on times when you were compassionate with someone who was very distressed, especially if this is the first time you've tried this exercise. It may help to write down the specific memory you want to focus on and to "risk assess" it first, making sure it's not too distressing for you to work with; otherwise you might find yourself focusing on the other person's distress and maybe your inability to entirely alleviate it, rather than bringing your attention to your own compassionate qualities. The aim is to focus on your feelings of wanting to help and your kindness.

So, once you have brought to mind an appropriate occasion, focus on how you felt as a result of being kind and compassionate. As you develop your image of you at your best, focus on your body position, facial expression, and tone of voice as you offer your wisdom, strength, warmth, and courage. Spend sufficient time on this exercise to really be able to explore it thoroughly and reflect on the experience.

Both of these exercises draw on Buddhist ideas having to do with developing key qualities of the self (such as mindfulness and compassion), which in turn give us new insights into the nature of the self.

When we see the compassionate self as the self we would like to become, in a way this is no different from wanting to develop any other aspect of the self. If we want to be good at sports, an accomplished pianist, a good cook, or well read in poetry, we know we would need to practice. The more we practice, the closer we get to being what we want to become. Some days your practice won't go very well, but this doesn't mean that over the long term, you can't move toward your goal of becoming the kind of person—sportsperson, pianist, cook, or literary scholar—you would like to be.

It's exactly the same with the self. You can make a decision to become more like the compassionate self of your imagination. You can practice what you would like to become by imagining, enacting, thinking, and playing with those compassionate qualities. If you have an argument with somebody, you can reflect with the compassionate self on how you might deal with that situation better in the future. If you have problems with food, you can learn to be compassionate rather than angry and critical, and gently and kindly think about how to help yourself next time. There's nothing fixed about your personality; you can make choices about it and, with practice, move closer to being the kind of person you want to be.

COMPASSION EVERY DAY

Ideally, try to practice becoming the compassionate self each day. As well as doing the exercises when you have time, you can also fit practice into even the smallest slots in a busy life. When you wake up in the morning, try to spend a few minutes practicing becoming your compassionate self. As you lie in bed, bring a compassionate expression to your face and focus on your real desire to be wise and compassionate. Remember, inside you, you have the capacity for wisdom and strength, but you have to create space for it. If you practice for even two minutes a day, every day, it's likely to have an effect. You can also practice while standing at the bus stop or taking a bath. You may then find you'll want to practice for longer periods of time and perhaps to make more time during your day for this. Meanwhile, whenever you are aware of the opportunity, even sitting in a meeting, you can use soothing rhythmic breathing and focus on becoming your wise, compassionate, calm, mature self.

Compassion Flowing Out from You to Others

The idea of the next three exercises is to focus on the desire to help and on feelings of kindness and warmth. If the feelings don't come easily, don't worry; it's your behavior and intentions that are important; the feelings may follow. In the first of this group of exercises, you simply get into your compassionate mind-set and imagine your compassion flowing into someone you care about, giving that person three key compassionate messages. In the second exercise, you will focus your compassion on helping a particular individual you care about who is struggling with something in his life and whom you would like to support using your compassionate self.

The final exercise in this group can be a little trickier for some people. Many people who overeat are actually critical of others who overeat and find it difficult to be compassionate with them. In a way they can be a reflection of ourselves and our own struggles, and if we are very critical of ourselves, we can also be very critical of what we see in the mirror! One way to overcome this obstacle is to personalize things; it can be far harder to be uncompassionate with a specific person than with an idea or abstract group of people. Exercise 5.8 builds on your innate wisdom and compassion for others by directly focusing your attention on offering compassion to people who overeat.

Of course, many people who overeat are very sympathetic with the struggles of others, but find it difficult to offer themselves the same level of compassion. Indeed, I find this all the time in the groups I run. Exercise 5.8 is the beginning of offering yourself compassion for your difficulties with overeating, but please only try to work on it when you feel you can do exercises 5.6 and 5.7 quite comfortably and are starting to feel your compassionate emotions coming into action, even if only a little.

Exercise 5.6 Focusing Compassion on Others

First find a time and place when and where you can sit quietly without being disturbed for at least ten minutes. Now try to create a sense of being a compassionate person as best you can, as you did in exercise 5.4. Some days this will be easier than others; even just the slightest glimmer can be a start. Now bring to mind someone you care about: this might be your partner; a friend, parent, or child; or a pet or other animal. When you have this individual in mind, focus on directing toward her three basic thoughts (if you're familiar with Buddhism, you may recognize this traditional text or mantra):

> May you be well.
> May you be happy.
> May you be free of suffering.

Keep in mind that it's your behavior and intentions that are important; the feelings may follow. Be gentle, take time, and allow yourself to focus on desires and wishes you create in yourself for the other person or animal. Maybe picture this being smiling or looking affectionately at you and feeling happy to receive your compassionate wishes. Spend time focusing on this genuine desire of yours for the well-being of another individual.

Do this exercise mindfully; that is, if your mind wanders, that's not a problem; just gently and kindly bring it back to the task. Try to notice any physical or emotional feelings that emerge from this exercise. Don't worry if nothing much happens at a conscious level; the act of giving it a try is the important thing. It's like getting physically fit; it may take several visits to the gym or training sessions before you consciously notice feeling different, but your body will respond straightaway.

Exercise 5.7 Compassion Flowing
Out to Others in Difficulty

In this exercise we will again imagine kindness and compassion flowing from you out to another person or animal, but in this case, that other individual will be facing a difficulty that you want to help with. As with exercise 5.5, try not to choose a time when that person (or animal) was very distressed, because then you will likely focus on the distress and possibly your inability to dispel it, rather than on your own compassionate feelings. It can help to prepare by jotting down the name of the person or animal you want to help and the difficulty you want to help with. Before you start, try to make sure that the issue will not be so distressing for you that you can't do the exercise.

Begin by establishing your soothing rhythmic breathing or your safe place as a basis for your compassionate mind-set. Now move into the following sequence of stages, trying to spend at least one minute on each element of the exercise.

1.   When you feel ready, bring to mind a time when you felt compassionate toward the person or animal you have in mind.

2.   Imagine yourself expanding, as if you were becoming calmer, wiser, stronger, more mature, and better able to help that individual. Pay attention to your body as you remember your feelings of kindness.

3.   Now imagine warmth spreading within your body and flowing over the other person or animal. Feel your genuine desire for this other individual to be free of suffering and to flourish.

4.   Now focus on your tone of voice and the kinds of things you would want to say or do to help this individual.

5.   Next think about your pleasure in being able to be kind.

6.   To finish, focus on combining all of these qualities in your compassionate self, and imagine them flowing into the other person or animal: your desire to be helpful and kind, feelings of expansion, the sense of warmth, your tone of voice, the wisdom in your voice and in your behavior.

When you have finished the exercise, you might want to make some notes about how doing this exercise made you feel.

Exercise 5.8 Compassion for People Who Overeat

There are several ways to do this exercise. The first step is to identify the person or people you want your compassion to flow toward. Some people find it easier to offer their compassion to someone they know personally who overeats; others find it easier to offer compassion to someone they don't know personally (for example, someone from a TV dieting program or someone they've seen in a newspaper); others find it easier to offer compassion to everyone who struggles with overeating. For the purposes of the exercise, it really doesn't matter which you choose. The key point here is to learn to feel compassion for people who struggle with overeating.

Then, having identified the person or people you want to offer compassion to, decide whether you would find it easier to offer them general compassion (exercise 5.6) or compassion for a specific difficulty (exercise 5.7) before you move on to offering them compassion for the struggles they may have with their eating. Start with the exercises you find easier and then build toward the practice you find more difficult.

So this is how you do it. Find a place to sit comfortably and then establish your soothing rhythmic breathing or your safe-place image. When you feel ready, imagine becoming a compassionate person: you at your best. Remember to keep a confident posture and an upright stance. Go through the key qualities of compassion in a secure and wise person, believing yourself to be strong, confident, and deeply kind. You realize how difficult life is because of the brain we have evolved with.

Now in your mind's eye, see somebody who overeats. Watch that person. Understand that the motives and desires causing the person to overeat are complex and can often cause him distress. You may also focus your compassion on the unintended consequences overeating can have for that person. Using your wisdom, recognize how the person is caught up in a pattern of feelings and behavior she didn't design and probably doesn't want. You're not trying to change anything about the person at this point; you're just learning to be compassionate for the person and to him. Imagine the person getting as much compassion as she needs. For example, you may see yourself beside the person, saying, "You're going through a tough time at the moment," "I can see how hard this is for you," or "I can see that food is a real comfort for you," or trying to help the person find ways to help himself manage the problems that cause him to overeat.

Give yourself plenty of time to just keep your compassionate mind gently focused on what you're seeing in front of you. As you do this, you may begin to have feelings about what would be helpful to the person you're watching. However, if you feel your mind becoming angry, critical, or irritated with the person, then break the image, pull back, and refocus on your soothing rhythmic breathing or safe place until you notice these feelings ease a little; then reengage with your compassionate self before recommencing the imagery. It's not unusual to have only fleeting feelings of compassion for people who overeat, and you may need to gently redirect your compassion for the person several times during the exercise.

When you have finished, bring yourself gently back into the room, and note how you feel now and how, from a more compassionate perspective, you might act differently toward people who overeat. You might also want to reflect on your experience from your own perspective. What came up for you? Was there anything that surprised you? What would you like to work on to improve your capacity to respond to overeating with compassion?

Compassion Flowing into You

Although many of us can see how being offered and being able to accept compassion can be helpful for other people, we can find it quite difficult to accept for ourselves. Our compassionate minds have the capacity both to give compassion to others and to receive it from them. As you have seen, your capacity to receive compassion is crucial to activating your affiliative soothing system and hence to helping you manage difficult events and emotions. In the next two exercises you will practice allowing compassion from others into your life. The first exercise is focused on helping you to remember times when other people offered you compassion. When we are distressed, the threat/protection system naturally focuses on things that are dangerous to us, which may mean we temporarily forget that some people in the world have been compassionate to us. The key here is to nurture those memories and use them as a basis for helping you to engage with those in your life who can be compassionate, to recognize compassion when it is offered, and to use it to help you.

Sadly, for a variety of reasons, sometimes people can't remember when others have been particularly compassionate toward them. Perhaps they are so distressed that it's hard to bring back any memory of kindness, or maybe they have just not had very many experiences of other people being compassionate toward them. Sometimes people struggle to recall these memories because the compassion they were offered was conditional, with a price tag they don't want to remember. For example, they might have been offered compassion at one moment and hostility the next from a very unpredictable person. Sometimes, too, memories of compassion from another are too painful to bring to mind because the person is no longer around.

So it's not always easy to find a memory of being offered compassion. If your experiences make this difficult for you for one reason or another, that's sad, but it's not something you can blame yourself for, nor is it a sign of any failure or personal inadequacy on your part. It is simply the way it is! It does, however, create a practical problem in that it means you will need to build from scratch an image of compassion flowing into you from others. The second exercise in this section is designed to address this need by developing an image of someone or something that can offer you compassion throughout your life, a compassionate companion you can always rely on. It's possible to do this even if you have limited experience of compassion from others, by drawing on your innate wisdom about compassion that you used in exercise 5.5 ("You at Your Best").

Exercise 5.9 Compassion Flowing into You: **Using Your Memories**

This exercise asks you to recall a time when someone was compassionate toward you. This memory shouldn't be of a time when you were very distressed, because you will then focus on the distress rather than the compassion; the point of the exercise is to focus on another person's desire to help and be kind to you. Try to spend a minute or so on each phase of the exercise.

To begin, engage in your soothing rhythmic breathing for a minute or so until you can feel your body slowing down.

1. When you feel ready, bring to mind a memory of a time when someone was kind to you.

2. Allow your face to relax into a compassionate expression and your body to adopt a posture that gives you a sense of kindness and a warm glow or a feeling of gratitude as you recall the memory.

3. Explore the facial expressions and body position of the person who was kind to you. Sometimes it helps if you see the person moving toward you, or see her face breaking into a smile or her head from one side.

4. Now focus on the important sensory qualities of your memory. First spend just one minute focusing on the kinds of things this person said and the tone of his voice. Then focus on the emotion in the person, what he really felt for you at that moment.

5. Now focus on the whole experience, maybe whether the person held you, touched you, offered you a tissue, or helped you in other ways. Notice how the person created in you a feeling of being soothed and connected, and a sense of gratitude and pleasure at being helped. Allow to grow the experience of soothing, connectedness, gratitude, and joy in being helped. Remember to keep your facial expression as compassionate as you can.

When you are ready, gently let the memory fade, come out of the exercise, and make some notes on how you felt. You may notice that bringing these memories to mind has created feelings inside you, even if they are just glimmers. What came up for you? Was there anything that surprised you? What would you like to work on to improve your capacity to receive compassion from others?

INVENTING THE COMPASSIONATE OTHER

Experiencing compassion and kindness from another person, feeling and sensing that another mind is focused on us with benevolence, can have quite a powerful impact on us. Our brains have evolved to be very responsive to receiving kindness from others. We want to develop exercises that will help trigger those responses, because in doing so, we create a sense of being soothed and also an inner security. So how do we do this if we can't recall any real experiences of receiving compassion? We practice using the idea of a compassionate other, whom we create for ourselves. Some people say, "Well, it's all very well imagining compassionate others, but I want real ones in my life." Of course, we all want compassionate relationships with other people. These exercises are not meant to replace real relationships. They are designed to stimulate your brain to help you with your feelings and emotions. Developing these aspects of your brain can also help you to feel safe enough to create and foster compassionate relationships with other people in the outside world. So it's not a matter of either-or. To use a sports analogy again, practicing in the gym is not the same as playing the real game. But it can help you when you do play the game for real.

Exercise 5.10 Creating a Compassionate Companion

In this exercise you will create your ideal compassionate other. If you could imagine or create a being that would encapsulate everything you could possibly desire from someone totally focused on your welfare, what kind of qualities would that person have?

Now, some people may, of course, dismiss this idea straightaway, with thoughts like, *I don't deserve that* or *If anybody got really close to me and knew me from the inside, they wouldn't like me*. However, for the purposes of this exercise, this is all beside the point, which is to *imagine* that you are the recipient of complete compassion from another mind without judgment in the present moment.

Whatever image that comes to mind or that you choose to work with is *your* creation and therefore your own personal ideal of who or what you would most like to care for and about you. It's not uncommon for people to choose an inanimate object (like a tree or a color). Some people prefer for their images to be those of animals or fantasy characters (like dogs or fairies). Some people can bring to mind a fictional character from a book or film (such as Gandalf from *The Lord of the Rings*), while some prefer to invent their own individuals or creatures. You can choose a real person you actually know, although in my experience, this can be a little tricky. Most people we know are not compassionate all the time; after all, they are only human, like us! Also, it's very tempting to choose someone who has been very caring but may no longer be with you, perhaps a teacher, friend, or relative who may have passed away or moved on and whom you no longer see. Thus your image can get mixed up with feelings of grief and longing, distracting you from the aim of this exercise, which is to experience receiving compassion from your ideal compassionate other.

Whatever your companion looks like, it's important that you give the person certain qualities, including the key qualities of the compassionate self we identified earlier in this chapter that are present in complete and perfect form in the ideal compassionate other:

- a deep commitment to you: a desire to help you cope with and relieve your suffering, and take joy in your happiness

- strength of mind that is not overwhelmed by your pain or distress, but remains present, enduring it with you

- wisdom that has been gained through experience and truly understands the struggles you go through in life

- warmth, conveyed by kindness, gentleness, caring, and openness

- an acceptance that's never judgmental or critical, but understands your struggles and accepts you as you are, while also remaining deeply committed to helping and supporting you

You can use worksheet 5.1, "Building Your Compassionate Companion," to help you with this exercise. The key is to focus on the feelings and on the experience of imagining another mind that fervently wants you to flourish. When you have completed the worksheet, you are ready to begin the imagery part of the exercise.

Sitting in a place where you won't be disturbed, first establish your soothing rhythmic breathing and allow your face to relax into a compassionate expression. Then bring to mind your safe place. This may now be the place where you wish to create and meet your compassionate image, or you can choose to meet your compassionate companion in another place; that's okay too. The key thing is to create the feelings of being safe and soothed before you meet your compassionate companion.

Now imagine your compassionate companion appearing in your safe place; this individual may materialize from the mist, walk in though a door, or appear in some other way. Imagine the person sitting or standing beside you. You may want to touch the person or be held by him, and that's okay, but only allow your compassionate companion to be with you in a way you feel comfortable with and that helps you to feel safe and soothed.

To begin with, simply practice experiencing what it's like to focus on the feeling that another mind really values you and cares about you unconditionally. Now focus on your compassionate companion and imagine that the person looks at you with great warmth. Imagine that your companion has the following desires for you:

That you be well.
That you be happy.
That you be free of suffering.

Try to allow yourself to open up to the experiences of compassion, in the knowledge that you can always rely on your compassionate companion to offer you her commitment to you, as well as her strength, wisdom, and acceptance.

You may notice that your mind wanders, perhaps to memories of times when people were not compassionate toward you. This is perfectly normal. Just gently bring your mind back to the task at hand, which is focusing your attention on experiencing compassion from your companion.

Try to do this exercise for about ten minutes; then gently bring yourself back into the here and now, and jot down what you felt during the exercise.

Worksheet 5.1 Building Your Compassionate Companion

How would you like your ideal caring, compassionate image to look or appear? What are the visual qualities?

How would you like your ideal caring, compassionate image to sound, for example, what tone of voice?

What other sensory qualities can you give to it, such as its smell or textures?

How would you like your ideal caring, compassionate image to relate to you? Example: In a caring, warm, understanding way.

How would you like to relate to your ideal caring, compassionate image? Example: Allow it to care for me, Listen to its wisdom and concern for me.

STRUGGLING WITH THE IDEA OF A COMPASSIONATE COMPANION

It's common for people to struggle to develop this image of an ideal compassionate other; for example, you might have thought, *Yes, but this is not real; I want somebody real to care for me.* That is, of course, very understandable. It's even possible that doing this exercise could make you feel sad, because we all have an innate desire for genuine connection with others. However, as I pointed out in the introduction to this exercise, in a way, these reservations are missing the point of the exercise. Of course, it's desirable to find people who care for us and to be able to accept their compassion. But sometimes, though we have these people in our lives, we can't allow their compassion in, because we haven't learned how to accept it. And at other times we could accept compassion, but just don't have such people available to us.

The aim here is to help you develop the compassionate aspect of yourself, which though you may already be able to direct toward others, you may struggle to direct toward yourself. Your ideal compassionate companion allows you to practice receiving compassion at a pace and in a way that feels safe for you, and from a source that's available to you whenever you need it.

Self-Compassion

This may be the hardest of all of the exercises we have introduced so far. Many of us struggle to be compassionate toward ourselves. In the next chapter we will take a closer look at why this may be. For now, you will simply try to practice directing compassion toward yourself, using the skills you learned in the exercises you have already done.

In these previous exercises you practiced offering compassion to a person or people who overeat. You may have found this tricky. If you are very critical of your own eating habits, this is probably not the best place to begin your journey to becoming self-compassionate. Instead, you may want to offer yourself compassion for other difficulties in your life, perhaps the things that trigger your overeating.

Sometimes people find it difficult to jump straight into offering themselves compassion. This is where your compassionate companion can be really helpful. You can imagine that person feeling compassion for you concerning another difficulty you have experienced, such as a loss or a health problem, ideally one that's not overwhelmingly distressing; otherwise you might get caught up in the distress rather than the feeling of compassion. As you become more confident in using your compassionate companion to support you, you can always increase the difficulty of the problems or situations you bring to this individual.

Of course, we know that your compassionate companion is not real; it simply represents the kindest, strongest, wisest, and warmest parts of you. However, it can be a useful bridge until you are able to offer yourself compassion directly. Try the following exercise to get you started.

Exercise 5.11 Using Your Compassionate Companion to Help Yourself

Find a time and place when you can sit quietly without being disturbed. Now establish your soothing rhythmic breathing and allow your face to relax into its compassionate expression. Then bring to mind the safe place where you want to meet your companion. At this point you are ready to begin the exercise; try to spend at least one minute on each element.

1. First, imagine spending some time with your companion and experiencing this individual's compassion flowing over and around you. You may want to touch the person or be held by her; this is fine, but remember only to allow your compassionate companion to be with you in a way you feel comfortable with and that helps you to feel safe and soothed.

2. Next, focus on your compassionate companion looking at you with great warmth. Imagine that this individual has the following wishes and hopes for you:

    That you be well.
    That you be happy.
    That you be free of suffering.

3. Allow yourself to sit with and open up to these experiences of compassion, in the knowledge that you can always rely on your compassionate companion to offer you his commitment, strength, wisdom, and acceptance.

4. Next, imagine telling your compassionate companion about the struggle you are having. Imagine the person's facial expression and body posture as she listens to you with concern and acceptance.

5. If you can, imagine what your compassionate companion would say to you to help you have the courage, wisdom, and strength to face your difficulty. Perhaps this individual will come up with other ways of seeing things or suggest other ways to help you. Perhaps he cannot. It doesn't really matter; what's important is that you experience this person's warmth and kindness, strength and wisdom, and that you feel you can express the worries or feelings that are troubling you without being judged or criticized.

6. Draw the exercise to a close by once more experiencing the compassion flowing from your companion into you. Allow yourself to take pleasure in the feelings of safeness, comfort, and connectedness for a while before you gently bring yourself back into the room.

You may want to note how you felt about this experience, and any new understandings or ways of coping you have learned from your companion.

Exercise 5.12 Being the Focus of Self-Compassion

This exercise is similar to exercise 5.6. The only difference is that you are focusing your compassionate attention on yourself, rather than on someone else.

Find a time and place when you can sit quietly without being disturbed. Now try to create a sense within yourself of being a compassionate person. When you can do this, bring to mind a picture of yourself. Sometimes it can help to use a photograph or look at your face in the mirror. If you have a strong sense of self-dislike or self-criticism for the way you are now, it may be helpful to use an image of you as a child.

When you have an image in your mind, focus on directing toward yourself the same three basic feelings and thoughts:

May I be well.
May I be happy.
May I be free of suffering.

Keep in mind that it's your behavior and intentions that are important; the feelings may follow later. Maybe you can picture the image of you smiling back at your compassionate self and feeling joy and gratitude.

As with the other exercises, try this for a couple of minutes at first, and then gradually build to about ten minutes when you feel ready. Your wandering mind is likely to be very active during this exercise, particularly at first. This is quite normal: just gently and kindly bring it back to the task.

When you have finished, note any thoughts or feelings that emerged while you were doing the exercise or after you completed it that you might want to take away from it.

Exercise 5.13 Focusing Self-Compassion on a Specific Problem

A variation on exercises 5.7 and 5.11, this is the final exercise and the most advanced so far in terms of self-compassion. In this case you are practicing offering yourself compassion for a specific dilemma or difficulty in your life. As with exercise 5.11, try to resist the temptation to choose something that's very painful for you at the moment. You can work your way up to this as you grow in confidence with the exercise.

In this exercise you will imagine kindness and compassion flowing from you toward yourself. It can help to prepare by jotting down the issue you want to work on. You may also want to use the photograph you used for exercise 5.12 or to look in the mirror while doing the exercise. Try to spend at least one minute on each element of the exercise.

Begin by establishing your soothing rhythmic breathing or your safe place.

1. When you feel ready, bring to mind your compassionate self. Imagine yourself expanding as if you were becoming calmer, wiser, stronger, more mature, and better able to help.

2. Pay attention to your body as you remember your feelings of kindness.

3. Now imagine expanding the warmth within your body and imagine it flowing over and around you. Feel your genuine desire for you to be free of suffering and to flourish.

4. Now focus on your tone of voice and the kind of things you would want to say or do to help you with the problem you are facing. If it helps, you can imagine having a conversation with yourself.

5. Next think about your pleasure in being able to be kind to yourself and to accept your own kindness.

6. To finish, focus on combining all these qualities of your compassionate self—the calmness, wisdom, strength, and maturity; the warmth, kindness, and genuine desire to help—in both voice and behavior, and imagine them flowing into you.

When you have finished the exercise, you might want to make some notes about how it felt for you and what you want to take away from it.

SUMMARY

The exercises in this chapter are designed to help you to develop and foster your capacity for compassion, and to learn to direct your compassionate attention toward yourself and others. You may find that these exercises take some effort at first, and you may well find that you do not actually *feel* compassionate, particularly toward yourself, for some time; however, it's crucial that you can at least *act* from a compassionate mind-set before you move on to trying to address your overeating. This is why I say in the exercises that it's important to focus on your intentions and behavior, and that the feelings can follow later. It's quite normal to find genuine feelings of compassion hard to generate, especially if you haven't had much experience of compassion from others, or if you have learned to be self-critical. Eventually, though, these feelings do emerge, usually for other people or things before ourselves. It's also normal for these feelings to come and go, particularly when we are distressed. The key is to continue to practice the exercises to gradually develop the habit of compassion, like a "mental muscle"; as you do so, your brain will gradually change to improve your capacity to give and receive compassion.

It's possible that these exercises may arouse strong feelings or memories. This, too, is not uncommon, and the important thing is to accept these feelings or recollections with compassion as part of you that may need to be cared for.

In the next chapter we will explore how you can use the habits of compassion you have learned to help you manage your emotions, including the more difficult ones, and to find ways to face life's challenges without using food as a source of comfort or solace.

CHAPTER 6

Developing the Skill of Self-Compassion

In the last chapter we explored ways to work on developing compassionate attention, thinking, feeling, and behavior, toward both others and ourselves. This chapter builds on that work in exploring how to use our compassionate focus in a range of practical ways to help us cope with difficult emotions and thoughts, especially those related to eating.

MANAGING DISTRESS COMPASSIONATELY

Many people find that they eat more when they are distressed and that doing this helps them to manage their emotions: anger, pain, sadness, guilt, shame, fear, and so on. Eating can indeed offer some respite from our immediate emotional distress; however, the relief is usually short lived because the underlying issues or causes have not been addressed or resolved. Now, sometimes the things that cause us distress resolve themselves, but even if they do, if we haven't explicitly addressed them and therefore don't know *how* they were resolved, the chances are that next time we are in distress, we will turn to food again for the same immediate relief, rather than tolerate the distressing feelings for long enough to investigate them and sort out where their real origins lie so that we can deal with them once and for all.

You might ask at this point, "Well, if eating works for me every time, why bother to work out what's going on underneath?" Sadly, these overeating solutions are not cost free; they can often lead to cycles of distress and potential health problems. An example of how this pattern can get established is shown in figure 6.1. Of course, it's perfectly understandable that we do our best to manage unpleasant feelings in any way we can, and in the next three chapters we will explore how overeating, often along with a dieting mind-set, has developed to help you do this. So we need to take a compassionate view of these ways of managing distress, not beat ourselves up for having used them. After all, until we have other ways to manage that we can really rely on, we would be very unwise to give up something we know works, even if it only works temporarily.

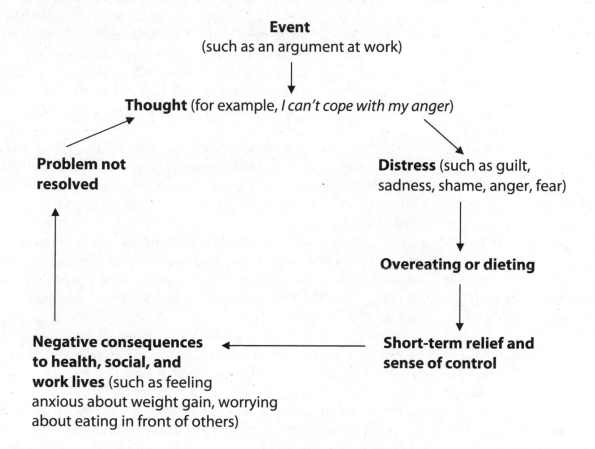

Event
(such as an argument at work)

Thought (for example, *I can't cope with my anger*)

Problem not resolved

Distress (such as guilt, sadness, shame, anger, fear)

Overeating or dieting

Negative consequences to health, social, and work lives (such as feeling anxious about weight gain, worrying about eating in front of others)

Short-term relief and sense of control

Figure 6.1   The Vicious Cycle of Distress and Overeating

It's also helpful to remember that, as we saw in chapters 2 and 3, our bodies do actually respond to overeating in a way that can help us to feel better, and indeed the food industry has made the most of this fact. So we're up against both evolution and big business! In exploring alternative ways to manage our feelings, we will look at both short-term solutions, for those times when our feelings are very intense, and longer-term solutions, in the form of ways to activate our affiliative soothing systems and work on our feelings and desires without using food.

LEARNING TO ACTIVATE YOUR AFFILIATIVE SOOTHING SYSTEM

As we saw in chapter 3, our emotional system for soothing and contentment has evolved to help us manage distress by seeking out and using support from others. When we are very distressed, this system can become overwhelmed so that we use other ways to manage the threats we experience or feel. We live in a world that can be very stressful, and where there can be very little space for us to experience soothing, or even acknowledgment that we might need it. Indeed, our culture often drives us to associate feeling contented with stimulation: buying new things, eating more food, or seeking new thrills and excitement—buzzes linked to the drive system in our brains. Sadly, we have lost touch with our need to keep our emotional systems in balance, and the skills of dealing with stress by calming our minds have been sorely neglected.

Imagine your mind as a hot-water boiler. Boilers have a thermostat that switches off the heat when the water is hot enough. Without a thermostat the water just keeps getting hotter and hotter until the boiler explodes. Our emotional regulation systems are a little like this: we have different ways of reducing the pressure. One is "letting off steam" through distraction, excitement, or eating; another is turning our boilers down by using our affiliative soothing systems.

A little later in this chapter we will consider why we should learn to tolerate our emotions when they are very "hot," and how we can do this. However, this takes confidence that we can manage our feelings, and developing the skill of self-soothing is a very important step toward learning to do this. So in this section of the chapter we will first explore how you can lower your overall "emotional temperature" by turning on your affiliative soothing system.

In the previous chapter you learned ways to bring your affiliative soothing system into action using your imagination. We will now explore how to use the things we can physically sense around us to do the same thing. We will go through various techniques; the key is to find the ones that help you.

Learning to use your senses of sight, hearing, smell, and touch, and mindfully focusing on your sensory experiences, can help you to activate your affiliative soothing system. Indeed, some therapy programs use the experience of nature walks specifically to do this. Here you are trying to immerse yourself in a sensory experience that helps you to feel calm and contented in a way that feels safe for you. It's likely that you will find that some sensory experiences do this better for you than others. Sometimes the experiences we focus on in our safe places can give us clues to what works best for us. Play with all of your senses to find which ones soothe you. You may well find that different sensory experiences affect you more strongly at different times; this is perfectly normal.

In the following exercises you will explore how to use your senses of sight, hearing, touch, and smell to activate your affiliative soothing system. Taste can also be a powerful way to bring the affiliative soothing system into play; however, as you are trying to break the association between eating and feeling soothed, it's more helpful to avoid this sense as a way to soothe yourself, at least until you are sure that it won't lead to overeating.

Using Your Senses to Activate Your Affiliative Soothing System

SOOTHING BY SIGHT

Sight, and the things we see, can be very powerful in triggering the affiliative soothing system. As with all the senses, to find out whether this works for you, the important thing is to try to immerse yourself in the experience, to pay mindful attention to the things you can see.

In choosing what you find soothing to look at, take care to avoid anything associated with unpleasant memories or events. People I have worked with have found it soothing to look at a beautiful flower, a lit candle or a burning fire, an intricate shell, or a smooth pebble. Alternatively, you may find it more soothing to look at a wider range of things, in which case you may want to visit a museum or gallery, sit in the lobby of a beautiful hotel, take a walk and look at nature around you, or go out in the middle of the night and watch the stars. Some people prefer to make their own scrapbooks, or even to make one space in a room visually appealing so they can control the range of things they want to look at.

Whatever you choose, it's likely that your mind will wander when you look at things you find soothing. Again, as with the breathing and safe-place exercises, you are not *forcing* yourself to concentrate. Rather, just notice where your mind wanders to and gently return to the visual experience you find soothing. As with all of these exercises, the more you practice, the better you will become at using your senses to soothe yourself. Some days you will find it easier than others to use your senses to soothe yourself; it can be particularly difficult if you are already close to "boiling over."

SOOTHING BY HEARING

We know that humans can be very sensitive to sound. Babies in the womb can be calmed by certain types of music or startled by loud noises. Again, the key is to discover the sounds you find soothing. You may be drawn to beautiful or soothing music, but again, we may need to be a little careful in what music we choose. Musicians throughout the ages have used music to create certain moods in us, so because the idea here is to call up a feeling of being soothed, it's probably best to avoid loud, invigorating, or sad music! Some people find the sounds of nature (waves, birds, rainfall, or rustling leaves, for example) to be soothing. I personally find some voices soothing and comforting; you may find that a particular actor's voice does this for you, or it may be the voice of someone you know personally. Some people I know use audiobooks to help soothe themselves.

SOOTHING BY SMELL

The fastest way to a man's (or woman's) heart—actually, his brain—is not through his stomach, as the popular saying has it; it's through his nose! Our sense of smell is our fastest-acting sensory system, which makes sense in evolutionary terms, because we can often smell danger long before we can see or hear it, let alone touch it. You may have tried to incorporate smells in your safe place and compassionate companion exercises. If not, this can be a good opportunity to try to discover what smells you find soothing. You could use your favorite perfume or lotions. To save money you can try them at the perfume counter first! You might find that natural smells are more soothing; you can experiment with the smells of different flowers, fruits, or other natural products (like pine).

SOOTHING BY TOUCH

Touch can be a powerful source of soothing. Studies of infant monkeys found that if they were fed without receiving comforting touch, they suffered serious difficulties in their development and grew up to be fearful. There's now a lot of evidence that affectionate touch has many positive effects on us. When we're anxious, being touched by another person who we feel cares for us can reduce our anxiety more quickly than even the most powerful antianxiety drugs. This is probably not news to you; it comes to us automatically to reach out and hold our children, friends, or partners if they are in distress. The key here is to allow yourself the opportunity to experience touch in a way that feels safe for you, which can include planning more hugs into your day or having a massage. Even if other people are not around, you can massage yourself or even imagine being held (for example, by your compassionate companion).

Human touch is not the only tactile experience that can soothe us. Pets can have a similar effect; indeed, some hospital wards even have a visiting-pet system, because stroking a pet can help soothe patients and even speed up their healing process. Even something that simulates the feel of a pet (for example, a fur-covered hot-water bottle) can be soothing for some of us.

Other tactile experiences you may find soothing include smoothing a creamy lotion on your hands or body, placing a cold compress on your forehead, or even brushing your hair for a long time. Physical warmth can also be soothing, for example, having a pleasantly warm bath, sunbathing (don't overdo this, though, and make sure to put on some sunscreen!), or cuddling a hot-water bottle. For other people the experience of slipping into fresh, clean sheets or silky clothes, or sitting back into a comfortable chair can be very soothing.

You may find that you prefer to be soothed by just one of your senses or a combination. The key is to be mindful of the experience and to allow yourself to take joy and pleasure from the experience of being physically soothed. Some people prefer to take a more active approach to being physically soothed, for example, by taking part in formal relaxation training or meditation classes. Again, this is absolutely fine, as long as you find that it activates your affiliative soothing system. Remember that your wandering mind may pull you away from any of these experiences and that you may need to gently refocus on the experience of being soothed.

Aim to practice your physical self-soothing skills every day. You may wish to draw up a list of the types of things you can try and to practice each one for several days before moving on to try another. Over time you will discover your own menu of things you find physically soothing. Sometimes you can get the best of both worlds by practicing your physical self-soothing and then moving into your compassion exercises.

Strategies for Coping with a Crisis

Practicing soothing skills is not a way to stop bad things from happening or stop yourself from feeling the ups and downs of life. No matter how good we have become at self-soothing, we are all bound at some time to experience events, emotions, or memories we find difficult to deal with. When this happens, it's easy to fall back on unhealthy eating, overeating, or dieting to get us through; so what we need are other compassion-focused ways of riding these waves of difficult emotions and situations. There are basically two ways of doing this: one is to try to *distract* yourself from the emotional distress you are experiencing; the other is to learn to compassionately *tolerate* that distress.

So let's explore some techniques you can use to help you distract yourself from your distress or to tolerate it, and thus enable you to cope in new ways with the ups and downs and crises of life. It's important to note that these skills are not about resolving the difficulty underlying your distress, but are designed to help you to cope with it and to support you while you try to deal with the underlying issue, that is, to give you some space for what may be a longer-term task. These are skills for handling painful events and emotions, accepting life as it is in the moment, when we can't make things better right away.

In the longer term it's more helpful to learn how to tolerate distress for at least long enough to understand what's causing it, and we explore how you can do this a little later in the chapter. However, this skill can take some time to develop, and even then you may still want to have confidence in your ability to manage your distress without using food.

DISTRACTION TECHNIQUES

Sometimes we can get as far as deciding we won't use old coping behaviors (such as overeating), but do not feel that we have gotten to the stage where we can tolerate our distress or rely on new ways of coping. At these times, distracting ourselves from our distress can be very helpful. Distractions, which can be practical, mental, emotional, or some combination, can be a great way of buying time to allow our impulses to subside (for example, the impulse to have an extra cracker as a treat) and help us realize we have more control over our impulses than we thought we had.

Practical distractions. Specific practical activities can include hobbies (such as knitting, craft work, or painting) or sports activities, going to social or cultural events, calling or visiting a friend, playing computer games, going for a walk, doing paid or voluntary work, reading, working puzzles, gardening, even doing housework! It can be helpful to make a list of all the activities you could use as distractions before you actually need them.

Of course, our minds will still tend to wander, and some things can be more absorbing than others. Some activities, too, have an inbuilt limited time span—for example, a movie on DVD comes to an end—and you may need to plan a variety of activities so that there's always something else you can do. It can also be very easy to take some distractions to extremes (for example, overworking or exercising excessively). So it's also important not to let any distraction become too much of a habit or to get too far drawn into something you can't afford to do because of either the time it takes or the money it costs. Remember, this is simply a short-term way to help you cope.

Practical activities that also help other people can have the double benefit of providing a useful distraction and also helping to activate your compassionate mind, for example, volunteering, giving something to someone, making something nice for someone, or planning and doing something surprising and thoughtful for someone that you know the person will like.

Simple physical sensations can be helpful as a very short-term distraction, for example, holding something cold, squeezing a rubber ball very hard, standing under a warm shower, listening to very loud music, dancing to a CD, or singing out loud.

If you have no planned distractions available or if you are in a place where it's hard to do any of them, you can still practice paying mindful attention to whatever day-to-day activities you're doing, for example, focusing your entire attention on the physical sensations that accompany tasks like walking to stores, hanging the laundry, doing the dishes, and so on. Again, the key thing is to pay mindful attention to the sensations or tasks.

Mental distractions. Paying mindful attention to your physical distractions can help shift your focus away from your distress. Your safe-place imagery can also be used to provide a soothing distraction from painful thoughts and feelings. There's also a range of other mental distractions people have found helpful.

Some of these are imagery exercises that focus on doing something with our distress to put it away from us, for example, imagining your painful emotions draining out of you like water out a pipe, or floating away like a balloon. Other people prefer the idea of putting their suffering away but knowing that they can come back to it at a later date, for example, imagining that it's in a box they can lock away. Some like to leave their suffering with their compassionate companions.

Another technique is to practice bringing other thoughts to mind to give yourself something else to focus on. These thoughts may be positive images of the future (for example, planning your next vacation) or the past (for example, happy memories). Alternatively you can work impersonal mental tasks or puzzles, like a difficult chess or sudoku problem, or a mathematical task; even counting the bricks in a wall takes concentration and thus can give temporary respite. Tasks that engage your imagination as well as your rational thoughts, such as following an absorbing book or TV program, can also help to distract you.

Emotional distractions. Often we find ourselves so caught up in our emotions that it's very difficult to find a way out of them or indeed to feel that we have any control over our emotional states. At these times it can be helpful to break up these feelings in some way so we can step outside them to explore compassionate ways to accept and manage them. Again, it can help to plan how you might do this before you get into an intense emotional state, and even to practice learning to switch your moods deliberately. This is very useful in giving you a greater sense of control over your feelings. You might want to start by getting into a positive mood, interrupting it for a little while, and then bringing it back again. A good way to do this is by using music or TV programs. Start by listening to or watching something that makes you feel happy, perhaps an upbeat piece of music you really like or a favorite comedy program; then switch to something a little more sad, perhaps songs of unrequited love or a tearjerker; and finally play something that makes you happy again. Notice how your mood can change and how you can choose to allow yourself to go along with this.

You may wish to put together an "emotional library" of music, films, books, soaps, or art that you know can influence your mood. You can use it when you feel stuck with an emotion you find distressing. It doesn't really matter what mood you use to switch out of this emotional state, as long as it's different from the one you are struggling with. For example, if you feel angry, try not to watch a revenge film; you could watch something that frightens you, makes you cry, or makes you laugh, as long as it doesn't exacerbate your feelings of anger, even on behalf of someone else!

The key to all of these distraction techniques is to find the ones that work for you, to have some available in advance, and to give yourself permission to use them whenever you need them. It can be really helpful to experiment with them when you don't need them. Avoid experimenting with them when you feel really upset. A good way to begin is to draw up a list of possibilities and try to practice a new one every day for a few days, until you find out which ones work best for you.

DECIDING TO TOLERATE DISTRESS

Distress tolerance is a key element of compassion (take a look back at the compassion circle in figure 4.3). It's also a skill that most of us have to learn. When we face difficult situations, setbacks, or disappointments, we are unlikely to think about how much distress we can tolerate; on the contrary, we are more likely to think about how to *stop* feeling bad. So we will tend to rely on whatever way of doing this we've gotten used to, and if this is overeating, reaching for the chocolate bar or potato chips, then so be it.

One of the things a compassion focus can help us with is tolerating some degree of suffering to help us gain more control over whether or not to eat when the impulse arises. Now, of course, the key reason for learning to tolerate distress is to find new ways of coping with it, not simply to prove how much pain we can take! There will be some kinds of distress or discomfort we can choose to subject ourselves to, such as those from giving up unhealthy eating habits, and there will be others we may be able to plan for in advance, such as those resulting from an argument at work. In both kinds of situation it can be helpful to use your compassionate mind to help yourself consider the pros and cons of tolerating the distress; for example, in the first case you might want to think about the possible benefits of tolerating the urge to reach for the chocolate bar without giving in to it. By acknowledging your desires in this way without responding to them, you can learn to act differently in the face of certain emotions.

Keep in mind that many different emotions, at a range of different levels of intensity, might be driving your eating. For example, we can feel angry, fed up, deprived and deserving of food, lonely, or simply desirous of a good time. And we can feel anything from mild irritation or frustration to utter misery or fury.

If you do decide to practice tolerating distress, be guided by the skills of self-compassion you learned earlier in this chapter. Don't set impossible goals or see a return to your previous coping strategies as a failure. Your ability to tolerate distress is another mental ability that you may need to develop slowly and to nurture. Here's an exercise that will help you to practice this useful skill.

Exercise 6.1 Learning to Tolerate Distress

Bring to mind your compassionate image; this can be either your compassionate self or your compassionate companion. Focus on a feeling of genuinely and kindly wanting to help yourself learn to understand the things that distress you, and to allow yourself to experience your emotions. What would your compassionate image say to help you allow yourself to face and explore your distress without resorting immediately to overeating or dieting?

You might want to include some of the things people I have worked with have found helpful, for example:

- *I am suffering these feelings for a reason, so in the future I will have these feelings less often.*

- *I can learn to experience and learn from my distress.*

- *My distress will pass; I can learn to ride the wave.*

- *I am strong enough to bear my distress.*

- *This work is part of the long-term changes I can make to turn overeating into a thing of the past.*

In the following space, add anything else your compassionate image can think of:

-

-

-

Thinking about the disadvantages of *not* tolerating your current distress can also be helpful. For example, you might call to mind what happened in the past when you used overeating or dieting to escape the distress of the moment, perhaps feeling cross with yourself and even more distressed after overeating, or feeling first elated and then miserable after a diet that didn't last. However, if you do this, it's also important to remember that at that time, you did not have the choices your new skills give you now; in other words, don't beat yourself up for having dealt with distress in the best way you could at the time.

So again, from the perspective of your compassionate image, try to write in the following space the downsides of not learning to tolerate your feelings:

-

-

-

-

-

Next, try to make a plan for the type of feelings you want to learn to tolerate and for how long. To start with, you may want to work on the less painful or distressing feelings you associate with overeating. For example, some people begin by working on tolerating the urge to overeat when they are happy or to reward themselves, and to aim at first to resist the urge to overeat for about five minutes. You may then decide to go ahead and eat, or you might decide to use some of the self-soothing or distraction activities we explored earlier in this chapter. The point here is not to *stop* yourself completely from overeating straightaway, but to learn at least to *postpone* overeating for a fixed length of time. As you develop your confidence in your ability to tolerate and explore your feelings, you can work on tolerating more-painful feelings and doing this for longer periods of time.

The key in this exercise is to use the time you are tolerating these feelings to be mindful of the things that caused you to overeat in the first place, perhaps even writing them down. Later in the book we will explore a more structured way of doing this by using a diary. Some days you will find tolerating your feelings easier than others; as always, just go at your own pace, and use your compassionate mind to guide you and help you to understand when and why your feelings arise.

COMPASSIONATE THINKING AND BEHAVIOR

As we discovered in chapter 4, the compassionate mind has a number of different elements, which we divided into attributes and skills. These elements relate to both our emotional and our rational minds, and to our actions, that is, to the way we feel, think, and behave. So far you have been learning to bring your affiliative soothing system and compassionate emotions into play, using imagery to focus your compassionate attention on yourself and others. In this section we will explore ways you can develop your ability to think and act compassionately.

Compassionate Thinking

You have seen how the mind-set you are in can affect the way you think about things. For example, if you are in a dieting mind-set, you are more likely to think about the achievements that dieting will bring you, but also all the reasons why you think you need to lose weight, and to be very self-critical if you break your diet. If you are in a compassionate mind-set, on the other hand, you are more likely to focus on your discomfort or distress and to look for ways to alleviate it with care and kindness. The aim of compassionate thinking is to help you stand back from the flow of your thoughts and think in a more balanced way, so that you are not too biased or at the mercy of your emotions.

Exercise 6.2 Compassionate Thought Balancing

One way to develop your capacity for compassionate thinking is to note the way you think when you are in different mind-sets. You can then use your compassionate mind to develop other ways of thinking. Challenging your thinking can be very effective in helping you to learn to think differently. The key is not only to come up with alternative ways of thinking but also to express them compassionately, which we can call "compassionate thought balancing." You might like to give it a try now, using the examples in figure 6.2. First imagine reading the "compassionate alternative thoughts" out loud in a very critical or cold voice. Do you think someone would find this helpful? Now read the same thoughts out loud again, this time as if you really wanted to help and care for someone who was struggling with overeating. Spend a few minutes thinking about the difference and how you would feel about being on the receiving end of these statements being said to you in the two different ways.

Of course, learning to think and talk to yourself in this way, and then learning to believe your new thoughts, is a skill you may need to practice. You can use the blank form in worksheet 6.1 for this (there are a couple of more blank sheets at the back of the book, which you can photocopy if you need more). First write down your overeating (or dieting) thoughts in the left-hand column. You don't need to develop alternatives straightaway. Sometimes we are so caught up in our usual mind-sets that it's difficult to think differently. However, if you focus on your compassionate image or your compassionate self using the exercises in chapter 5, you will probably then be able to come back to your list and come up with alternative ways of thinking about these things. When you have finished, you can then practice reading them aloud. Choose the alternatives you think are most likely to help you, and perhaps keep them with you, either written down on little flash cards in your wallet or purse, or as text messages to yourself, so that you have them at hand to help you practice these new ways of thinking whenever thoughts crop up that are likely to make you think about overeating.

Overeating Thoughts	Compassionate Alternative Thoughts
There's something wrong with me because I overeat.	Overeating is very common. People overeat for a whole lot of reasons: because they are hungry, tired, upset, or happy. Humans evolved to overeat, so it's normal to have the urge to do so.
I'm weak because I overeat.	There are lots of reasons why I don't want to overeat, but stopping this is pretty tricky. It's a sign of how difficult my brain and body are to manage that I overeat, not a sign that I am weak. It takes a lot of strength and courage to want to work on giving up overeating.
I'll never be able to stop overeating.	It is sad and frustrating that stopping overeating has been so difficult for me in the past. People can and do learn to change the way they eat and deal with their feelings, but this will take some time. I can give myself the chance to see if the ways of doing it in the book can help me.
When I lose some weight, I will start to make changes in my life and be happy.	Losing weight might happen if I stop overeating and dieting, but it's not fair to stop living my life until I lose some weight. I deserve to be happy and as healthy as I can be, whatever my weight, and I will start doing things to care for myself regardless of my weight!
If I don't overeat, I can't cope with my feelings.	It is okay to be worried about this; I have used overeating for years to help me manage my feelings. I can gradually learn to change this, but it's not the end of the world if I do need to overeat from time to time. I will get better at learning to manage my feelings the more I work on it.
I can't refuse to eat when everyone around me is eating.	Most people find this hard; after all, eating is a very social thing. But I can choose when I eat; other people around me do choose not to eat at times, and I don't think they are bad or rude. I can also choose to eat with them if I want, but perhaps eat a bit less than they do.

Figure 6.2   An Example of Compassionate Thought Balancing

Worksheet 6.1
Compassionate Thought Balancing

Overeating Thoughts	Compassionate Alternative Thoughts

Exercise 6.3 Getting Outside Your Mind-Set

Another way to develop your compassionate thinking is to explore the ways you normally think when you are in a particular mind-set. For example, what kinds of thoughts do you have when you are in a dieting mind-set or a food-as-fun mind-set? You can start by jotting them down now. For example, in a dieting mind-set you might think, *I deserve to eat if I'm unhappy*, *Dieting will make me feel better about myself*, *Overeating is something I can never resolve*, and so on. Gently explore these thoughts, and see if you can develop compassionate alternatives by using your compassionate mind to try to answer the following questions.

- *Is this thinking helpful to me?*

- *Would I think like this if I weren't in this* (comfort-eating, dieting, food-as-fun, and so on) *mind-set?*

- *Would I teach a child or friend to think like this?*

- *If not, how would I like to teach a child or friend to think about these things?*

- *How might I think about this when I am at my compassionate best?*

- *What would help me in the long run?*

- *Is this thinking compassionate?*

The key point in this exercise is to try to be mindful of your thoughts and to see how they can be pulled in certain ways, depending on how you feel. This exercise will help you to stand back a little and observe your thoughts, enabling you to find a compassionate, fair, and balanced approach.

SELF-CRITICAL THINKING VS. SELF-COMPASSIONATE SELF-CORRECTION

Some people believe that self-criticism is the only way to make themselves do things, succeed, or be good. For example, a person might say, "If I didn't kick myself, I'd never stop eating." Or some people might believe that unless they are critical and keep themselves on their toes, they will be lazy, so they use self-bullying and self-criticism to drive themselves. Some people learn self-criticism in childhood, if they have had parents and teachers who tended to focus more on their errors than on the things they did well and the good things about them. As a result, these people, as children, become good at self-criticism and self-punishment, but poor at seeing their own good points and unused to rewarding and valuing themselves. However, it's not always the case that self-criticism is learned in childhood; it's important to remember that criticism based on shaming is very common in our society. We are likely to experience it at school, but we can also see it in our treatment of the mistakes of politicians and celebrities in our daily papers. So even if we didn't have direct experience of frequent criticism while growing up, there's so much of it around us that it can be hard for us to develop other ways of relating to ourselves.

Of course, there will be times when things we do don't go as we would like them to, and when we want to change what we do for the better. Compassion is certainly not about an "anything goes" approach! So what we are aiming at is a way of correcting ourselves kindly and gently, with compassion and understanding that change is often a difficult and long-term process.

It can be helpful to keep the differences between shame-based self-criticism or self-attacking and compassion-based self-correction at hand so that you can more easily figure out which one you're using when you try to correct yourself. The key differences are summarized in figure 6.3.

Compassionate self-correction is focused on:	Shame-based self-criticism is focused on:
• The desire to improve	• The desire to condemn and punish
• Growth and enhancement	• Punishing past errors and often looking backward
• Looking forward	
• Encouragement, support, and kindness	• Anger, frustration, contempt, and disappointment
• Building on positives (such as seeing what you did well and then considering learning points)	• Focusing on faults and fear of being found out
• Focusing on specific areas and qualities of self	• Focusing on the whole self
• Focusing on and hoping for success	• Focusing on fear of failure
• Increasing the chances of engagement	• Increasing chances of avoidance and withdrawal

Source: Adapted with permission from Gilbert, P. 2009. *The Compassionate Mind.* London: Constable and Robinson.

Figure 6.3   Compassionate Self-Correction vs. Shame-Based Self-Criticism

You can see that shame-based self-criticism involves the emotions associated with the threat/protection system, such as anger and fear. Letting go of this type of self-criticism can help you to learn new ways to manage your feelings and to deal with the urges and desires that cause you to overeat. Compassionate self-correction focuses on and encourages your real desire to do your best and to improve.

To see how this works, consider two sports coaches teaching a young child. One focuses on the child's faults and picks on her when she makes mistakes. The other focuses on what the child does well, encourages the child to improve and learn from her mistakes, and offers clear guidance. Which one will foster the child's confidence? Which one is the child more likely to want to work with? Which one do you prefer? Attacking self-criticism can often make us feel disheartened so that we just want to give up and hide away. If we really want to reduce our overeating (or correct other aspects of our behavior), we stand a better chance of doing so if we get into the habit of using *compassionate* self-correction when things go wrong or when we start to feel frustrated with ourselves.

Compassionate self-correction is based on being mindful, openhearted, and honest about our mistakes, acknowledging our genuine wish to learn from them. No one wakes up in the morning and thinks, *Oh, I think I will make a real mess of my eating today, just for the hell of it.* Most of us would like to eat healthily, most of us would like to avoid mistakes, most of us would like to avoid being out of control with our temper, and so on. Compassionate self-correction recognizes this. Self-criticism, on the other hand, deals in fear and anger; it's concerned with punishment for things we have already done. The problem is that we can't change a single moment of the past; we can only change the future, and beating ourselves up is really not the best way of helping ourselves to do better.

Making the transition from shame-based self-criticism to compassion-based self-correction can be difficult at first, but with practice it will become easier. You may well already be turning more readily to compassionate thoughts as a result of your imagery work, and it can be really helpful to keep a note of such thoughts as they develop, perhaps even keeping a list with you to look at when you are tempted to return to self-criticism. Later on we will look at how you can develop this supportive practice of compassionate self-correction using techniques such as compassionate letter writing, described in detail in chapter 14.

Compassionate Behavior

Behaving compassionately is doing helpful, kind, or thoughtful things to help ourselves and others deal with difficulties, setbacks, and suffering; and develop, flourish, and improve.

Many people with eating problems have told me that they have been able to *act* in more compassionate ways before they can routinely *think* in a compassionate way. This takes us back to the comparison with "method acting" I suggested when introducing the imagery work in chapter 5; it's often the case that *doing* things compassionately for ourselves will not necessarily be associated with the *feelings* of self-compassion, at least in the early stages. As I stated earlier, this is just fine; it is our intentions and behaviors that matter; the feelings can and will come along later.

Learning to behave compassionately toward yourself can help maintain your compassionate motivation. There will, of course, be times when you're angry or frustrated and don't want to follow through on your commitment to look after yourself properly. This is entirely understandable, but if you can, to the best of your ability, just notice and be compassionate to your anger and frustration, and act compassionately toward yourself; it will be easier to pick yourself up and carry on. Sometimes we just need to ride the waves of emotion and wait for the intensity of our feelings to subside.

In later chapters of this book, you will work on developing compassionate behavior in relation to your eating habits and your body's needs for activity and rest. For now, you might want to try to practice acting compassionately toward yourself for perhaps five minutes every day. If you are one of the many people who find it harder to be kind to themselves than to others, you might find it easier to approach this by doing something compassionate for another person or animal for the first week and then gradually adding things you do for yourself.

Before you actually try to do this, it can be helpful to put together a list of things you have done or seen others do that you consider to be compassionate. You might also find it helpful to talk to people you know or to notice what they do, to find out how they are kind to themselves. Following are some ideas to get you started:

- Do one thing, no matter how small, that's specifically designed to be enjoyable (for example, take a warm, scented bath).

- Make time to speak kindly to someone. Try to find out a little bit about the person.

- Each day do one spontaneous act of kindness for someone that doesn't involve food or eating.

- Practice one act of forgiveness to yourself, no matter how small, especially if you tried something and weren't as successful as you wanted to be, or if you had a relapse of some kind.

- Set aside time to practice some of your self-compassion or distress management exercises.

- Spend five minutes remembering kindnesses that occurred in the day.

KEEPING DIARIES OF YOUR PRACTICE

People often keep diaries to record their thoughts and feelings, especially if they're feeling low. Keeping a diary of all your practice with compassion can be really helpful in enabling you to see how you are doing. You can use it to record the specific exercises you do from this book, but also to keep notes of your occasional practice, your personal observations, what your compassionate mind says, and your successes, no matter how small. This can help you to keep track of your progress and to see which of the exercises are turning out to be most helpful for you. Figure 6.4 shows an example of a week's completed practice diary, and worksheet 6.2 gives you a blank form you can use for your own diary if you wish. (There are a couple of more copies at the back of the book.)

BLOCKS TO COMPASSION

Remember David, from chapter 3? He lost a lot of weight after a period of illness and then got stuck in a cycle of yo-yo dieting and self-recrimination. When he began to work on self-compassion, his reactions were typical of many. David recognized that dieting had made him feel better about himself, helping him feel in control and more confident. Looking back at the past, he came to see how his eating habits had changed alongside the events in his life, and this helped him to realize how he had come to rely on overeating to manage some very difficult experiences in his past. However, although he could see the logic of why overeating had helped him, he could not stop criticizing himself for his "weakness" in needing food to comfort him or for the unintended consequences of overeating, such as weight gain. David also found it very difficult to be compassionate with himself over the difficult events in his life. He could see that if they had happened to someone else, he would feel sad for them and angry on their behalf, and would want to help them, but he felt nothing for himself. When I expressed my compassion for his difficult experiences, David found this very difficult to accept; he even talked about ending our work together, as he felt he didn't deserve and couldn't cope with other people caring for him.

Fortunately, David was able to explore and overcome some of his blocks to compassion using the exercises in this section of the chapter. At first he was not able to *feel* compassion for himself, but he was prepared to give *behaving* compassionately a try. He found that this helped him to recognize the positive changes in his mood and eating that caring for himself gave him, and he gradually learned to value his capacity for self-compassion.

Just like David, many of us are not used to thinking compassionately about ourselves, and some of us find it difficult to accept and use compassion offered by others. There can be many reasons for this. Some of them are the result of the culture we live in; others may be related to painful experiences in our pasts

Day	Type of Practice, Time, and Duration	Comments: What Was Helpful?
Thur.	10:00 a.m. Soothing rhythmic breathing Compassionate self	Felt calmer, less stressed. Noticed mind wandering, but managed to keep focusing on breathing. Tricky to get started, but began to see the point; thought about someone I wanted to be compassionate to.
Fri.	Soothing rhythmic breathing in bed Compassionate self on the bus	Mixed today as busy. Useful to slow down, refocus, and think about the self I would like to be. Able to get in touch with a desire in myself to be kind and calm. Recognized that I can be quite self-critical, but can slow down and refocus.
Sat.	Very busy In bathtub, 15 min. compassionate relaxing	Did occasionally think about being mindful and taking a moment to slow down. Also thought about my compassionate color, but lots to do with the family. Only thought about it toward the end.
Sun.	Very busy with family, so no specific time	Trying to think about compassion at different points in the day.
Mon.	11:00 a.m. Half hour focused on both compassionate self and compassionate imagery	Recognize I need to spend time practicing. When I can make time, it does help. Working with my image was difficult; it tended to come and go, but I just allowed that to happen and began to have a sense of an image rather than seeing anything clearly.
Tue.	Similar to Monday	
Wed.	2:00 p.m. Compassionate self	Have a friend who's been having difficulties, so practiced imagining compassionate self and just being compassionate to her. Felt I could sense this desire in me for her to feel better. Recognizing I do have compassionate feelings.
Comments on week's practice		Trying to bring my practice into everyday life as well as set time aside. Recognizing that it's about remembering to attend and focus on compassionate things.

Source: Reproduced with kind permission from the Compassionate Mind Foundation website (www.compassionatemind.co.uk).

Figure 6.4   Sample Compassion Practice Diary

Worksheet 6.2 Compassion Diary

Day	Type of Practice, Time, and Duration	Comments: What Was Helpful?

Source: Reproduced with kind permission from the Compassionate Mind Foundation website.

or the present. In this section we will explore some of the most common blocks to allowing ourselves to accept compassion from others, and to offering it to ourselves.

These common blocks to compassion include:

• Confusing compassion with pity

• Feeling that people who need compassion are weak

• Seeing acceptance of compassion as self-indulgent or selfish

• Seeing compassion as a soft option

• Seeing compassion as letting your guard down or letting yourself off the hook

• Believing that compassion means getting rid of feelings (for example, never feeling angry if people upset or hurt you)

For some people, the idea of compassion can trigger difficult, emotionally charged memories or strong feelings that can also act as blocks, including:

• Anger for a lack of compassion experienced either now or in the past

• Grief for pain they have been through or are going through now

• Fear or anxiety, either that compassion will be taken away or that it will come at a cost

Many people find one or more of these blocks getting in the way of their work on developing self-compassion skills and accepting compassion from others, even others they know they can trust. Of course, some people may simply never have thought they might be able to use this aspect of their personalities to help themselves as well as other people, possibly because they have found other coping strategies (like comfort eating or dieting) to be effective. If this is the case for you or if you don't have any blocks to compassion, you may wish to skip the exercises in the rest of this chapter and move straight on to the next chapter. However, if you have any concerns about developing your compassionate mind, for any reason, it might be a good idea to try these four exercises before you move on. Also, if you find that blocks come up when you try any of the other exercises in the book, you can come back to these exercises to help you work through them.

Before using the exercises to explore your own blocks to self-compassion, it may be helpful to consider some of the common blocks in a little more detail.

Confusing Compassion with Pity

Although compassion can bring to the fore our sympathy and desire to alleviate distress, unlike pity it also recognizes our own and other people's wisdom, courage, and resilience. Compassion starts from recognizing that in our common humanity, we all, at times, struggle to cope with life. Pitying other people, by contrast, tends to be associated with feeling superior to them. Thus many people have a strong aversion to being pitied, associating it with being seen as inferior or weak. Compassion combines sympathy with respect.

Feeling That Those Who Need Compassion Are Weak

Interestingly, we tend not to think in this way when we offer compassion to others. We see them as being in a temporary state of suffering, which we may be able to help relieve. We are more likely to think *we* are weak if we need compassion. This may be related to the emphasis our modern culture places on self-sufficiency or to concerns about what other people will do if we show them any sign of "weakness." This is often related to the confusion of compassion with pity, noted previously.

Seeing Acceptance of Compassion as Self-Indulgent or Selfish

When we are compassionate toward others, we tend to put their needs first. Thus many of us recoil from the idea that self-compassion may involve putting our own needs first, having been brought up to believe that this is wrong. In fact, allowing ourselves to experience compassion from others or give it to ourselves is often an important step in enabling us to be *more* concerned for others. For example, when we are stuck in a comfort-food mind-set, we can be very single-minded about eating, and when we are stuck in a dieting mind-set, we may think about little other than our diets. In both cases, this narrow focus may mean that we unintentionally neglect the needs of others, because we are just not aware of them. Opening ourselves to compassion, as we have seen, can also mean that we will be more open to being compassionate with others.

Seeing Compassion as a Soft Option

Actually, developing self-compassion is hard work! Self-compassion requires us to develop the courage to address our difficulties, which often involves facing problems we have used our dieting or comfort-eating mind-sets to avoid because we felt we couldn't cope with them. It also encourages us to face and take responsibility for our actions, including those that hurt ourselves or others. Self-compassion can also require us to be assertive with others, for example, resisting the urge to eat if they offer us food we don't want to eat.

Before you begin the next group of four exercises, you may want to start with a brief period of reflection, just a minute or so, on a time when you experienced compassion from others or tried to offer yourself compassion, as in exercises 5.9 and 5.12 in the previous chapter. Notice the thoughts and feelings that come up as you do this and try to jot them down. After about a minute, use your soothing rhythmic breathing to help refocus your attention, and step out of the reflection.

The four exercises are presented here as a group, but you may want to do each one separately and to plan to do something soothing or distracting after you finish each exercise.

Exercise 6.4 My Personal Blocks to Experiencing Compassion from Others

Please list here any thoughts or ideas you think might stop you from letting other people offer you compassion. You might find it helpful to review the common blocks listed at the beginning of this section.

-
-
-
-
-

Exercise 6.5 My Personal Blocks to Developing Self-Compassion

Please list here any thoughts or ideas you think might prevent you from being compassionate toward yourself. Again, you might find it helpful to review the common blocks listed at the beginning of this section.

-
-
-
-
-

When you have done both of these exercises, it can be helpful to consider the blocks you have identified from the perspective of your compassionate image. What might your compassionate image suggest as reasons why you have these blocks? You might even try writing a compassionate letter about the blocks you have to allowing yourself to experience compassion. (For detailed guidance on how to go about this, see chapter 14.) Your letter may help you find ways around these blocks.

If you wish, you can use the next two exercises to draw together your thoughts on how you might manage these blocks. Again, you can use you compassionate image to help you.

Exercise 6.6 Coping with Blocks
to Compassion from Others

Try to list anything you could do or say to help you cope with your blocks to accepting compassion from others.

-
-
-
-
-

Exercise 6.7 Coping with Blocks to Self-Compassion

Try to list anything you could do or say to help you cope with your blocks to accepting compassion from yourself.

-
-
-
-
-

Another way around these blocks is to simply note these beliefs as common, but to practice compassion anyway. Think of it as being like physiotherapy. If you had a weak muscle in your leg, perhaps as a result of injury, you wouldn't tell yourself you didn't deserve to have a stronger muscle. So why not build your compassionate skills anyway, and then, if you decide you don't want to use them, that's up to you. However, you can only *choose* not to be self-compassionate if you have the ability to be self-compassionate, so to make that genuine choice, you will need to learn the skills.

Earlier in this chapter we explored learning how to tolerate distress. If you are not used to receiving compassion or have a lot of blocks to this, you may also find that this skill can help you to "get used to" compassion. Perhaps you can work out how much compassion you can let yourself have by using exercise 5.9 from the previous chapter or deciding to tolerate other people's kindness to you.

SUMMARY

In this chapter we have explored some additional ways of managing feelings of discomfort and distress. It can be useful to keep a record of ways you find most helpful and the situations in which they're most likely to be effective. This way you can build a tool kit of new ways to cope with the situations and experiences that trouble you, before you begin working on changing your eating habits.

Many of us find it difficult to allow ourselves to experience compassion from other people and, particularly, from ourselves, and we have also explored this difficulty a little further in this chapter. It's important to remember that though it's very common to experience blocks to compassion, we can learn to think and behave in more compassionate ways even before we learn to feel compassion, so we can make progress in developing these key skills that will help us to deal with the problem of overeating.

CHAPTER 7

Why Do We Overeat? A Compassionate Approach

Before you start working on a more compassionate approach to your eating and your body, it can be very helpful to understand why you overeat now. The particular reasons that apply in your individual case may include events and influences in the past, as well as factors present in the here and now. This chapter guides you through a way of identifying these influences and making sense of them. In the next chapter we will focus more on how things in your past may have made you vulnerable to overeating; then, in chapter 9, we will look more closely at the here-and-now factors before moving on to consider how you can put all this information together into a personal formulation that will be the basis of your work to beat your overeating for good. The idea of developing a "formulation" of your difficulties is to help you gain a compassionate perspective on your experiences.

This chapter is a little different from the previous ones, in that it involves your doing quite a lot of thinking and reflecting on how and why you eat. This can be an emotional journey for some people. Coming to an understanding of how and why we sometimes eat too much can involve remembering difficult experiences with food and our bodies in the past, and perhaps grieving for the pain and distress we have unintentionally put ourselves through in trying to follow eating regimes that were—unbeknownst to us at the time—inevitably doomed to failure. You may also find that you have used food to punish or reward yourself for things that have happened in your life. Because these explorations are likely to bring up quite a lot of emotion, it's really helpful to approach them with compassion, and this is where you'll see all the work you have already done pay off in helping you through the next stages.

So, with each of the exercises in this chapter, only go at a pace you can manage. Kindly and gently accept your emotional reactions: if you're upset, confused, or angry, or even proud of the short bursts of control you have had over your use of diets in the past, that's fine. But remember, although there will come a time for compassionate self-correction, there's no place in the compassionate approach for shaming self-criticism. Beating yourself up for the way you have felt, or for the ways you have tried to manage your feelings in the past, *will not help* and can make you feel worse. Compassionately acknowledge that you are showing strength and courage now in trying to find new ways of dealing with the challenges of life, including managing your see-food-and-eat-it brain in a world of plenty.

So this may be a difficult journey, but the rewards can be amazing. Many people say that this process of self-discovery has been crucial in helping them to understand their relationships with food and eating, and from there to take responsibility for changing those relationships.

There are six golden rules for undertaking this journey:

- Make practical and emotional space for doing each exercise.

- Expect the exercises to be challenging but not overwhelming.

- Be as honest with yourself as you can.

- Use other people to help and support you if they are available and interested; this can include family, friends, or medical professionals.

- Expect it to take time to use your new knowledge to change the way you act.

- Remember that understanding things now does not mean you could have changed the way you behaved in the past, or altered the events that happened to you.

You might find it helpful to write down these rules or make a copy of them and just remind yourself of them each time you move on to tackle a new exercise.

WHAT A COMPASSIONATE FORMULATION FOR OVEREATING INVOLVES

In approaching overeating with compassion, we are trying to understand the factors that have influenced who we have become and why we act as we do. We know, for example, that if you grow up in a particular, say, religious group, it's likely that you will adopt values and attitudes shared by that group. If you grow up in a loving environment, it's likely that you'll feel confident about yourself, whereas if you grow up in a hostile or neglectful environment or are bullied at school, you're likely to feel less confident about yourself and more fearful or suspicious of others around you.

Now, of course, not all our difficulties are related to our childhoods—many relate quite simply to where we are now—but childhood is important and can create in us certain assumptions and values, ways of behaving and dealing with emotions, such as fear, loneliness, anxiety, and anger; and these emotions can affect our attitudes and values related to eating.

The compassion-focused approach to therapy considers how our current emotional and psychological problems may have developed through a series of experiences and reactions over time. In this approach we begin by considering some of the key childhood experiences that might have had an influence on your sense of self and the things you are sensitive to. Anything you felt as threatening can be especially significant, for example, criticism from or rejection by others. Also, anything that aroused feelings of shame—a sense that you are inferior, inadequate, or no good in some way—is also significant, because once you have learned to feel ashamed, you can carry this feeling, or a fear of its returning, around with you for a long time. And the shame, or the fear of it, can very easily come to the surface when you make mistakes, get criticized, or lose control of your eating.

So our compassion-focused approach will first try to establish what your underlying feelings about yourself are and where they might have come from. The next part of the exploration concerns the *safety strategies* you have developed to defend yourself against these unpleasant feelings, for example, of threat, fear, or shame. These are ways in which your mind will try to avoid experiencing these uncomfortable emotions or avoid coping with them if you can't prevent them. So, for example, somebody who was bullied at school and felt ashamed of her body weight might learn to become quite submissive in order to avoid making others angry. She might also become preoccupied with her appearance. If someone feels overwhelmed by painful emotions, he might try to avoid them by turning to food (or other substances, such as alcohol) to calm and distract himself. If these safety strategies work, even if only in the short term, people will tend to use them over and over again. This is, of course, very understandable, but it prevents them from addressing the original difficulty and also tends, as we saw in chapter 6, to reinforce the mistaken belief that those painful emotions should not, indeed cannot, be tolerated.

In addition to identifying safety strategies, a compassionate formulation of the reasons for overeating will investigate the ways in which we try to correct our mistakes, avoid problems, or deal with frustration. It's sadly very common for people to become very self-critical when things go wrong for them, particularly if they can't work out why this is happening. For example, we may often criticize ourselves because we're disappointed that we can't *make ourselves* do better. This self-criticism can be partly linked to fear of the consequences of not dealing with the problem. It can also be linked to memories of people being critical and cruel in the past. Sometimes your own critical voice sounds remarkably like that of a parent or teacher, or school bully. We often think self-criticism will somehow improve ourselves, but in fact it's more likely to just make us feel more ashamed.

EATING AS A SAFETY STRATEGY

We create safety strategies to deal with things in our internal world, things that go on in our own heads, such as avoiding difficult emotions or trying to stimulate pleasurable ones, and, of course, things that go on in the outside world, such as trying to avoid rejection or getting people to like us and be kind to us. The trouble is that the safety strategies we come up with as solutions can also become part of the problem. For example, imagine the difficulties somebody who's always submissive will run into or those that will confront somebody who never wants to face an uncomfortable emotion. So safety strategies can have *unintended consequences*.

Now, as you have already seen, you may overeat or diet and find your weight going up and down like a yo-yo for a variety of reasons. This may happen, for example:

- Because you don't know enough about the way your eating patterns affect your weight

- Because of how the things that you consume other than food affect your appetite and your ability to regulate it

- Because of habits you learned while you were growing up

However, overeating can also be a *safety strategy*, which can serve a very useful purpose in helping us to regulate our emotions, particularly in helping us to manage the things that bother us most, our key threats, if you like. When overeating has become a way of dealing with your emotions, it's important to recognize this, because if you're going to have a good chance of succeeding at changing your eating habits, you'll need to work on the issues that drive it. For example, if you have an underlying sense of shame or of being out of control, simply trying to change your eating behavior without changing those feelings may by tricky. Indeed, when you begin to challenge and work on your safety strategies, some of the key threats they were designed to deal with can resurface, so you'll have to deal with them!

As the term implies, "safety strategies" are designed to keep us safe in some way. They can be deliberate and thought out, or they can also be things we find ourselves doing without really knowing why. They fall into two categories: *external safety strategies*, which are aimed at managing how other people will see us or treat us, and *internal safety strategies*, which are about managing our own emotions and how we think or feel about ourselves.

Figure 7.1 shows you how safety strategies are developed in response to key threats, both past and present; how they have both intended and unintended consequences; and how these consequences keep the safety strategies in use. We can call the overall pattern a compassionate formulation for overeating. To give you a better idea of how this works in practice, we're now going to look at Alison's compassionate formulation for overeating, which is summarized in figure 7.2.

Figure 7.1   A Compassionate Formulation for Overeating

1 Key Threats

Past influences
Criticism from others
Bullied about weight
Other people's needs more
important

Current triggers
People who are critical
Conflict with others
Feeling ignored

2 Safety Strategies
Externally focused
Trying to please others
Being unassertive

Internally focused
Comfort eating
Dieting and planning dieting

3 Intended Consequences

Avoid conflict/criticism
Feel good when dieting
Feel soothed when comfort eating

4 Unintended Consequences

Of pleasing others
Feel not doing enough
Resentful of others

Of comfort eating
Weight gain
Fear of being bullied about weight gain
Feel inferior and out of control
Angry at self for comfort eating

Of dieting
Fearful of hunger responses
No other ways to manage difficult emotions
Become more critical of weight and eating

Others
Remain fearful of being criticized or upsetting others
Angry at self for being unassertive
Hard to trust others care for me when not at my best

Figure 7.2   Alison's Compassionate Formulation for Overeating

EXPLORING ALISON'S COMPASSIONATE FORMULATION FOR OVEREATING

Key Threats: Past Influences

Alison recalled that when she was growing up, her parents were very loving but set quite-high standards for her. They appeared disappointed if she failed at things and, at times, were difficult to please. They were busy people, and she had to work hard to earn their attention. She remembered dreading any criticism intruding on the precious moments of loving attention she had from them. She doesn't recall much open or affectionate discussion of her feelings in any depth, learning that in life you "just get on with things." She also remembered that she had to work quite hard to succeed at things, because she wasn't a naturally gifted student. Alison recalled that her parents were proud of her when she achieved things, but she was always worried that they would criticize her if she failed.

So Alison developed a belief that people liked and cared about you if you weren't a nuisance to them, and just got on with things and achieved things. She was very anxious about what other people thought about her when she wasn't able to do this. In her heart she felt that other people saw her as a disappointment and wanted to distance themselves from her rather than help if she failed or made mistakes.

Sadly, the belief that love, approval, or support will only be offered to us if we "deserve" it is very common, a lot more common than most of us imagine. Many of us worry that if we struggle or fall, very few genuine helping hands will come to our aid.

We can think of the beliefs Alison developed in terms of the three systems of emotional regulation discussed in chapter 3. (You might want to review figure 3.1.) Alison's sense of security has come to be based on her ability to maintain her drive system. Only then does she begin to feel safe and less fearful of others. She doesn't find it easy to get access to her affiliative soothing system (through being kind to herself or expecting others to be kind to her).

Alison also remembered being slightly overweight as a child and being bullied for several years when she moved to high school. She felt that she was a very caring person and that other people's needs should take priority over her own.

Key Threats: Current Triggers

By exploring her personal history in this way, Alison came to recognize that as an adult, she found it very difficult to deal with being criticized or with situations where she might be criticized. She found conflict with others very difficult and struggled to be assertive about her needs. She also noticed that feeling that other people had overlooked or ignored her left her feeling angry toward them.

Alison began to recognize that one of the reasons why she didn't like any kind of conflict and could easily feel overwhelmed by it was that she had different feelings going on at the same time. For example, she was clearly anxious about the rejection of being put down, but there was also an element of anger in the background, because she wanted to defend herself; and yet she was also anxious about this anger in case other people might see her as silly. So she also tended to criticize herself for feeling angry. So you won't be surprised to hear that anger was a feeling Alison struggled with and tried to avoid. And you can probably guess what she did if she got angry: she ate.

Safety Strategies

Alison saw that she had tried to avoid conflict and criticism mainly by trying to predict the needs of others, especially those in authority or who had some power over her, and to please them. Typically, she found that if the emotional temperature in a potential conflict was rising, she would immediately get anxious and back off, falling into a submissive attitude. That safety strategy was so well rehearsed that it was automatic for her, and even though she found herself battling with it, at times she was also frightened to overrule it. She also recognized how both comfort eating and dieting had helped her to manage the threat of criticism.

So Alison noticed that she had three main safety strategies, which she called pleasing others, comfort eating, and dieting. Pleasing others is an example of an external safety strategy. Comfort eating was an internal safety strategy, designed to help Alison cope with or turn off painful feelings. Dieting was both an external safety strategy (helping her to manage her fear of criticism from others) and an internal safety strategy (helping to improve her feelings about herself and to give her a sense of achievement).

Intended Consequences

The consequences Alison intended to follow from dieting were feeling better about herself and avoiding distressing thoughts about feeling inferior, out of control, criticized, or in conflict with others. Comfort eating had the intended consequences of helping her to deal with distressing emotions (particularly anger) by soothing her whenever these thoughts arose. Being unassertive helped her to avoid conflict with and criticism from others.

Unintended Consequences

Let's look at the unintended consequences of Alison's safety strategies in more detail. It's common for these consequences, which we don't plan or foresee, to maintain or even worsen our difficulties.

PLEASING OTHERS

Alison found that pleasing others covered a numbers of things she did to avoid being criticized. These included overworking, trying to predict and meet the needs of others, always putting her needs second, being unassertive, and avoiding conflict. The unintended consequences of these strategies were that she felt hurried and put upon, as if she could never achieve quite enough, as if she were somehow a failure and inadequate, yet also resentful of the demands that others put on her and the effects that meeting their needs had on her physical, emotional, and social life.

COMFORT EATING

Alison noticed that comfort eating really helped her to soothe her distress (an intended consequence). Looking back, she noticed that this pattern had begun relatively early in life and may have contributed to her being slightly overweight between the ages of ten and sixteen (an unintended consequence). She worried that gaining weight through comfort eating would lead to being bullied again, and these worries often brought back the memories and associated distress of the times when she had been bullied about her weight in the past. As her weight increased, so her mood would dip. The self-critical voice within her would start up again, and she would be angry with herself for being unable to control her urges to eat.

DIETING

Alison remembered that dieting was initially a way to help her to lose some weight to avoid being bullied, and to give her a feeling of being in control and to some degree a sense of pride and pleasure in her appearance. Her plans to diet would be triggered by becoming more aware than usual of her weight and shape (noticing, for example, that her jeans and dresses were getting tight), and more critical of her appearance. However, she also found it difficult to cope with feeling hungry, and would get angry with herself when she was tempted to break her diet.

When Alison was dieting, she could not turn to comfort eating to cope with difficult emotions in her life, which meant that her feelings of anger and irritation with herself (either because of her weight or hunger) were with her even more. Alison found that planning a diet could give her hope about managing her weight, and distracted her from these feelings temporarily. But then thoughts about dieting tended to intrude at other times in her life. For example, her mind often wandered to thoughts about losing weight when she was trying to concentrate on tasks at work, and often she would find herself seeking reassurance from her partner that her diet was working, which he found quite irritating!

All Safety Strategies

Alison recognized that together, her safety strategies had the unintended consequence of not allowing her to develop other ways to manage her fear of being criticized, her inability to assert herself, and her anger and irritation toward others. She also noticed that she was often angry or disappointed with herself for needing to comfort eat, diet, or avoid conflict and criticism, and that this tended to lower her mood, even when she had supportive friends or family around her. These unintended consequences left Alison feeling even more distressed and needing her safety strategies even more to help her to cope with her emotions.

Working out this formulation of threats, safety strategies, and intended and unintended consequences helped Alison to understand where her tendency to overeat had come from, but also, and more important, it helped her to make sense of why it had been so difficult to give it up over the years, even though she really wanted to.

Having come to this point, Alison could begin to offer herself compassion for her past pain and to recognize that overeating had been the best way she could help herself cope with that pain, and function in the world. Having compassionately acknowledged this, she could go on to explore new ways of addressing her key fears, without using her old safety strategies, and thus work toward breaking out of the vicious cycle of overeating.

WHY CREATE A COMPASSIONATE FORMULATION FOR OVEREATING?

It's important to think through why we want to set out a formulation like this and how it relates to the compassionate approach discussed in earlier chapters of this book. We begin with a genuine desire to develop wisdom and insight into our difficulties. The process of building your formulation allows you to stand back and see how different pieces of your life fit together. When we began to put together Alison's formulation, she could see how the difficulties she came across arose from the combination of her experiences in life. By the time the formulation was complete, we could also see that Alison was likely to become even more stuck in her current vicious cycle if she went on criticizing and blaming herself for her difficulties and how she copes with them.

To sum up, setting out a compassionate formulation for your overeating has a number of benefits:

- It allows you to be open and honest without blaming yourself.

- It can help you to recognize that your overeating is the result of many complex and interacting factors.

- It can help you to see more clearly how your overeating works, including all the intended and unintended consequences of overeating.

- It can help you recognize that although it's not your fault you overeat (because you are "set up" for it in so many ways), it *is* your responsibility to resolve it.

- It can help you to think carefully, from a kind, encouraging, and supportive perspective, about how to move forward to be the kind of person you want to be and cope with things in your life in a way that you're happy with.

- It can help you to acknowledge the need for compassion, understanding, and encouragement on your journey toward becoming that person.

- It can help you to think about and plan which aspects of your overeating to work on first.

- It can help you to see if the work you are doing is successfully tackling the factors that trigger your overeating and keep it going.

Always keep in mind that this is a *compassionate* formulation, developed from within a compassionate mind-set, that is, from a genuine intention and desire to understand and care for yourself. It's not another tool with which to beat yourself up for failure or nonachievement!

MAKING YOUR OWN COMPASSIONATE FORMULATION

A compassionate formulation is always a "best guess" at how our difficulties have evolved and what keeps us stuck. In the coming chapters we will explore in more detail different ways to make sense of the past and present influences on your overeating. For now we will work through the process of constructing a compassionate formulation for your overeating, using things you already know about yourself. So we will spend a little time thinking about how some of the things that trigger your overeating or shift you into dieting are related to underlying fears and worries you might be carrying from the past.

Bear in mind that these thoughts are just ideas to help you think through your own formulation. Keep in mind, too, that this is a *compassionate* approach, so you will be thinking about this in a compassionate, friendly way, curious and open to discovery rather than judgmental and critical, recognizing that all human beings struggle with a combination of the same range of emotions and their own individual life histories. See your discoveries as ways of understanding yourself better and also perhaps working step by step toward making decisions about how you would like to change things, how you would like to become kinder and more forgiving to yourself while being more encouraging, more supportive of change and growth, giving yourself that kind arm around your shoulder.

Three exercises follow that you might wish to do to help yourself develop your own formulation. Take a little while to read through them first. And take your time working through them; there's no rush. This framework will be the basis for much of the work you will do to change your eating, so you deserve the time and space to put it together thoughtfully and, if this is more comfortable for you, bit by bit. So do the following exercises at a pace you can manage.

Before you attempt any of the exercises, be sure to bring your compassionate image with you. If, while completing an exercise, you find that you are becoming self-critical or that the exercise is too much for you to manage, step away from the exercise and bring your compassionate mind back to the fore before going any further. Just to remind you, the best way to do this is to begin by establishing your soothing rhythmic breathing or safe-place image. When you feel ready, you can then bring up your compassionate image (either you at your best or your compassionate companion). When you have the image in mind, spend a little time exploring what it feels like to step into the shoes and role of your compassionate image, what it feels like to be strong, warm, caring, and interested in developing and fostering the potential of another human being. Notice how this changes your emotions, the things you would pay attention to, and the ways you would think and act. When you have a sense of this, you can then imagine what answers your compassionate companion would give to the questions in the exercises as this individual tries to help you develop a personal formulation for your difficulties.

Exercise 7.1 Talking to Your Compassionate Image

Imagine that you're talking to your compassionate image or your very best friend, and explaining to this individual some of the things in your early life that you think might have set you up for the difficulties with eating you have now. Remember, if this becomes overwhelming or too upsetting for you, then it's quite okay to back off for a while and return to it when you are ready. The idea of the task is not to distress you, but to give you a compassionate lens through which you can look at possible connections between your past and your present. This is why imagining you're talking to a deeply compassionate person can be very helpful.

Exercise 7.2 Writing a Compassionate Life Story

It's sometimes helpful to write a compassionate life story, as if you were writing a letter to someone about yourself. If you want to try this, you might find it helpful to have some questions in your mind to get you started, possibly including:

- *What were the most important influences on me while I was growing up?*

- *What are the key distressing emotional memories that may have affected me?* (These are memories of important events or relationships in your life; they often come to mind when you are threatened, and may be linked to your drive system or trigger difficult feelings in you, such as shame or anger.)

- *What threats, worries, and uncertainties about myself carry through to today from my early life?*

- *How have I learned to cope with things that frighten me? If I had to guess, what might my basic safety strategies be?*

- *When confronted with setbacks, difficult emotions, or conflicts with other people, what are my typical ways of dealing with them?*

- *When I think about these ways of dealing with such challenges, what are they intended to do?*

- *What are their unintended consequences?*

- *How do I acknowledge, face, and work on those unintended consequences from now on?*

Exercise 7.3 Using a Compassionate Formulation Form

This exercise is designed to help you work through the elements of the formulation outlined in figure 7.1, in a similar way as we did for Alison in figure 7.2. You can use worksheet 7.1 to summarize your formulation.

Step 1: What are my key threats? The first step is to identify the things that trigger your threat/protection system. Remember, these may be associated with a range of different emotions, including sadness, anger, disgust, grief, and so on. Try to think of both situations and events in the past that tended to bring up these emotions, and ones in the present that have the same effects. Now try to list them:

The past influences on my key threats

1.

2.

3.

4.

(and any others)

The current triggers to my key threats

1.

2.

3.

4.

(and any others)

Step 2: What are my safety strategies? These are the things you do, feel, or think to help you manage your key threats. They might be directed outward (external safety strategies), for example, trying to influence other people's judgments of you, or inward (internal safety strategies), for example, trying to influence your own feelings about yourself and your emotions.

These strategies can be a little tricky to identify at first. The key is to ask yourself what you do, feel, or think to protect yourself from reexperiencing things you found distressing in the past or to avoid painful experiences in the future. It can sometimes be helpful to think about the things other people might notice that you do to protect yourself; perhaps you can even talk this through with someone close to you, whom you trust to have your best interests at heart. Now try to list them:

My external safety strategies

1.

2.

3.

4.

(and any others)

My internal safety strategies

1.

2.

3.

4.

(and any others)

Step 3: What are the intended consequences of my safety strategies? Sometimes we are very aware of the pain and distress that our safety strategies have evolved to help us manage, and we use our safety strategies in a very deliberate way. Sometimes, though, these strategies have become more of a habit, with their original

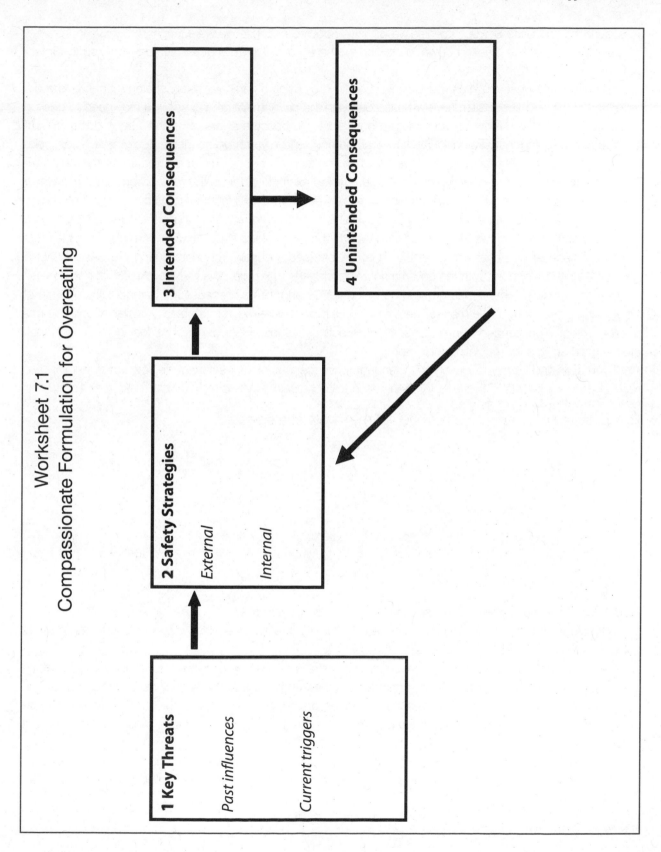

Worksheet 7.1
Compassionate Formulation for Overeating

1 Key Threats

Past influences

Current triggers

2 Safety Strategies

External

Internal

3 Intended Consequences

4 Unintended Consequences

purpose lost in the past. Some strategies we will have adopted because we were taught to behave in this way, as a family or social rule passed down to us, and we have no real idea what the strategy is trying to protect us from.

If you do know what you're aiming to achieve or avoid by using a particular safety strategy, it can give you a head start in thinking about alternative ways to cope with the problem. At other times you may need to give up the strategy a little (even if only in your imagination) before you become aware of what it's been doing for you.

You may also find that strategies you have learned and believe you have needed actually have no association with your personal threat/protection system when you start to change. This may be particularly true if your safety strategy was "inherited" from someone else. A good example of this is the rule: *I need to eat everything on my plate, even if I feel full.* My own grandparents followed this rule and taught it to us every time they visited. You can see that it was a perfectly understandable safety strategy for ensuring that no food was wasted in a poor family living between the First and Second World Wars, when food supplies were unreliable and the most had to be made of whatever was available. This rule became nationally important during the Second World War in the United Kingdom, with the government reinforcing the message, "Waste Not, Want Not." It was a less useful eating strategy when I was growing up in the 1960s and 1970s, because my parents (although still of the working class) were a little more affluent and food supplies were much more readily available, and this rule has the potential unintended consequence of contributing to subsequent generations losing touch with their internal mechanisms for regulating their eating.

If you don't find it easy to identify the intended consequences of your safety strategies, it may help to take each of your key threats in turn and try to link each to a particular safety strategy. Now make your list:

The intended consequences of each of my safety strategies

1.

2.

3.

4.

(and any others)

Step 4: What are the unintended consequences of my safety strategies? As you saw in Alison's story, it's likely that our safety strategies really do help us cope with our key threats; otherwise we would give them up pretty quickly!

Sadly, though, as we have also seen, some of our strategies can have unintended consequences, which may lead to difficulties later. It's really important to remember that this exercise is designed to help you explore the complexities of your emotional systems and develop greater control over your threat/protection system so that you can beat overeating for good; the idea is *not* to use this new information as a stick to beat yourself with!

As with the previous step, it can be helpful to separate your safety strategies and to work out the unintended consequences of each of them separately, perhaps with the help of someone else who cares for you. Now write your list:

The unintended consequences of my safety strategies

1.

2.

3.

4.

(and any others)

Finally, you can explore whether these unintended consequences actually increase the level of threat you experience or mean that you use your safety strategies even more. You may wish to use worksheet 7.1 to help you do this. As we saw in Alison's example (figure 7.2), her unintended consequences led to further problems with assertiveness, comfort eating, and dieting.

When you finish this section, you can then explore whether any of your unintended consequences leads you into further problems that your eating (or other safety strategies) evolved to help you solve. If they do, you can then draw some lines to represent these connections on worksheet 7.1.

SUMMARY

In this chapter we have explored a way of making sense of the factors that may have made you likely to overeat in the past and that may keep your overeating going in the present. Using Alison's example, we have also explored how the strategies we use to protect ourselves from unpleasant events or emotions can be helpful to us, but can also have unintended, and sometimes unwanted, consequences. Blaming ourselves for these things can often keep us trapped in a vicious cycle of threat and response, and can even make things worse. Creating a compassionate formulation for these influences and processes helps us to explore them without blame or criticism so that we can start to think about how to move forward in a more caring, kind, and supportive way that takes into account the problems that changing may pose for us.

The chapter has also introduced a number of exercises to help you develop your own compassionate formulation for overeating. When you have completed these exercises, you can then move on to developing alternative strategies for managing your threat/protection system and to help with any difficulties that may arise as you give up your old safety strategies. This new and more sensitive way of understanding your relationship with eating will help you to predict the types of problems you will need help with and the possible unintended consequences of changing your relationship with food.

In the following chapters we will explore ways of building on this formulation to develop a deeper and more detailed understanding of both the past and present influences on your eating.

CHAPTER 8

Understanding Your Current Eating Pattern

Making sense of your past can help you to make sense of your current relationship with food and to stop criticizing yourself for the way you eat now. It's equally important (and sometimes easier), if you aim to stop overeating in the future, to understand your current eating habits and the things that influence you now.

USING AN EATING DIARY

A helpful way to understand your eating habits is to learn to observe and become mindful of your eating patterns in a structured way, by keeping an eating diary. This can be a really helpful tool in changing your relationship with food. So the first part of this chapter will suggest what information you might record and how to make sense of the information you gather. But first it's useful to be clear about the main purposes of learning to monitor your eating habits and the thoughts and emotions that affect them, which are:

- To get an overview of your difficulties

- To look for and make sense of patterns in triggers to overeating

- To look for and make sense of things that protect you from overeating

- To help slow down the "inevitable" rush to overeat

- To record your coping thoughts and strategies

- To record and understand your progress in addressing overeating

As for how to keep an eating diary, there are only two rules for monitoring your eating:

- Do it in real time, as you eat or as soon as possible afterward, not at the end of the day.

- Be honest!

The amount of time it takes to get the hang of keeping an eating diary will vary from one person to another, but you'll probably want to spend several weeks or even a few months doing it so that you get a really good overview of your basic eating style.

Worksheet 8.1 is a form you can use to monitor your eating. Take a few moments to read through the headings. It might look a bit daunting at first, so after looking at it section by section, we'll go through a real-life example using a day of Alison's diary. (Copies of the blank worksheet are available at http://49776 .nhpubs.com and you can download as many more copies of these as you need or just copy the headings onto fresh sheets of paper.)

Before Eating

The first column is designed to help you make sense of the circumstances that lead to overeating or that protect you from either dieting or overeating. Sometimes overeating can be triggered by being in particular places or can be more common at different times of the year, month, or day. Some people can help us avoid overeating, while others may deliberately or accidentally encourage it. Some of our relationships can be difficult, so our emotions when we're with these people, or after we've been with them, can lead to overeating.

At this point there are two types of feelings we are interested in. The first is your *physical sensations*, which include whether you feel hungry or full, although if you have been dieting or overeating for some time, you may have lost touch with these bodily sensations, so it may not be easy to determine at first. You can also record here whether you feel tired, restless, agitated, and so on.

The other type of feeling we are interested in is your *emotions*, whether you feel anxious, sad, bored, angry, irritable, or any of the many other possibilities. You may, of course, feel pleasant emotions, such as joy, pleasure, or excitement. Usually you will feel a mixture of emotions; it's common to feel several emotions at the same time or to have rapid changes in your emotions.

As for what you're thinking at this point, this, too, may not be easy to pinpoint at first. Sometimes we can be unaware of our thoughts, and it's a skill to be able to recognize them. You may find this easier as you get used to keeping your eating diary. If you do notice yourself thinking in a particular way or about particular things, this can give you a clue to what triggers your eating.

We can break thinking into three areas:

- Memories, positive or unpleasant, that you have before eating

- Thoughts about problems you are facing or will face in the future

Worksheet 8.1 Eating Diary

Day and Date: _____

Situation Where were you? Who were you with? How were you feeling? What were you thinking before you ate?	What You Ate or Drank Type and amount Physical Activity Type and duration	Overeating? Yes/No	Dieting or Comfort-Food Mind-Set Active When Eating? Yes/No	Thoughts and Feelings During or after eating, about doing the diary, or anything else you think is important

• Thoughts about eating, including the possible benefits of overeating or problems that overeating may create for you

You may, of course, have other types of thoughts that are not related to overeating, and again it may be helpful to write them down too.

What You Eat and Drink, and Your Physical Activity

In the second column, you can write what you eat and drink. Ideally you will also record roughly how much you have eaten; however, don't worry about recording or adding up calories at this point. You will only do this when you review your diary, and we'll explore how to do this a little later in the chapter. This column will be very helpful later on, when you are discerning whether your overeating is actually related to not giving your body enough food during the day. It may also help you notice whether any particular types of food are more likely to be associated with overeating. Remember that there are a number of nonfoods that are also associated with overeating, including alcohol, medications, and some illegal drugs. It's also important to list what and how much of these substances you take every day to help you understand whether they affect how much you eat.

It's also useful to keep a brief note of the types and amount of physical activity you do, for example, noting whether you do an hour of housework or go to the gym for thirty minutes each day. The information in this column can help you understand your energy and nutritional balance, and notice whether particular types of food trigger overeating.

Have You Overeaten?

The third column asks you if you believe you have overeaten. This is important, because sometimes we think we have or haven't overeaten because of the types of foods we eat or our feelings at the time, rather than as a result of an objective decision about what our bodies needed at a particular time or how our eating compares to that of people who are more in touch with their bodies' needs and appetites.

What Mind-Set Are You in While Eating?

The fourth column prompts you to consider what kind of mind-set you are in when you are eating, which will help you to recognize what kind of eating you're doing and also to think about what problems this mind-set is trying to help you manage. The main types of mind-set we are interested in here are the ones that are most likely to influence your eating: the comfort-food and dieting mind-sets. However, you may also find that other types of mind-sets, such as being in an anxious, depressed, or angry state of mind, can also influence your overeating.

What Are You Thinking and Feeling?

The final column explores your thoughts and feelings while you're eating and afterward. In a more advanced version of this diary, you can also use this column to record thoughts, feelings, or things you do that help you manage your urges to overeat or limit overeating. In your early diaries, you may find that you have a lot of self-critical thoughts and feelings about overeating, or find that overeating helps you to manage some difficult thoughts or feelings.

In figure 8.1 you can see one day of Alison's completed diary.

As with all the exercises in this chapter, it's important that you keep the diary at your own pace. To begin with, it may be easier just to record what you eat, the time of day, and whom you are with. When you are used to doing this, you can then start to include your feelings and thoughts before and after eating. You can leave it until you feel fairly used to doing this, before you try to decide whether you actually overate and whether you were in a dieting or comfort-food mind-set before, during, or after eating.

BLOCKS TO MONITORING

Monitoring may look like a pretty simple exercise; after all, it only has two rules: complete it in real time, and be honest! In practice, however, many people find that they come up against obstacles when they start trying to monitor their eating. These blocks generally fall into one of two categories: practical and emotional.

Practical blocks to monitoring include:

- Difficulty with learning to use the form

- Difficulty with keeping the diary private

- Problems keeping the diary when other people are around

- Finding the time to keep the diary

Emotional blocks to monitoring include:

- Resenting doing the task

- Worrying that being more observant and mindful of your difficulties will make your eating or feelings worse

- Feeling more self-critical or ashamed on seeing what you eat written down

- Worrying about what others will think if they see you keeping the diary

It's helpful to identify any of your own blocks to monitoring and to try to find solutions to them, before you begin to keep your diary. Worksheet 8.2 is a form you can use to help you do this, or you can, of course, create your own. Figure 8.2 shows a worked example of the form.

Monday, March 23

Situation Where were you? Who were you with? How were you feeling? What were you thinking before you ate?	What You Ate or Drank Type and amount **Physical Activity** Type and duration	Overeating? Yes/No	Dieting or Comfort-Food Mind-Set Active When Eating? Yes/No	Thoughts and Feelings During or after eating, about keeping the diary, or anything else you think is important
8:00 a.m., at home, alone A bit hungry, tired Not really thinking about anything	Cereal, two slices of toast, tea	No	No	Felt okay about eating, a bit worried about going to work today
10:00 a.m., at work, with colleagues A bit anxious Worried about difficult meeting later today	Tea and five ginger cookies	Yes	Comfort food	Felt a little worried that colleagues would think I was greedy, but felt I needed the food to calm me down
12:30 p.m., at work, alone A bit queasy, not hungry More anxious abut meeting	Tea and ten more cookies; had planned to have lunch but couldn't face it	Maybe?	Comfort, but also thought I would cut back on the cookies for the rest of the week	Felt greedy
1:45 p.m. at restaurant at work, alone Very upset by meeting, felt angry with boss and useless Mainly thinking about meeting and worried about what other people thought about me	Burger meal, large milk shake	No	Mainly comfort but planned not to eat for the rest of the day	Felt okay about eating, but very down about myself, worried about going back to work
10:30 p.m., home, with partner Still upset about work Felt I deserved a treat	Four glasses of wine, take-out meal, plus leftovers Individual tub of ice cream	Yes	Dieting mind until just before the meal, but partner came in from work late and brought in take-out	Didn't want to eat, but when I did, felt out of control and could not stop Felt angry with myself for overeating, planning to eat a lot less tomorrow

Figure 8.1   Alison's Eating Diary

My Personal Blocks	Compassionate Things I Can Say to Myself or Do to Get Past the Blocks
It brings attention to my overeating.	It's understandable to feel a bit upset when I become aware of the difficulties, but in my heart, I would like to move forward on this, so learning how to face my embarrassment or distress can be helpful in the long run. Maybe I can try it a few times and see how it goes.
This is boring, and I really don't like having to do this kind of monitoring activity.	t's true, this can be boring, but maybe I could just have a couple of tries to get going and see how I do. Perhaps I could put a small note on the fridge to remind myself. To be honest, there are lots of things I do in my life that I find boring, so this doesn't have to be a block. I am quite capable of doing boring things if I recognize that they can be helpful in the long run.
I guess I feel bad because I'm being quite critical really; I don't like myself because of my overeating.	I should remember that this is not my fault. I have a see-food-and-eat-it brain, and the food industry has encouraged me to want certain foods. I also learned to use eating to support myself emotionally because it helped at the time. It's more important to be kind and understanding, and recognize that there is a problem here and that if I am gentle and kind with myself, I can begin to find new ways forward.

Figure 8.2   Example of Managing Blocks to Monitoring

Managing Emotional Blocks to Monitoring

Practical blocks sound easier to address but are, in fact, often easier to manage once you have worked though emotional blocks. So let's start with some of the most common emotional blocks.

For most people, the first emotional block is finding a reason to keep the diary that will prompt you to fill it in even if it's a struggle. We will explore motivation to change in chapter 10, but for now you might try thinking of keeping a diary as a leap of faith, something that's worth a try to see if it can help you. Again, you may wish to explore the idea of keeping a diary from the perspective of your compassionate image. What would "you at your best" or your compassionate companion say to help you take this leap of faith? How would this individual express understanding of and care for your real and honest concerns that the diary could be emotionally challenging for you? What would this person say about the advantages of keeping a diary for you personally? What kind of compassionate plan might this person come up with to help you deal with your emotional blocks?

Many people worry that keeping the diary will be upsetting. Well, this can happen, particularly as you begin to make connections between eating and your thoughts and feelings. However, this distress tends to be temporary and can help to remind you that what you're doing has a purpose, that if you can learn to tolerate a certain amount of distress now, you're likely to be better able to prevent yourself from overeating in the future, and to learn new ways to manage your thoughts and feelings. Even so, keeping the diary short, not rereading it at the end of the day, or even keeping each eating episode written in

Worksheet 8.2 Managing Blocks to Monitoring

My Personal Blocks	Compassionate Things I Can Say to Myself or Do to Get Past the Blocks

a separate place (so you don't have to see your day's eating all in one go) can help you to avoid getting upset. You may also wish to plan soothing and distracting exercises to do after you have written in your diary. By using whichever of these techniques suits you, you can put together a plan for making your diary emotionally manageable.

It's also important to make sure you tackle your diary from a compassionate mind-set. People who diet or overeat often use diaries as a way of beating themselves up for what they have eaten or why they eat, which is absolutely *not* the idea here. Remember all that you discovered in the earlier chapters of this book about where your impulses and habits related to eating come from, way back in our common ancestry and also in your early personal history. The habits and practices you've been using are just the best ways you've found so far to deal with your own circumstances; the aim now is to give you new and better ways to do this with information and understanding you haven't had before.

Managing Practical Blocks to Monitoring

The eating diary form in worksheet 8.1 may look a bit cumbersome; still, many people get used to it fairly quickly and become happy to fill it in using this format. However, this is certainly not the only way to do it. Several people I have worked with prefer to keep the information in their own personal diaries, which can help the task to feel more private and special to you. By all means, buy yourself a nice diary or notebook, ideally one that can be locked or is inconspicuous, to use as your monitoring record.

I have found that people can be really ingenious in managing this task. For example, texting the information to your cell phone can be a good way to both get the information down quickly and keep it private.

As for the time it takes, monitoring is designed to be done quite rapidly; I would suggest taking no more than a minute or so for each episode of eating. So it shouldn't take any more than ten to fifteen minutes a day. It's important, however, not to leave this until the end of the day, doing it all at once then. It really does help to have the information recorded as you're eating or at least immediately afterward. Most people can remember what they ate and when at the end of the day, but it's not so easy to remember accurately how you were feeling and what you were thinking at the time. You might want to use a personal code to note your feelings and thoughts; like texting, this can be a good way to get the information down privately and quickly. Other ways of doing this are to record a few short lines as a phone message or e-mail, or on a scrap of paper. It doesn't matter how you get the information down, really, as long as you do it as soon as possible. If you end up with a collection of what seem like scrappy notes, you can always write a neat copy at the end of the day. But here's a word of warning: I suggest you try to do this fairly rapidly, because dwelling for too long on a whole day's eating, feelings, and thoughts might leave you feeling a bit upset or uncomfortable.

USING YOUR DIARY TO MAKE SENSE OF YOUR EATING

Once you've gotten used to keeping your eating diary, you can start using the diary review sheet provided as worksheet 8.3 to help you draw together the information you've collected and start to identify the things that protect you from, as well as those that put you at risk of, overeating. Again, when you set about reviewing your diary, it's important that you do so from the perspective of your compassionate mind, exploring the patterns you find in a genuine spirit of concerned curiosity, wanting to understand and then find ways to alleviate the uncomfortable and perhaps painful emotions that your overeating both helps you with and causes for you. It's also a good idea to plan to set aside time to soothe any distress the reviewing process causes.

When I review diaries with my clients, we set aside at least an hour or so at the end of the week and review a whole week's worth of diaries. This gives us a much better idea of patterns; indeed, sometimes we review four weeks' worth of diaries together to get a longer-term perspective. It can take a week or two to get the hang of keeping the diary, so you might want to wait until you feel you have a week's worth of complete daily records before starting your review.

As you have seen in previous chapters, there's a whole range of factors that can affect your eating habits. When we are reviewing a diary, we aim to cover as many of these factors as possible, including the following.

Eating Pattern

As you found in chapter 3, eating patterns can significantly affect your risk of overeating. When looking at your diary, it's important to look for the spaces between eating episodes. Your body can last for about three or four hours before it starts getting hungry. Eating more frequently than this can put you out of touch with your hunger; leaving longer gaps puts you at risk of overeating at the next meal.

Energy Balance

As you saw in chapter 2, our bodies need a certain amount of energy every day just to keep our physical systems going, and we need a variable amount on top of this to fuel our activities during the day. If you overeat, you can lose touch with your bodily needs; if, on the other hand, you are trying to eat less than your body needs, you are likely to overeat, as well as to experience a range of psychological and physical side effects. So you'll want to aim for energy balance: eating just the right amount to support your physical systems and your activities.

Many people who overeat are quite good at estimating their energy intake (in the form of calories), although they may be less aware of the amount of energy they use or need. Unless you have access to a dietitian who can figure this out for you, this is a skill you will need to develop. We'll explore how to do this in more detail in chapter 11, but it's worth taking a look at the basic principles here.

The easiest (but by no means, easy) way of estimating your energy intake is to become familiar with the calorie content of what you eat and drink. There are many commercial calorie-counting books and websites that can help you to do this. Again, you might find adding up your calorie intake to be an uncomfortable exercise at first; try to view it as a necessary step in helping you to gain control over your eating and support yourself compassionately while you do it.

Ideally you are aiming for an energy intake of 2,000 calories a day if you are a woman and 2,500 calories if you are a man. It's normal to have a variation of about 200 calories a day—your body is more than capable of adjusting to this—but your overall aim is a balance in your energy over the week, which means an energy consumption of around 14,000 calories a week if you are a woman, 17,500 if you are a man.

Worksheet 8.3 Diary Review

Eating Pattern

How long do I leave between eating episodes?   _____ hours

How many times a day do I eat more often than every three to four hours?   _____

How many times do I eat less often than every three to four hours?   _____

Energy Needs

What is my daily energy need?   _____ calories

How much energy do I take in each day?   _____ calories

How much energy do I use up each day?   _____ calories

Am I eating more or less than I need each day?   More/Less

What I Eat and Drink

Are there specific types of food that trigger overeating?

Are there any foods that help me to avoid overeating?

Are there any things I take into my body that affect my appetite (such as medication, drugs, alcohol)?

Times, People, Places

Are there any times, people, or places that make overeating more likely?

Are there any times, people, or places that protect me from overeating?

My Feelings and Overeating

Are there any feelings that make my overeating worse?

Are these physical sensations, such as hunger?

Are these emotions (such as sadness, boredom, anger, anxiety)?

My Thoughts and Overeating

Am I in a dieting mind-set before, during, or after overeating?   Yes/No

Am I in a comfort-food mind-set before, during, or after overeating?   Yes/No

Do I give myself permission to overeat as a treat?   Yes/No

Do I use overeating to punish myself?   Yes/No

Do I hope that overeating will help me manage difficult feelings, memories, or events?   Yes/No

Do I follow certain rules or habits that I have been taught about eating?   Yes/No

Do I criticize or bully myself about what I have eaten or the way I eat?   Yes/No

Am I worried about what other people will think about my overeating?   Yes/No

If you answered yes to any of these questions, try to be as specific as you can about exactly what you are thinking and, if you can, where you learned to think in this way.

Keeping an eye on your calorie intake to try to establish an appropriate energy balance can really help you to tackle overeating. It's likely that if you are using this book to help you beat overeating, you may find it difficult to balance your energy at this stage. Don't worry; we will work on how to do this in more detail in chapter 11.

What You Eat and Drink

Many people find that specific types of food act as a trigger to overeating. These may be foods that we associate with comfort, that are usually "forbidden" in some way, or simply that we really like! Learning to eat and enjoy these types of foods in moderation can be really important in managing overeating.

Times, People, Places

Often, overeating happens in a regular or predictable way; for example, many of us overeat on the weekends or when we are with others who overeat. Understanding these patterns can help us plan to manage these situations in another way.

Your Feelings and Overeating

As we explored earlier, it can be helpful to divide feelings into physical sensations (including hunger) and emotions (such as anger, boredom, or anxiety), although, of course, our physical sensations and emotions are often mingled together. It can sometimes be difficult to identify both kinds of feeling, particular if eating helps you to manage them. Sometimes you may have to delay responding to the urge to overeat for a little while to be able to identify your feelings more clearly. We will explore how to do this in chapter 12. Once you can identify these feelings, you are on your way to learning to understand and manage them in a more compassionate way.

Your Thoughts and Overeating

There are many ways in which your thoughts can lead to overeating. They can:

* Give you positive permission to overeat, telling you, for example, that you "deserve food" because you have been good or had a hard time

* Allow you to punish yourself with food

* Encourage you to hope that eating will help you to manage unpleasant feelings or experiences

* Encourage, support, or bully you into dieting, thus increasing your risk of overeating later

- Provide rules that lead to accidental or habitual overeating (such as *I must always clean my plate*)

Our thoughts are also very likely to be intertwined with our feelings. Sometimes our thoughts have less to do with eating itself than with how we think about ourselves, or how we think others will think about us after we have overeaten. As we have seen, these patterns can lead us into vicious cycles of secret eating or dieting to deal with the painful feelings this type of self-criticism and shame can lead to.

All of these ways of thinking are understandable and very common, and it's important to understand and be compassionate with the way these thoughts develop.

Our thoughts can also help us to manage our urges to overeat or to cope when we have overeaten. Recognizing, supporting, and encouraging the thoughts that can help us to manage overeating is a major step in controlling overeating. Your diary can help you to identify and build on these thoughts, and to develop new ones.

Here's one cautionary note: I encourage my clients not to review their diaries if they have had a particularly difficult day or to do it just before bedtime, when they will probably be tired and may be tempted to brood critically on what they recorded rather than analyze it compassionately. It's better to do the review when you are feeling relatively calm and alert, and able to learn from your diary.

MAKING SENSE OF ALISON'S DIARY

In the final section of this chapter, we will review the sample day of Alison's eating diary shown as figure 8.1 to give you an idea of how reviewing a diary works in practice and how what you learn can help you to beat overeating for good.

As I mentioned earlier, usually the more information we have, the easier it is to make sense of a diary, so it's a good idea to review a whole week's records together. There may also be monthly or seasonal patterns to your relationship with overeating that you can only see when you look at a sequence of diary records over a much longer period. However, even looking at one day can be very revealing, and that's what we're going to do here.

When we review Alison's diary, we see that four of her eating episodes occurred relatively close together (at 8:00 a.m., 10:00 a.m., 12:30 p.m., and 1:45 p.m.) but that there was then a very long gap until her final meal of the day at 10:30 p.m. On reflection she noticed that she wasn't particularly hungry at 10:00 a.m. or 12:30 p.m., but in the evening had been fending off feeling hungry from about 6:00 p.m. By looking over a lot of similar days' records, Alison became aware of a couple of issues that she decided to work on. The first was learning to eat when her body was more likely to be hungry and to avoid eating when she didn't need to, even if that meant not eating at times when other people were. The second one, which was related to the first, was a long-standing pattern of trying not to eat in the evenings, which in fact amounted to a "rule" that she should not eat in the evening. This left her feeling deprived, hungry, and likely to overeat if she did break her rule.

Alison also noticed that both having other people around and being alone increased her risk of overeating, in different ways. She found it hard not to overeat when she was with work colleagues or if her partner offered her food to cheer her up. However, when she was alone, she also tended to comfort-eat. Alison was able to identify both anxiety and anger as feelings that she managed by using food.

Before starting to keep a diary, Alison believed she overate all of the time. She was surprised to find that some of her meals (such as breakfast) were actually normal portions. Later on, when she worked out her energy intake for this day, she found that she had eaten at least 1,500 calories more than her body needed. This wasn't really news to Alison, although she did find it upsetting to see it written down. What was more interesting was that at lunchtime, she couldn't face eating the sandwich, bag of potato chips, and apple she'd brought to work because it felt like overeating, but actually these added up to fewer calories than the cookies she had eaten out of her desire to avoid overeating.

As she thought more about what she ate that day, Alison remembered that she had always been offered cookies to help her manage being upset when she was growing up. This helped her to consider the urge to eat cookies as a good warning sign that she might need to deal with her feelings, as well as to focus on eating foods that would be more filling, like her sandwich and chips (even if they felt too fattening), to help her avoid overeating later.

The final thing Alison realized about what she was eating and drinking was that alcohol tended to make her feel hungrier and less able to control her urges to overeat. This helped her to think about changing her drinking habits and, in particular, trying to reduce the amount of alcohol she drank if she was upset, anxious, or angry.

Alison was particularly skilled at recognizing the type of mind-set she was in when eating. She fluctuated between her comfort-food and her dieting mind-sets. She noticed that these mind-sets often clouded her whole day, but also helped her to deal with threatening events, for example, the distressing meeting she had at work that day. Thinking about food in one way or another helped her to avoid thinking about the meeting for large parts of the day. She was also able to notice that she often struggled with feeling greedy after eating, became worried about what other people thought about her if they saw her eating, and could get very angry with herself when she overate. She noticed that her anger was helpful in fueling her urges to diet and to avoid being seen as greedy, and in preventing her from overeating later, but often led to her feeling even worse and needing to comfort-eat to manage this.

It took Alison several weeks of diary keeping to clearly identify these patterns and some time after that to decide which areas to work on first in trying gradually to reduce her overeating. In the next chapter we will explore how you can use the information from your diary to develop a compassionate understanding of your own difficulties and to set realistic goals for addressing your overeating.

SUMMARY

This chapter has explored a practical way of recording and exploring the current patterns and triggers that may influence your eating habits now. In the next chapter we will put this information together to help you develop a personal understanding of your eating and how your eating habits help you to manage your threat/protection system. We will also explore how to put all of this information together by revisiting the compassionate formulation for your overeating.

CHAPTER 9

How Does Your Overeating Work Now?

In the last chapter we explored how keeping an eating diary can help you to become more observant of your overeating and how you can begin to make sense of the information you gather in this way by reviewing your diary. Now, drawing on both that chapter and the previous one, in which we explored how both events in the past and things you are dealing with in the present can affect how and what you eat, we will work on putting all this information together to see how you may have been using overeating to help manage your very complex emotional systems and see-food-and-eat it brain.

It's worth pausing here to repeat that if you're struggling to deal with overeating, you are certainly not alone: overeating is a problem for over half the Western world. Nor does it mean that there's anything wrong with *you*. Overeating is likely to be the outcome of the complex interactions among your genetic make-up, biological mechanisms that helped us all successfully survive famine, and events in your own life that have either taught you to overeat or taught you that overeating could help you in some way.

In the first three chapters of this book, we explored these mechanisms in some detail and introduced the three-systems approach to understanding how we regulate our emotions. In chapter 7 we introduced the idea of a compassionate formulation for overeating. We will now revisit all of these ideas and draw them together to help you construct a new and more developed formulation for your difficulties with overeating.

OVEREATING AND THE THREE SYSTEMS OF EMOTIONAL REGULATION

The three-systems model of emotional regulation can be a very helpful way of thinking about the ways in which you can use your overeating (deliberately or accidentally) to manage your emotional life and to think about how overeating can affect your emotional life.

As you may remember, we are interested in three main systems:

- The threat/protection system, which is mainly about helping to stop us from doing, or get us away from, things we believe are unpleasant or dangerous to us

- The drive system, which is concerned with helping us reach specific goals

- The affiliative soothing system, which focuses on making us feel calm, soothed, and cared for

We need all three systems to help us manage the challenges of life, and all three of them can be affected by, and can in turn affect, the eating habits we learn and get used to. As we have seen, feeling soothed by food (the comfort-food mind-set) can replace other ways of feeling cared for, soothed, and contented. The dieting mind-set is often connected with the drive system, so that we feel that dieting can both be an achievement in itself and help us get closer to other life goals. Both the comfort-food and dieting mind-sets can be turned on when we feel under threat in some way. These threats can be either external (things that are happening to us) or internal (from our memories, thoughts, and feelings). Often a threat has elements of both types. Once our threat/protection system is active, we tend to see things we would normally feel okay about as threats too. Remember that this rapid escalation of the threat/protection system is perfectly normal; after all, it evolved to protect us, and it wouldn't have been much good at that if it had been easy to ignore! But because this system is so active and powerful, it can quickly become difficult for us to see the forest for the trees, so to speak, as we seem to be surrounded by threats and under pressure to respond to or retreat from them. So it can be helpful to understand in advance what triggers the system and then what additional issues arise once the system has been activated.

In a compassion-focused approach to overeating, we are particularly interested in helping you understand whether the balance among these three systems has become skewed. We also want to see if comfort-food, dieting, or other overeating mind-sets (such as eating for fun or eating to belong) have become entangled with these systems. Finally, we want to see if the ways you have been using to try to manage these systems have had unintentional side effects that are making it even more difficult for you to manage your emotions.

HOW OVEREATING MAY HELP US MANAGE EMOTIONS

In the next section of this chapter, we will explore how overeating may help you to manage your three emotional regulation systems. This analysis, involving a series of key questions, will provide you with a deeper understanding of how eating helps you in the here and now. Combined with the information you began to gather in chapter 7 about past and present influences on your eating habits and why you may be sensitive to particular types of threats, it will give you the basis for a new, personal compassionate formulation for overeating.

This analysis revolves around nine questions that help us to make sense of the reasons why we overeat and the unintended consequences of overeating:

- *Am I at greater risk of overeating when my threat/protection system comes into play?*

- *What types of threats are most likely to trigger my overeating?*

- *Are there any other threats that I pay attention to once my threat/protection mind-set is active?*

- *How does eating help me to cope when my threat/protection system is switched on?*

- *Does eating help me to feel soothed?*

- *Does eating help me turn off or tone down the threat/protection system?*

- *Does eating activate my drive system?*

- *How do I hope eating will make me feel safer (the intended consequence of eating)?*

- *What are the unintended consequences of overeating?*

We will work through these nine questions, using Alison's thoughts and responses, to show you how they can help guide your exploration, before trying to analyze how your three systems relate to your own overeating habits.

Alison's Analysis of Eating and the Three Systems

Using her first compassionate formulation for overeating, which we saw in chapter 7, and the completed pages of her eating diary (one of which we looked at in chapter 8), Alison began to develop her analysis of how her overeating related to her three emotional systems, taking the nine key questions in turn, sometimes singly and sometimes in groups, starting with the first three questions.

Key Questions

- *Am I at greater risk of overeating when my threat/protection system comes into play?*

- *What types of threats are most likely to trigger my overeating?*

- *Are there any other threats that I pay attention to once my threat/protection mind-set is active?*

Alison noticed that the biggest trigger to overeating on the day she completed her diary was the meeting with her boss just before lunchtime. This was a routine meeting to review her work performance. Alison wanted to use it to make her boss aware that she had taken on a lot of work recently that was beyond both her pay grade and training. She had spent a lot of time planning how to let her boss know she was upset about this additional burden and wanted the company to reduce the demands made on her.

However, Alison had found it difficult to be assertive with her employers in the past and already expected that, even if she told her boss about the problem, the company would do nothing to rectify the situation. Alison recognized that her problems with assertiveness cropped up in many relationships, and believed they dated back to her childhood. She noticed that both anticipated and actual experiences of trying to be assertive with others tended to activate her threat/protection system.

Alison also noticed that when her threat/protection system was in play, she was likely to remember times in her life when others had not met her needs. She was also likely to be angry with herself for finding it difficult to be assertive.

Key Questions

- *How does eating help me to cope when my threat/protection system is switched on?*

- *Does eating help me to feel soothed?*

- *Does eating help me turn off or tone down the threat/protection system?*

Alison noticed that eating helped her to deal with feelings of anxiety about the meeting in several ways. First, the food helped to soothe her anxiety. She also noticed that the types of food she ate reminded her of people who had cared for her; for example, the smell of the ginger cookies she ate at 10:00 a.m. reminded her of her grandmother, who used to bake with her when she was growing up.

Alison also found that focusing on the taste and pleasure of eating her burger helped to take her mind off the meeting after it happened. It also temporarily distracted her from self-critical thoughts about her performance in the meeting.

Key Question

- *Does eating activate my drive system?*

Some people who overeat are proud of their ability to eat more than others. There are even world records for the most hot dogs you can eat! However, for most people this is not the way their drive systems are activated when they overeat. More commonly, it is either anticipation of the pleasure of eating or planning to diet that will activate the drive system.

Alison had both of these experiences. She had not planned to have a burger and milk shake for lunch that day; indeed, she had actually brought a sandwich to work. But once the meeting was over, she told herself she deserved something nice to eat because she had survived what she thought would be a very difficult meeting (in fact, her boss praised some of her work and wasn't as critical as she had predicted). She spent the hour between finishing the meeting and her lunch break anticipating the flavors of her favorite food and the pleasure it would bring her.

Once she had finished eating her burger, she then spent a lot of time thinking about how she needed to diet to manage the extra food she had eaten that day. She remembered the times she had dieted and lost a little weight in the past, and the sense of achievement that eating less would bring her.

As we can see, the drive system can be turned on by the things we actually do, but a lot of the time, the focus is on how we will feel when we have achieved our goals; to this extent the drive system can often be driven as much by hope and wanting as by actually getting what we want.

Key Question

- *How do I hope eating will make me feel safer* (the intended consequences of overeating)?

Alison hoped that eating would both calm her anxiety and reward her for facing a difficult situation. She gave herself permission to overeat by telling herself she would diet later. Planning her diet also helped reduce her anxiety and manage her self-criticism by giving her something else to focus on. She also hoped dieting would make her happier in the longer term, particularly because it helped to boost her self-confidence.

Key Question

- *What are the unintended consequences of overeating?*

This question took Alison a little more time to explore. She noticed that although eating did help her feel a little less anxious, after overeating she often felt greedy and out of control (that is, self-critical). She worried that other people would also think she was greedy and out of control. Alison was worried about the effect of overeating on her health, but this concern tended to be less important than managing her fear of being criticized when her threat/protection system was more active.

On further reflection, Alison noticed that although eating helped her to reduce her anxiety before the meeting, it meant she had given less thought to how she was going to be assertive with her boss or to addressing this very important issue in her life in the longer term. And after the meeting, her focus on rewarding herself with food for surviving the encounter meant she didn't really compassionately listen to her sadness over the impact of being unassertive on her life, or make sense of her anger and grief for having her needs ignored for so long.

Your Own Analysis of Eating and the Three Systems

Having read Alison's analysis of how her eating related to her emotional systems, you may now wish to develop your own. You can use the information you have gathered from your diary and the first draft of your compassionate formulation from chapter 7, as well as any other observations you (or other people) have made about your eating, to help you answer the nine questions.

The nine key questions are set out next with some brief comments that may help you answer them, and again in worksheet 9.1, with space for your answers. Before you start trying to write down your answers, once again spend a few moments slowing your breathing and bringing to mind your compassionate sense of self so that you are looking at these questions from a compassionate frame of mind, with a genuine curiosity based on a desire to understand in order to be helpful, not critical. Now spend some time writing out your own thoughts in response to each of the questions.

- *Am I at greater risk of overeating when my threat/protection system comes into play?* If so, what ideas do you have about why this might happen?

- *What types of threats are most likely to trigger my overeating?* Try to think about what reasons there may be for this, perhaps by thinking about your personal history or current circumstances.

- *Are there any other threats that I pay attention to once my threat/protection mind-set is active?* Often when the threat/protection system comes into play, we can end up in threat spirals, feeling more and more threatened. This type of threat escalation is very normal. It can be useful to identify any new types of threats that emerge and how your eating may help you deal with them as well as with the original threat that was triggered.

- *How does eating help me to cope when my threat/protection system is switched on?*

- *Does eating help me to feel soothed?* If you feel that it does, think about in what way it does this; for example, does it help you to feel numb, bring in other soothing memories, and so on?

- *Does eating help me turn off or tone down the threat/protection system?*

- *Does eating activate my drive system?* For example, is it linked to having fun, or does compensating for overeating by dieting give you a feeling of pride, achievement, and being in control?

- *How do I hope eating will make me feel safer?* What are the intended consequences of overeating for you?

- *What are the unintended consequences of overeating?*

Sometimes it's helpful to do several separate analyses, to further explore the different threats overeating helps us with. For example, Alison could have worked through one to help her explore her feelings of being criticized by people she worked with, and another to explore concerns she had about upsetting other people in her life. If there were any differences between the two analyses, this might have suggested approaches she could take to managing the key threats she experienced and the safety strategies she used.

PUTTING IT ALL TOGETHER: A NEW, COMPASSIONATE FORMULATION FOR YOUR OVEREATING

In chapter 7 we introduced the idea of a compassionate formulation to help you make sense of your overeating. Building on this with the work we did in chapter 8 and what we have done so far in this chapter, you can now put together the information you have gathered about your history and your current eating habits, and the analysis of how your eating habits relate to your three emotional systems, to generate an overview of why your overeating developed, how it may be helping you now, and how the unintended consequences of eating may trap you in cycles of overeating that can be very difficult to escape.

As you may recall, the compassionate formulation is made up of four elements:

- Key threats, and the past and present influences that activate them

- Safety strategies, which we can use to provide us with a sense of external or internal safety

- Intended consequences of our safety strategies

- Unintended consequences of our safety strategies

Worksheet 9.1 Nine Key Questions for Analyzing the Relationship Between Eating and the Three Emotional Systems

1. Am I at greater risk of overeating when my threat/protection system comes into play?

2. What types of threats are most likely to trigger my overeating?

3. Are there any other threats that I pay attention to once my threat/protection mind-set is active?

4. How does eating help me to cope when my threat/protection system is switched on?

5. Does eating help me to feel soothed?

6. Does eating help me turn off or tone down the threat/protection system?

7. Does eating activate my drive system?

8. How do I hope eating will make me feel safer?

9. What are the unintended consequences of overeating?

We are also interested in how the unintended consequences of our safety strategies can lead to further difficulties that we end up using our safety strategies to solve, setting up vicious cycles.

It's important to remember that our formulation is always a "best guess" at explaining our eating habits. As you come to understand your overeating better, you can always update your formulation by adding new things or taking parts out.

Exercise 9.1 takes you through the same four steps to construct a new compassionate formulation for overeating. Just as you did the first time around, take your time with this. Work at a pace you can manage, and always bring your compassionate image to mind before you attempt to answer the questions. You can use worksheet 9.2 to record your formulation as you build it.

If you find yourself becoming self-critical or if the exercise is too much for you to manage, step away from the exercise and, before going any further, bring your compassionate mind into play again, using your soothing rhythmic breathing or safe-place image, and spend some time focusing on your compassionate image.

Exercise 9.1 Creating a New Compassionate Formulation for Your Overeating

Step 1: What are your key threats? This is where you identify the things that trigger your threat/protection system. Remember, these triggers may involve a range of different emotions, for example, sadness, anger, disgust, or grief. You may find it helpful to use any notes you have made about your personal history and your eating diary to identify times when you had to deal with events and emotions you found difficult. You can then look for patterns and triggers to your threat/protection system. Now try to list them:

The past influences on my key threats

1.

2.

3.

4.

(and any others)

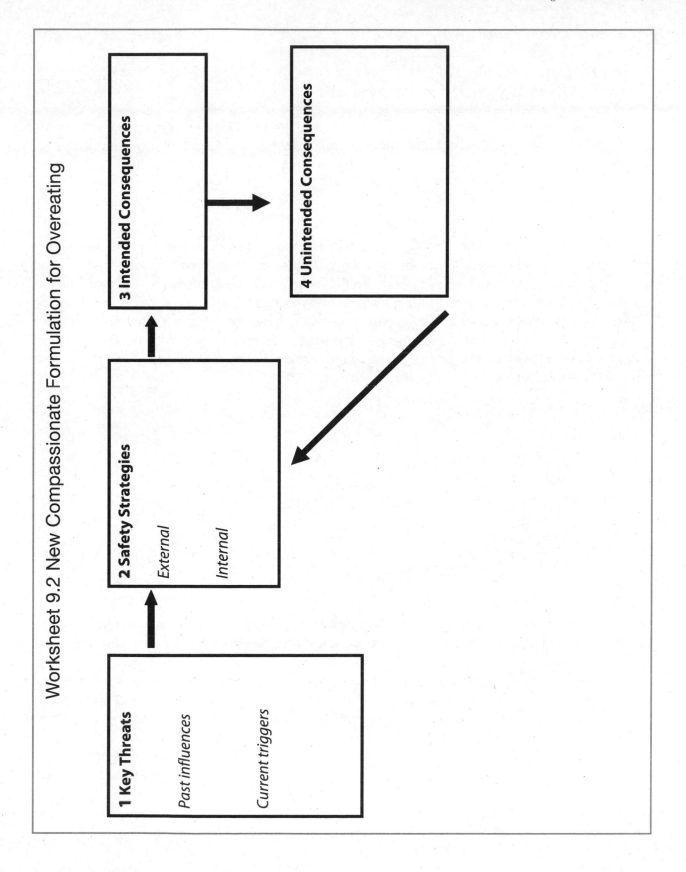

Worksheet 9.2 New Compassionate Formulation for Overeating

1 Key Threats

Past influences

Current triggers

2 Safety Strategies

External

Internal

3 Intended Consequences

4 Unintended Consequences

The current triggers to my key threats

1.

2.

3.

4.

(and any others)

Step 2: What are your safety strategies? These are the things you do, feel, or think to help you manage your key threats. Alison's example mainly explored her behavioral safety strategies: trying to please others, comfort eating, and dieting. Other strategies can include thoughts that protect you from powerful emotions, such as not allowing yourself to get close to others or always blaming yourself when things go wrong. They can also include habitual emotional reactions, such as disgust, to keep us away from things we find threatening.

If you find it difficult to identify these thoughts and emotions, it may be helpful to consider what other people might notice that you do to protect yourself; you might perhaps be able to talk this over with someone you trust. Now try to list them:

My safety strategies

1.

2.

3.

4.

(and any others)

Step 3: What are the intended consequences of your safety strategies? We may use our safety strategies in a very deliberate way, or we may find that these strategies have become something of a habit, with their original purpose lost in the past.

Knowing what you aim to achieve or avoid by using a particular safety strategy makes it easier to start thinking about alternative ways to cope with the problem. However, sometimes you may actually need to give up the strategy a little before you become aware of the role it has been playing and become able to start considering other ways to perform the same function.

You might find that working on your key threats individually, linking each of them to a safety strategy, helps you to understand what the intended consequences of each of your safety strategies are. Now try to list them:

The intended consequences for each of my safety strategies

1.

2.

3.

4.

(and any others)

Step 4: What are the unintended consequences of your safety strategies? You have now seen some of the unintended consequences of your strategies that can lead to further difficulties. It can be helpful to work on each strategy separately, using your personal history, your diaries, your own wisdom, and the helpful observations of others who care for you to understand the unintended consequences of your own safety strategies. Now try to list them:

The unintended consequences of my safety strategies

1.

2.

3.

4.

(and any others)

Finally, you can explore whether these unintended consequences actually increase the level of threat you feel or encourage you to intensify your safety strategies.

Once you have completed your formulation, you are then in a position to start developing alternative strategies to managing your threat/protection system. Your new understanding of your relationship with eating will help you to predict the types of problems you will need help with and the possible unintended consequences of changing your relationship with food. In the next chapter we will explore how we can use this new understanding to motivate you to make changes in your eating.

SUMMARY

In this chapter we have worked on expanding your personal formulation to explore the ways in which it may help you to manage key threats that have arisen from your past or present experiences, by exploring how your eating works now. Although it can be a little daunting at first, learning to use and analyze your diary can be a valuable way of recording your here-and-now relationship with eating. It can help you to identify a wide range of influences on your eating and will be the basis of your plan to overcome overeating, which we will explore in the final chapters of this book.

CHAPTER 10

Motivating Yourself to Change

In this chapter we will explore a way of understanding how the process of changing our behaviors, thoughts, and feelings works. If you are reading this book, it's likely that you are at least considering changing your eating habits. Indeed, you may well have tried to do this in the past. As we shall see, change can be difficult, and sometimes we can feel as if we are taking one step forward and two steps back. It's really easy to get disheartened and give up, or blame ourselves for our "weakness." This chapter will help you understand why "failure" and setbacks are normal and to be expected as an inevitable part of the process of change. We will explore how to make the most of these setbacks and beat overeating for good.

This chapter is all about preparing you to make changes. By the time you have worked through it, you will have the tools to keep you motivated, to understand how and why setbacks take place, and to respond to them compassionately.

THE SEVEN STAGES OF CHANGE

Psychologists have been very interested in how people change. The good news is that people can and do change, and we have much better ideas about how to make this happen than we used to. Two pioneers in this field, James Prochaska and Carlo DiClemente (1983), were particularly interested in helping people give up physically and psychologically addictive behavior, such as smoking and alcohol misuse, and they worked out a model of how change happens that has now been widely applied to a range of difficulties, including eating problems. Many people I have worked with have found this useful in helping them understand where they are in relation to the stages of change and to work out how to move toward permanently overcoming overeating.

Prochaska and DiClemente (1983) identified seven stages in the change process from not thinking about change to changing for good. Let's take a look at how these stages may apply to overcoming overeating.

Precontemplation

In this stage, we are not trying to address our overeating. We are likely to be caught up in a comfort-eating or dieting mind-set. We may become quite defensive or dismissive if people talk to us about our overeating, express concern, or try to stop us from comfort-eating or dieting.

Contemplation

Here we are likely to be thinking about or discussing our overeating. For example, you may have been in this stage when you were reading the early chapters of this book. This stage can often be quite distressing, as we think about the impact that overeating has had on us and the various reasons we have needed overeating to help us cope with our situations or emotions. This is a stage that can often be difficult to tolerate, and people often move back into precontemplation to avoid this distress. If we are going to beat overeating (or any other problem in our lives, for that matter), it's really important to remember that this suffering is a purposeful step on the journey to change and avoid beating ourselves up for having needed to overeat in the past.

Preparation

This is a stage in which we are planning to make change and getting ready to move forward. The more time we put into this stage, the better chance we may have of success in making the changes we need to beat overeating. Sometimes we can feel in a rush to do something about our difficulties; though understandable, this can lead to unintended consequences of change that can accidentally sabotage things later on. The work you have done in completing your personal history, eating diaries, and compassionate formulation is part of this stage.

Your compassionate formulation should help you manage some of the unintended consequences of change, but it's important to remember that there is no such thing as "perfect preparation." This stage can sometimes feel rather overwhelming, as we notice the many things overeating may have helped us with. So as part of preparing for change and the distress it may bring with it for a time, we need to prepare for making small and achievable changes, and to be aware that sometimes change will have unintended consequences or help us to learn something new about ourselves that will need to be incorporated in our revised formulation and action plans.

Action

In this stage, covered in the following three chapters of this book, we are putting our plans into action. This is often hard work that can be quite frustrating, but it can also be very satisfying and empowering to learn new ways to manage life's challenges. Change can be quite a slow process, and there can be unintended consequences or obstacles we didn't plan for. To have the best chance of coping with these challenges, which may seem disheartening at the time, it's really important to have reasons for making this change that are important to you and ideally also to have support from others. This does not mean we can't change if we don't have external support. For example, developing a compassionate relationship with yourself and having a strong compassionate image can give you someone in your corner who's cheering you on and commiserating when things get tough.

Maintenance

In this stage we tend to find that the changes we've made have become easier to manage. However, sometimes this can lull us into thinking that our old coping styles are changed for good. It can be relatively easy to forget the things that are helping us to beat overeating, and to see any setback as a sign that the work we did before was wasted or anything going wrong as a sign that we are weak in some way.

Lapse

It's almost inevitable, when we are trying to change previously successful coping strategies and to develop new ways of managing our emotions or overcoming old habits, that we will have a lapse or setback at some point. Lapses are more likely to be triggered when our new coping strategies are becoming established. However, they can also occur when we face new or unfamiliar situations. For example, we may have managed to reduce our overeating at home very well, but then go on vacation with friends who encourage us to overeat. Lapses can also occur when we try to push changes too fast, for example, moving quickly from establishing a structured approach to managing our eating to learning to rely on our hunger to inform us when we are full. They key thing here is to have a plan for managing lapses that sees them as part of a normal learning curve rather than as taking you back to square one.

It's likely that we will sometimes move from a lapse back into a period of precontemplation or even into a prolonged period of overeating. Don't worry; we all go through these times when we are making changes. The key is to learn from our lapses and, when we are ready, to move on to the next phase of the process of change. With practice this process of recovery becomes quicker each time, and indeed you may even learn to welcome the occasional lapse to remind you that you do have the skill and courage to overcome setbacks. Many people find that they feel better about themselves for knowing that they have the strength to do this.

Termination

At this point we find that our new strategies have stood the test of time. We have learned to manage and overcome the obstacles to changing our eating habits.

WHY THINK ABOUT THE PROCESS OF CHANGE?

The key reasons to think about this process are:

- To remind us that we are only human, that change takes time, and that we will all have setbacks

- To help us recognize what stage we are in and to work with, rather than against, it; for example, it's okay to think about changing (contemplate) for some time before taking action, but we may need to plan to support ourselves through any distress this may cause us

- To help us develop realistic expectations of the amount of time and energy we may need to devote to making changes

- To develop a sense that facing obstacles and making mistakes is normal and okay

If we are in the contemplation stage, we may need to spend more time thinking about the potential benefits of change, as well as the costs, before we are ready to move on.

If we are in the preparation stage, we may need to think about our plans for beating overeating: how we can develop small and achievable targets that will help move us toward our goals, any potential obstacles we're aware of at this stage, the support we might need and where we might get it, and the skills we may need to develop to help us put our plans into action.

If we are in the action phase, we may need to think about the amount of time and energy we can devote to changing, how we will keep ourselves motivated, and how we will manage lapses.

In the maintenance phase, we may need to work on recognizing the changes we have made and encouraging ourselves to maintain them, reminding ourselves of the benefits of change, and again to think about how we manage lapses.

COMPASSIONATE MOTIVATION

As you may recall from chapter 4, one of the key attributes of a compassionate mind is compassionate motivation, which comes from a deep caring for our own and others' well-being that generates a decision and commitment to help care for and relieve suffering. As we have seen, sometimes other mind-sets can block us from alleviating our suffering or divert us to short-term solutions to our distress that can inadvertently lead to further suffering in the long run. Compassionate motivation tends to take a longer-term view of caring for ourselves and others, and is also interested in helping us manage the unintended consequences of the ways we manage distress (such as overeating) and interested in caring for us as we make these longer-term changes.

When we bring this type of motivation together with an understanding of the process of change, the combination can be very powerful in helping us remain motivated in our quest to overcome overeating and in finding ways to give us the best chance of succeeding. It can also help us to understand and deal compassionately with the inevitable lapses and setbacks that occur for everyone who changes their relationship with food.

The following exercises are designed to help you explore and develop your motivation to change. However, before you begin to work though them, it's really important to bring your compassionate mind into play. What we are mainly interested in here is helping you to develop your sense of caring for yourself and your desire to reduce any difficult emotions you may feel, particularly in the long term.

So, before you begin each of the following exercises, set aside some time to bring your compassionate image into mind, either your compassionate self or your compassionate companion. Begin by establishing your soothing rhythmic breathing. When you are ready, imagine yourself as a deeply compassionate person who fully understands why we overeat, for reasons beyond our control, and why managing eating is hard.

Focus on a sense of warmth and kindness. Let your face settle into a compassionate expression. Imagine how you might speak to someone with gentle understanding and encouragement, and consider what your compassionate tone of voice might sound like.

If you prefer, you can imagine how your compassionate image or companion would motivate you to resolve overeating. In that case you would imagine this individual's dedication to you, wisdom, kindness, and strength. Pay attention to really trying to imagine this person's compassionate tone of voice.

When you think you have created this mind-set at least to some extent, then you can begin the exercises. Try to spend a couple of minutes on each of the following exercises at first and write down whatever comes to mind. You can return to the exercises whenever you find any new things that might motivate you or if you find yourself losing motivation to work on your overeating.

Exercise 10.1 At What Stage of Change Are You, and How Can You Move Forward?

This first exercise helps you to think about what stage of change you are in at the moment. You can then use your compassionate image to help you consider what would help you move into the next phase. Imagine considering and answering this question with kindness, openness, honesty, and understanding.

The next exercise is designed to help you if you find that you are in the contemplation and preparation stages of change. It will help you to identify reasons for changing your overeating as well as the benefits of keeping overeating a part of your life.

Exercise 10.2 Recognizing the Benefits and Costs of Overeating

Using all of the information you gained from your personal history, eating diaries, and any other sources, try to complete the following statements 1 through 5. Your personal compassionate formulation for overeating really comes into its own here in helping you to explore your reasons for change. Remember, your compassionate mind knows overeating may have been your best coping strategy in the past and won't criticize you for it, but will only help you to take responsibility for seeking better coping strategies in the future. Keep your compassionate mind uppermost as you then answer questions 6 and 7 with kindness, openness, honesty, and understanding.

1. My overeating helps me to manage:

2. My overeating has had the following unintended consequences on my health:

3. My overeating has had the following unintended consequences on my mood, thoughts, and feelings:

4. My overeating has had the following unintended consequences on my social life and relationships:

5. My overeating has had the following unintended consequences on my occupational or academic life:

6. In what ways would my life improve if I changed my eating habits?

7. What would motivate me to give up overeating?

When you can answer the last two questions from a compassionate perspective, you are on your way from the contemplation to the preparation stage.

It can be useful to keep your answers to these questions—we can call them your "motivational lists"— somewhere to provide a daily reminder of why you want to change. People I have worked with have found various ways to do this, including:

• Keeping motivational lists where you can easily see them (such as on the fridge door or the bathroom mirror, or even as a computer screen saver!)

- Keeping them in a "beating overeating" scrapbook to which you can add pictures, poems, or letters that can motivate you to change

- Sharing your reasons for changing with someone who cares about you and giving that person (or people) permission to remind you of why you want to change

- Spending some time each day thinking about the reasons to change from the perspective of your compassionate image

Please remember that the things that will motivate you are personal to you. They may not always make logical sense, and they certainly won't be exactly the same for everyone picking up this book! Different things will motivate you at different times, and again this is perfectly normal. The only real rule we have about motivation is that it must be compassionate. It must have our best interests at heart and should not involve bullying, cajoling, or scaring us into change. This type of behavior can work in the short term but, farther down the line, is only likely to result in our being more self-critical and miserable or even rebelling against the very changes we want to encourage ourselves to make.

IMPROVING YOUR CHANCES OF SUCCESS: PLANNING FOR BLOCKS TO CHANGE

The final element of the preparation stage is to plan for potential blocks to change. Some of these blocks will be specific to the activities and exercises we will use to help us beat overeating, and we will explore them as we introduce each activity. However, there may be more-general blocks that we can address before you decide to begin changing your relationship with food and eating.

To resolve overeating, you will need to make time for yourself to work on the exercises in the book. On average, this will take about an hour a day, usually in short bursts (for example, spending a minute of so after each eating episode recording the details in your diary). However, sometimes you may need to set aside an hour to plan your eating or write a compassionate letter (which we will look at in chapter 14). Finding this time can be very difficult, even if we really want to, so it's important that you see the work from the perspective of caring for yourself and truly wanting to alleviate your suffering, rather than as something you have to criticize or bully yourself into doing!

Sometimes the commitments we have in our lives or the people around us can make it difficult to make the changes we want to. Again, it can be helpful to think about this in advance, especially if we can break this obstacle down into practical difficulties that we could find ways of working around to give us the best chance of making permanent changes in our eating habits.

You can use the next two exercises to think about any practical difficulties before we move toward developing the first phase of your action plan for beating overeating: planning to eat differently. Again, your compassionate image's perspective will be helpful here; it knows the difference between your fears of change and the real obstacles we can all face in dealing with our problems in the longer term. It is wise enough to help you manage some of these practical problems without blaming you or being angry with you for the things that may slow you down as you overcome overeating. Imagine doing this with kindness, openness, honesty, and understanding.

Exercise 10.3 Identifying Practical Problems

Make a note of any practical problems your compassionate image can see that may make it difficult for you to make time to change your overeating. For example, you may be just starting a new job or moving to a new house or apartment, which may leave you very little time to do your compassion exercises or to plan your eating.

Exercise 10.4 Overcoming Practical Problems

Now use your compassionate image to help you plan how you might overcome some of these practical difficulties. So, you may decide to postpone starting your journey of eating compassionately until your move is complete or until you have settled into the new job. Or, knowing that the upcoming events will be stressful, you may decide to take some time out to do your exercises and to eat regularly. Both are examples of a compassionate solution if they recognize your limitations and support you to work with them, without criticizing you for the solution you have chosen.

Some Things to Try

While I can't know, of course, what your personal obstacles are, it might be helpful for you to consider how people have managed to overcome some of the common obstacles you may well encounter.

MAKING TIME TO PLAN

In the early stages of this process, you may need to learn to make time and space to eat and to reflect on your feelings. Start to make this time before you start changing your eating habits; for example, plan a few more breaks in the day, don't rush straight to the next thing after you finish the meals you already have planned, and try to create five minutes of "me time" every couple of hours.

FOCUS YOUR ATTENTION ON CHANGING

This can be difficult, too. There are so many other things that can pull us away, and it's very easy to fall back into old habits. Try to set up reminders of the times that you plan to eat (perhaps as an alarm call on your phone).

MAINTAINING ATTENTION ON THE REASONS AND TRIGGERS FOR OVEREATING

For example, you might put a note on your fridge that says, "Do I really want to eat now?" Perhaps you can keep a notebook or send yourself a text message for when you spot an urge to overeat or when you have found a new way to cope.

STAYING FOCUSED ON WHY YOU ARE DOING THE WORK

Many people, perhaps most, get disheartened when they're trying to change things, and it will be relatively easy to go back to not working on overeating, especially at first. Keep the motivational lists you made in exercise 10.2 somewhere you can look at them; maybe even do them again when you notice that you want to give up or have had a lapse.

Another way to stay focused is to keep a scrapbook of the reasons why you want to change, possibly including pictures, drawings, poetry, artwork—anything you like. The key is to make it personal to the reasons you want to change and to the kind of person you want to become.

FOCUS ON SUCCESS

People who overeat are often quite self-critical and tend to focus on their mistakes. It can help to get into a daily habit of writing down each small (or big) step you have taken in improving your eating and becoming more compassionate. You might want to keep this list in your scrapbook and look at it each morning when you get up!

Sometimes what we initially think are practical blocks (such as *I don't have time*) turn out to be linked to emotional blocks (such as *I'm worried about what people will think of me if I make more time for myself*) or to other worries about changing (such as *How will I deal with my feelings if I can't use food when I'm upset?*). It's absolutely normal to have both practical and emotional blocks to change. They key thing is to be compassionate about our limitations and with our concerns about changing.

It's helpful to be aware that the more blocks there are to our progress, the longer it may take us to beat overeating, but that doesn't mean we can't do it. The biggest single factor in predicting whether we will succeed is our desire for and commitment to change. This is why it's important to understand why you want to change your overeating and what will help keep you motivated when the going gets tough.

GETTING SUPPORT TO HELP YOU RESOLVE OVEREATING

Overeating is something many people feel ashamed of, which can stop them from seeking appropriate support. This is something else that can undermine our chances of beating overeating, or at least lengthen the time it takes. The next exercise involves using your compassionate image to help you make a list of all of the people who might support you. Again, your image will be wise enough to know the difference between the fears that may stop you from asking them to help, and the reality of whether these people would genuinely want to help and support you.

Your list could include family, friends, colleagues, your doctor, and perhaps a therapist. Of course, you may not wish to share everything about yourself with everyone on your list; in fact, some people can help without ever knowing you have a problem. For example, you may arrange to go out with someone because you enjoy the person's company, and when you are with that person, you are less likely to overeat. There may be other people in your life who care for you and perhaps have a more compassionate view of you than you have of yourself. People like this can be really helpful in steering us away from the urge to beat ourselves up for overeating, or drawing our attention to aspects of ourselves that our self-critical or dieting mind-sets do not.

As with all the exercises, consider the task with kindness, openness, honesty, and understanding.

Exercise 10.5 Identifying Sources of Help

Use your compassionate image to help you list the people who could help you beat overeating and what kind of help they may be able to give you (for example, practical, emotional, distraction, and so on).

Person   Kind of help

When you have developed your own plan for overcoming overeating, you may wish to talk with some of these people about how they can help. You may also wish to share this book with them and let them see your compassionate formulation or other elements of your action plan to beat overeating.

COMPASSIONATELY MANAGING SETBACKS

As we saw earlier, setbacks are to be expected when we try to change the way we eat (or anything else, for that matter). Again, we need to bring our compassionate minds to bear when we have a setback or lapse into overeating. If you were truly motivated to care for yourself, and to learn from and move forward from a setback, what kinds of things would your compassionate self say? Would it blame you, see you as inadequate or weak in some way? Or would it want to comfort and support you, to help you understand and learn from your setbacks?

Of course, in the disappointment of having experienced a setback, it may not be easy to maintain your compassionate mind-set. So it's a good idea to practice in advance how you might respond when it happens. To do this, first bring your compassionate mind into play. Now imagine that you are supporting a friend who has tried to change his overeating but has had a setback, perhaps has lapsed back into overeating because he went to a party or found out some upsetting news. How would you feel if you wanted your friend to do well but saw him struggling? What sort of thing would you like to say to your friend to help him be compassionately motivated to learn from the experience and to make a renewed commitment to continuing to work on his overeating?

When you have some idea of the things your compassionate self would like to say to someone else, you could try writing a short compassionate letter to yourself that you can keep to read when lapses occur. (We'll look at writing compassionate letters in detail in chapter 14.) This might include expressing your appreciation for your courage and wisdom in working on overeating, your sadness and your disappointment for the lapse, but also your support and encouragement for continuing the journey. You may also want to put down some ideas for the things that can help remotivate you and the names of people who could support you.

SUMMARY

In this chapter we explored the process of change and, using your compassionate mind, helped you to develop an understanding of your current stage of motivation and to identify ways of supporting yourself as you move forward. We have also explored how to deal compassionately with the lapses that are inevitable as you change your eating habits, and how to treat them as important new learning opportunities, rather than see them as failures or insurmountable obstacles.

In the next chapter we will work on the first stage of a compassionate action plan to address the practical elements of changing your eating patterns: finding out the amounts and types of foods you eat, and how to provide your body with the physical activity and rest it needs to keep you healthy.

CHAPTER 11

Determining What Your Body Needs

In the last chapter we explored how to develop your motivation for working on overeating. By now I hope you are clearer about the reasons why you overeat and the intended and unintended consequences of overeating, the reasons why you want to change your eating habits, and some of the blocks that may get in the way. As the next step forward, this chapter focuses on our physical needs for food, activity, and rest. It will show you how to figure out your own personal energy needs so that in the chapters that follow, you can use this information in developing a new approach to eating.

Caring for ourselves and others involves, among other things, a concern for our and their physical and emotional well-being. Therefore a compassionate action plan to address overeating needs to take into account both of these areas of our lives in aiming to develop a new relationship with our eating and our bodies. This plan will include aiming to stop using food to manage our emotions.

Caring about your physical well-being includes:

- Eating as much as your body needs

- Balancing your energy intake throughout the day

- Providing your body with the nutrients it needs

- Providing your body with foods that will help you to feel full and satisfied

- Providing your body with enough physical activity to keep it healthy

- Providing your body with adequate time to rest and repair itself

Caring about your emotional needs includes:

- Managing your emotional regulation systems (the three cycles)

- Developing a range of coping strategies to deal with various kinds of threats

- Developing emotional resilience to manage life's challenges and setbacks

- Allowing yourself to experience joy and pleasure, including enjoying eating

LOOKING AFTER YOUR PHYSICAL NEEDS

As we have seen, our comfort-food, dieting, and other eating mind-sets can lead us to eat in ways that do not meet our physical needs. To recap, unless we eat enough satisfying food on a regular basis, we are very likely to overeat (as well as to experience a whole range of physical and psychological problems), but if we regularly eat more than we need, we are likely to weigh more than we should and be at greater risk of developing certain health problems. Therefore the ways we eat, and the amount and types of food we eat, can be critical in addressing overeating.

We are a species that evolved to be physically active; indeed, physical activity can have the same effect as antidepressant medication in improving our moods. Yet in the West many of us have become very sedentary. If we are aiming to develop a compassionate approach to our bodies, we may also need to think about our relationships with physical activity. We need about an hour of physical activity a day that raises the heart rate but leaves us able to hold a conversation while we are doing it. However, it's important to take medical advice before you start exercising more, particularly if you have been inactive for a while.

Many of us lead very busy lives that do not take account of our bodies' needs to rest and repair. Indeed, lack of sleep has been associated with mood problems and a tendency to overeat. Again, we will need to take this into account as we develop a compassionate relationship with our bodies. It's recommended that most adults have seven or eight hours' sleep a night.

Many of you who are reading this book will be looking to it to help you lose weight. That is absolutely okay as long as you are *actually* overweight. As we have seen, being overweight can pose physical health problems, although perhaps not as many as we are often led to believe. A compassionate approach to our bodies may result in our losing weight if overeating leads us to consistently eat more than our bodies need, or if we have experienced the yo-yo weight loss and gain that's usually associated with dieting. However, that is not the main aim of taking a more compassionate approach to your body's needs. The main aim is to learn to feed your body and provide it with appropriate activity to keep it as healthy as possible, and to help you to find and live with the body your genetic history meant for you to live in. This can be a difficult journey because our emotions and eating habits can become very entangled, so it's also likely we will need to address our emotional needs along the way.

WHAT DOES YOUR BODY NEED?

Determining *exactly* what any individual's body needs is quite a complex activity, taking into account that particular body's energy requirements by the hour; the person's exact weight, gender, metabolic rate; and a whole range of other variables. This is achievable, and indeed the guidelines we will work from now are based on these types of calculations. But, of course, the level of expertise and time required to do this individually is unlikely to be available to most of us. The good news is that there's relatively little difference in our energy needs, leaving aside those of us who have severe medical conditions or who are elite athletes. This means that it's okay for the rest of us to work from general guidance about our nutritional needs, which indicates, as we have already seen, that most women need about 2,000 calories a day, and most men about 2,500 calories a day.

But the number of calories we eat is only part of the story. Our bodies also need a range of foods to keep us healthy. Nutritional guidelines place these foods into five categories and suggest the approximate balance among these categories that will help keep us healthy. These groups are:

- Starchy foods (carbohydrates)

- Fruits and vegetables

- Meat, fish, eggs, and beans (proteins)

- Milk and dairy foods (or substitutes, such as soy milk)

- Foods containing fat and sugar

Starchy foods include breads, cereals, potatoes, pastas, and corn; there is also starch in beans, lentils, and peas. All of these foods contain carbohydrates, which are an essential source of energy. In a healthy diet, starchy foods should make up around a third of everything we eat.

Fruits and vegetables are a vital source of vitamins and minerals, and nutritional guidelines suggest that we eat five portions of them a day. One apple, banana, pear, or similar-sized fruit is one portion. A slice of pineapple or melon is one portion, and three heaping tablespoons of vegetables is another. A glass of fruit juice also counts as one portion. Juice only counts as one of your five portions a day, no matter how much you drink.

Meat, fish, eggs, and beans are all sources of protein, which is essential for the growth and repair of the body. Around 15 percent of the calories we eat each day should come from protein. Meat is a good source of protein, as well as many vitamins and minerals. Fish is another important source of protein. There is evidence that people who eat two portions or more a week of oily fish (such as sardines, mackerel, herring, and salmon) are at lower risk of heart disease. That's because oily fish contains high levels of a "good fat" called omega-3. Eggs, pulses (such as beans and lentils), nuts, and seeds are also great sources of protein.

Milk and dairy foods, such as cheese and yogurt, are other good sources of protein. They also contain calcium, which helps keep bones healthy.

Fats and sugar are powerful sources of energy for the body. Fat has been divided into two groups:

- Saturated fats are concentrated in such foods as pies, meat products, sausages, cakes, and cookies, which can raise your cholesterol level and increase your risk of heart disease. Most of us eat too much saturated fat, putting us at risk of health problems.

- Unsaturated fats, on the other hand, provide us with the essential fatty acids needed to stay healthy and can actually lower your cholesterol level. Oily fish, nuts and seeds, avocados, olive oil, and other vegetable oils are sources of unsaturated fat.

There are two kinds of food containing sugar, too:

- Naturally occurring sugar, in foods such as fruit and milk, tends to be released slowly from food.

- Added sugar appears in processed foods, such as carbonated drinks, cakes, cookies, chocolate, pastries, ice cream, and jam. It's also in some ready-made savory foods, such as pasta sauces and baked beans. This added sugar tends to be released more quickly from food and thus can lead to rapid swings in blood sugar, which can leave us feeling tired and hungry.

Table 11.1 sets out how the recommended proportions of these different types of food in a healthy diet translate into the calories you need from each type every day. These are amounts for the average woman or man; of course, if you are very physically active, you will need to add additional calories to meet increased demands on your body.

Table 11.1 Approximate Daily Calorie Needs and Balance of Food Types

Food Type and Ideal Proportion of Daily Calories	Calories per Day (for a Woman)	Calories per Day (for a Man)
Starch (30 percent)	600	750
Fruits and vegetables (30 percent)	600	750
Protein: meat, fish, eggs, and beans (15 percent)	300	375
Milk and dairy (15 percent)	300	375
Fat and sugar (10 percent)	200	250
Total (100 percent)	**2,000**	**2,500**

If you find visual images easier to remember than numbers, you may find the "eatwell plate" shown in figure 11.1 helpful. This is another way of showing the same information about the proportions of the various types of food we need.

Interestingly, these different types of food have different effects on our satiety system, the system that makes us feel full and satisfied so that we know when we have eaten enough. Some foods are better than others at doing this. Protein is the most effective such food, followed by starchy foods; both are better at helping us feel full and satisfied than foods whose calorie content consists largely of sugar or fat. In fact, eating sugary foods can lead to a temporary rise in blood sugar, followed by a rapid drop, leaving us hungrier, low in mood, and more tired than before!

Figure 11.1   The Eatwell Plate

To help you overcome overeating, it's really important that you eat:

- Enough calories for your body's needs

- Regularly, to avoid the blood sugar drops that provoke overeating

- A varied range of food, with a healthy balance among the types of food you eat

Doing all three of these things will help you to learn to recognize and respond to your body's sensations of feeling hungry and feeling full.

MOVING TOWARD BALANCED EATING THAT MEETS YOUR NEEDS

Ideally, eating compassionately means we understand what our bodies need and when they need it, and allow ourselves to enjoy the foods we like in a way that does not affect our health or lead to overeating. That can feel like a really tall order if we have been struggling with overeating or denying ourselves food for any length of time. Sometimes even thinking about compassionate eating as a goal can lead us to give up, believing that this *may* be possible for some people but certainly isn't for us!

If you're thinking this, you certainly are not alone. Remember, our see-food-and-eat-it brains and the comfort-eating, dieting, and other eating mind-sets we develop may take us a long way from compassionate eating. So although it may be our goal, it's unlikely that any of us will be able to do this 100 percent of the time. The good news is that occasionally eating in a less compassionate way (for example, overindulging on holidays) is something our bodies can cope with relatively well; they just can't cope if we do it a lot of the time.

Many people I have worked with have found it very helpful to use a structure to guide them in learning to eat compassionately. This involves putting some time into planning what and when we will eat, gradually learning to recognize our bodies' signals for hunger and fullness, and responding to these signals. Making these changes can provoke a whole range of thoughts and feelings that can stop us from compassionately caring for our bodies. We will explore ways to work on these changes in more detail in the next chapter. For now, we will just work on developing your skills in estimating how much you need to eat and how much you eat at the moment.

FIGURING OUT WHAT YOU'RE EATING NOW

In the early stages of learning to eat compassionately, you will need to devote a little time to figuring out what you are currently eating and how this compares to what you need. This can be a little unnerving at first, especially if you are used to calorie counting as part of a dieting mind-set or if you are unused to being aware of what you eat. However, if you are going to determine what your body needs, you will need to know how much energy you take in, how much energy you use up, and how the types of food you eat relate to the types of food your body needs.

If you have worked through the book to this point, you will already have tried keeping an eating diary. We can now use this, along with a calorie-counting book or website, to estimate your energy needs and your energy intake. There are many commercial and open-access Internet sites that give the calorie values of a wide range of foods, as well as a range of calorie-counting books in the shops and libraries. Many also tell you how many calories you use up doing different kinds of activities or exercises. I suggest looking at a few so you can choose one you find easy to use.

Like all tools, knowledge about the calories of the food you eat and the energy you use can potentially have some unintended consequences, including:

- Activating your dieting mind-set

- Reminding you of negative experiences in the past with calorie counting

- Leading you to become obsessed with the calories you eat

- Allowing you to use calorie estimating to beat yourself up for being greedy, out of control, and so on

So, before we begin, it's really important that you explore and manage these possibilities from the perspective of your compassionate mind. Take a little time to engage your affiliative soothing system by using your soothing rhythmic breathing; then, when you are ready, bring your compassionate image to mind. Allow yourself to experience its care and warmth for you, and then gently try to "step into" its shoes.

Let yourself imagine that you truly want to care for yourself, to offer yourself the benefits of the strength, courage, and wisdom of your compassionate image in exploring the next two exercises.

Exercise 11.1 Identifying Difficulties in Calorie Estimating

Allow your compassionate image to identify any difficulties it can foresee if you were to figure out the calories you have eaten, and jot down these difficulties in the following space:

-

-

-

-

Once you are aware of these risks, you can then use your compassionate image to help you to develop a plan to manage them. Please remember that the aim of estimating calories here is to help you to understand and to care for your body's needs; it is not about losing weight or beating yourself up for overeating. If you notice your critical mind-set chiming in, it's really important to slow down and return to your compassionate image before you go on with the task. You may wish to do this in the form of a compassionate letter (see chapter 14 for more on how to do this), or just to jot down the main points in the following space in exercise 11.2.

Exercise 11.2 Compassionate Thoughts and Actions for Estimating Your Energy Intake

-

-

-

-

The benefits of spending a short period of your life becoming more aware of what you eat and learning to eat in a way that cares for your body's needs can really be worth the time and effort it takes. People I have worked with have told me that this knowledge gives them control over what and how they want to eat, and makes it far easier to manage their biological urges that used to cause them to overeat. The good news is that you will only need to estimate your calories in a lot of detail once during the whole program, when you are designing your first meal plan. You can use the information you have gathered from your diaries so far to do this. Ideally, use at least two weeks' worth of diaries, particularly if there are big variations in how much you eat or how much activity you do.

It's a lot easier to estimate your energy balance when you have a meal plan in place, because you can simply add or subtract calorie estimates for foods you eat in addition to the plan, or for foods you leave out, as well as increases or decreases in your activity levels.

You can use the following guidelines to help you with this task:

- Estimate calories. You don't need to weigh out to the ounce everything you eat; a good estimate is usually good enough.

- Make a note of all the physical activities you do in fifteen-minute episodes.

- Make a note of the types of food you eat and approximately how many calories a day of each of the five main food types you eat.

Let's think about what this would look like in practice by exploring Alison's eating diary again. To save you from going back to chapter 8, the same day's diary is reproduced again here as figure 11.2. Alison was not particularly active that Monday, so her energy requirement would have been the normal 2,000 calories. However, if Alison were more active, we would have to raise her energy need to take this into account. For example, let's say that on Tuesday she spent four hours doing housework and two hours exercising. Suppose we use a calorie-counting book to figure out her energy needs for three hours of housework (720 calories) and two hours of exercise (two aerobics classes at the gym: 840 calories). We do not include one hour of the housework, because this would be included in Alison's routine energy needs. So on Tuesday Alison needed around 3,560 calories to meet her energy needs.

You can see from this calculation that physical activity can make a big difference to how much we need to eat. It's really important to take this into account when you are trying to understand daily fluctuations in your energy needs and how hungry you are likely to be!

If we go back to Alison's eating diary for Monday, we can add up approximately how many calories she ate and drank:

1 bowl of cereal with skim milk and sugar = 200 calories

2 slices of toast and butter = 300 calories

15 ginger cookies = 750 calories

Burger meal (small cheeseburger, no fries), large milk shake = 700 calories

4 (small) glasses of red wine = 350 calories

Take-out meal (pizza, 4 slices) = 1,280 calories

Individual tub of ice cream = 180 calories

3 cups of tea with skim milk = 30 calories

Total calories = 3,790

This would have been only a little more than she needed on Tuesday, but was 1,790 calories more than the 2,000 her body needed on Monday. One of the typical patterns we can fall into when we overeat is to try to make up for it the next day (hence Alison's very active day on Tuesday, after she had overeaten on Monday). Although Alison's energy intake across the two days more or less balances out, the problem was

Monday, March 23

Situation	What You Ate or Drank	Overeating?	Dieting or Comfort-Food Mind-Set Active When Eating?	Thoughts and Feelings
Where were you? Who were you with? How were you feeling? What were you thinking before you ate?	Type and amount / Physical Activity / Type and duration	Yes/No	Yes/No	During or after eating, about keeping the diary, or anything else you think is important
8:00 a.m., at home, alone A bit hungry, tired Not really thinking about anything	Cereal, two slices of toast, tea	No	No	Felt okay about eating, a bit worried about going to work today
10:00 a.m., at work, with colleagues A bit anxious Worried about difficult meeting later today	Tea and five ginger cookies	Yes	Comfort food	Felt a little worried that colleagues would think I was greedy, but felt I needed the food to calm me down
12:30 p.m., at work, alone A bit queasy, not hungry More anxious about meeting	Tea and ten more cookies; had planned to have lunch but couldn't face it	Maybe?	Comfort, but also thought I would cut back on the cookies for the rest of the week	Felt greedy
1:45 p.m. at restaurant at work, alone Very upset by meeting, felt angry with boss and useless Mainly thinking about meeting and worried about what other people thought about me	Burger meal, large milk shake	No	Mainly comfort but planned not to eat for the rest of the day	Felt okay about eating, but very down about myself, worried about going back to work
10:30 p.m., home, with partner Still upset about work Felt I deserved a treat	Four glasses of wine, take-out meal, plus leftovers Individual tub of ice cream	Yes	Dieting mind until just before the meal, but partner came in from work late and brought in take-out	Didn't want to eat, but when I did, felt out of control and could not stop Felt angry with myself for overeating, planning to eat a lot less tomorrow

Figure 11.2   Alison's Eating Diary

that she swung between overeating one day and then not eating enough for her needs the next day. By the time she reached Wednesday, she was back to overeating because she had become very hungry after leaving herself so short of the energy she needed on Tuesday. We will explore how to address this issue when we come to meal planning in the next chapter.

The other interesting thing Alison discovered from her diary was that most of her calories came from foods high in fat and sugar, such as cookies, or high in carbohydrates, like cereal, bread, and pizza. She also tended to have quite a lot of dairy products, such as milk and milk shakes, and a significant percentage of her calories came from alcohol. Her protein intake was relatively small (mainly the meat in her burger), and she had no fruits or vegetables on Monday. The difficulty here was that the high-energy foods she ate were also the foods she found least filling, so she tended to eat more of them.

Ideally, Alison needed to significantly increase her intake of foods that were less high in energy but would help fill her up (such as fruits and vegetables). She also needed to swap her high-energy foods for others that included more protein, which again would be more filling than fatty and sugary foods, such as cookies. This was bound to be difficult, because sweet and fatty foods can directly soothe us and thus tend to be the comfort foods of choice for most of us. Still, with time and perseverance Alison was able to make significant changes in her energy intake and to change the balance of the types of food she ate.

Alison also learned to develop other ways to cope with the low moods and distress she had become accustomed to relieving by eating. She learned to lower her "emotional temperature" by introducing a number of self-soothing activities into her daily routine, such as ensuring that she had at least a thirty-minute "me time" bath every evening. She also practiced using her safe-place imagery to help her regain some emotional stability when she got upset; in fact she got so good at this that she was able to summon up a feeling of being soothed by just imagining a peaceful beach for a couple of seconds! Alison also built a number of distractions into her routine, even taking a salsa dance class with her partner.

Like many of us, Alison tended to estimate the calories she had eaten in relation to how she felt about food. For example, she believed her cookies, which were high in fat and sugar, contained far fewer calories than her breakfast, because breakfast tended to be more filling. She was feeling quite upset when she had her burger, and greedy when she had her take-out, so she tended to overestimate what she had eaten on these occasions. She often associated feeling full with feeling greedy or having overeaten. She found it really helpful to figure out realistic calorie estimates for these eating episodes and to see how they differed from her "feeling-based" calorie estimates.

FIGURING OUT YOUR ENERGY BALANCE

Our energy balance is the difference between the amount of energy we take in, and the amount of energy we need to fuel our bodily systems and whatever else we do. Most people who overeat will have a positive energy balance (they eat more than they need), but on some days they may have a negative energy balance (eating less than they need). A long-term positive energy balance leads to weight gain, while severe short- and medium-term negative energy balances tend to lead to overeating. In this section we are interested in helping you develop a more neutral energy balance to help reduce overeating that's based on feeling hungry. This will also help to stabilize your weight so that you do not need to get into a dieting mind-set to manage it.

As we have already seen, there are two elements in our daily energy needs: our basic energy needs (2,000 calories for a woman, 2,500 for a man) and the energy we use up above our normal energy needs (for example, through housework, walking, or formal exercise, such as playing football or going to the gym).

It's best to determine your energy balance over a week, because it can fluctuate quite a lot from one day to the next. The easiest way of doing this is to calculate energy intake and energy used for each day, and then add them up at the end of the week. You can record these details in worksheet 11.1. (A couple of more blank copies are available at http://49776.nhpubs.com that you can download if you wish.)

As well as the amount of food we eat, we are also interested in eating more of the foods that can keep us healthy and feeling satisfied. So worksheet 11.1 also gives you space to record what you are eating and the type of food it is. You can then figure out the approximate proportion of each type of food you eat in your total intake.

We are also interested in the amount of activity you undertake, because the other half of your energy-balance equation is how much energy you use up. You can then figure out whether you are eating more or less than you need each day and throughout the week.

When you have all this information, you will be able to use it as the basis for the next stage in changing your eating habits, which is planning your meals to incorporate changes in the amounts and types of foods you eat. This will be the focus of the next chapter.

Exercise 11.3 will take you through some steps to help you complete the worksheet. You might also like to look at figure 11.3, which is a sample completed copy of the worksheet based on Alison's eating diary for Monday.

As you can see, the first part of worksheet 11.1 has spaces for you to record the food you eat, your approximate energy intake (in calories) from it, the type of food it belongs to, and any physical activity. This includes formal exercise, but also day-to-day activities like housework or walking. In the second part of the worksheet, you can note your calorie totals (both consumed and used) to arrive at energy-balance figures for each day, and then for the whole week.

We are particularly interested here not only in whether you end up with a positive or negative energy balance, but also in what types of food you're mostly eating. You can use the eatwell plate (review figure 11.1) and the information in table 11.1 to guide you in allocating a type of food to what you eat. For example, ginger cookies do contain a lot of starch, but they are designated as "fat and sugar" for Alison's worksheet, because this is where they appear on the eatwell plate.

When you are figuring out your energy balance, you will need to spend a little time reflecting on the types of activities you did each day. Many people are surprised by just how active they are, which in itself can sometimes account for some apparent overeating. As we saw in chapter 2, if you merely lie in bed doing nothing all day, you need around 1,550 calories just to keep functioning. If you do a sedentary job with about an hour's worth of physical activity (say, walking to the office and back, and around the stores at lunchtime) you will need 2,000 calories if you are an adult woman and 2,500 calories if you are an adult man. So if you are more active than this, you will need to increase your energy intake accordingly, keeping roughly to the same proportions of food types as shown in table 11.1. For example, if you do an extra hour in the gym, you may need an extra 300 calories during the course of the day, ideally in the form of 90 calories of starch; 90 calories of fruits and vegetables; 45 calories of meat, fish eggs, or beans; 45 calories of dairy products; and 30 calories of fat and sugar. You will also need some extra fluid to replace what you will lose though perspiration—and a bit of rest to let your body recover!

Worksheet 11.1 Daily Food Intake and Energy Balance

(a) Daily record

Food Eaten	Approximate Energy Intake (Calories)	Main Type of Food (Starch, Fruit/ Veg., Protein, Dairy, Sugar/Fat)	Activity and Approximate Energy Used

(b) Daily and weekly summary

	Mon	Tue	Wed	Thur	Fri	Sat	Sun	Weekly Summary
Total calorie intake								
Starch								
Fruits and vegetables								
Protein								
Dairy								
Sugar and fat								
Alcohol								
Energy need (approx. 2,000/2,500 + extra for energy expended in activity)								
Energy balance (= calorie intake – energy need)								

Food Eaten	Approximate Energy Intake (Calories)	Main Type of Food (Starch, Fruit/Veg, Protein, Dairy, Sugar/Fat)	Activity and Approximate Energy Used
Cereal	120	Starch	30 minutes walking to work (100 calories)
Skim milk (breakfast and teas)	80	Dairy	30 minutes housework (100 calories)
Two slices toast	220	Starch	
Butter	80	Dairy	
Sugar	30	Sugar	30-minute exercise video (only did 10 minutes: 120 calories)
Ginger cookies	750	Fat and sugar	
Burger bun	300	Starch	
Burger	100	Meat	
Milk shake	300	Dairy	
Pizza	1,280	Starch	
Ice cream	180	Dairy	
Wine	350	Alcohol	

(a) Daily Record

	Mon	Tue	Wed	Thur	Fri	Sat	Sun	Weekly Summary
Total calorie intake	3,790							
Starch	1,920							
Fruits and vegetables	0							
Protein	100							
Dairy	640							
Sugar and fat	780							
Alcohol	350							
Energy need (approx. 2,000 + extra for energy expended in activity)	2,000+ 120							
Energy balance (= calorie intake − energy need)	+1,670							

(b) Daily and Weekly Summary

Figure 11.3   Alison's Daily Food Intake and Energy Balance

When you are familiar with the worksheet and have looked through Alison's example in figure 11.3, you are ready to think about doing exercise 11.3.

The key to this exercise is to use your compassionate mind to explore your food diary and complete worksheet 11.1 with an approach of gentle curiosity:

- Gentleness is important because this exercise can lead us to feeling disappointed, angry, or ashamed of what and how we eat, so we really do need to be kind to ourselves and compassionate toward our struggles with eating. Your compassionate mind can use your personal formulation to help you understand why you eat the way you do and to support and value your commitment to changing the way you eat.

- Curiosity is also important, because exploring the types and amounts of food we eat can often provide us with new insights into and understanding of our relationships with food and the areas we feel we can begin to work on. Many people I have worked with have found that taking a gentle, inquiring perspective can help them overcome their usual patterns of either avoiding thinking about what they eat or attacking themselves for what and how they eat.

Remember, you only need to figure out your energy balance and the types of food you have eaten in detail once during the whole process of overcoming overeating, to give you an idea of your current eating pattern so you can design your first meal plan. Doing it in this degree of detail for any longer will become a chore at the very least and, at worst, can be counterproductive, because constantly counting the calories of everything you eat is likely to activate your dieting mind-set. Once you've done this one-time exercise, it's far more helpful to begin to plan your eating in advance, and then review it at the end of the week to see if there are times when you varied from your plan so you can refine it or address things that have led to overeating as part of the plan for the following week.

Only begin exercise 11.3 when you feel emotionally ready and practically prepared to start to make changes in your overeating. It is designed to help you make sense of some of the changes you may need to make. You may need to do a little preparation before you begin. The exercise can take about two hours, so you need to set aside time when you can work on it, either all at once or in several shorter sessions. It can also activate difficult thoughts, feelings, and memories in us, particularly if we have dieted a lot in the past or are critical of our eating. So you will need your compassionate mind to guide you, support you through the process, and help you to tolerate any distress the activity may cause you. Your compassionate mind will be wise enough to know how much of this you can manage at any one time. It can also be helpful to have some self-soothing or other distress-management activities prearranged for when you finish the exercise.

Exercise 11.3 Determining Your Own Energy Balance

Begin by using your safe-place image or soothing rhythmic breathing to bring your affiliative soothing system into play. It's common for people doing this exercise to find that their minds wander even more frequently than usual; this may be because they have associated looking at what they eat with the urge to diet or self-criticism.

If your mind wanders in this way, remember to use our motto "notice and return" to gently refocus your attention on the task in hand.

When you can feel that your affiliative soothing system is uppermost, you are ready to move on to the next stage of the exercise: activating your compassionate image. Allow yourself to experience its compassion for your courage and wisdom in taking on the task of exploring your diary. What sort of things would it say to support you in exploring your diary? How would it encourage you to explore it compassionately rather than use it as a way to motivate you to eat less or punish you for eating too much?

You can then, supported by your compassionate image, explore your eating diary from the perspective of your compassionate mind or, if you find it easier, your compassionate image. This may enable you to explore the diary in a more detached way, almost as if it were someone else's, but still with gentle, compassionate curiosity. Either of these approaches is fine. You may find it easier just to work though one day at a time and to do the exercise over several days, before you add up your week and summarize the information on worksheet 11.1.

However you do this, take your time over it. It's an important part of the groundwork for all the other things you will do to change your relationship with food, eating, and your body, so you deserve some time to spend doing it at a pace you can manage.

When you have finished filling in the worksheet, you can explore what your compassionate image would say about what you have learned and what changes in the amount you eat, the types of food you eat, and your activity levels you could work on. You may wish to jot down these thoughts, perhaps in the form of a compassionate letter (see chapter 14 for more on how to do this), to guide your efforts to address your overeating, which you are now ready to begin.

SUMMARY

This chapter has explored what it means to be compassionate with your body's needs, particularly in terms of your need for energy, activity, and rest. We have explored a way of using a week's worth of records from your food diary to help you figure out your energy balance and the types of food you eat. You can now use this as the basis for developing your plan for changing your eating and, of course, working on the thoughts and feelings that lead to overeating or that may follow from changing your eating. The next two chapters will guide you though a step-by-step approach to compassionately achieving this end.

CHAPTER 12

Toward a New
Way of Eating: The First Steps

This chapter combines all the work you have done so far to put together a practical plan for addressing overeating and caring for your body. It shows you how to establish a basic structure for eating that includes managing foods that can put you at risk of overeating. As always, the key is to use your compassionate mind—based on wisdom, kindness, and a genuine desire to be encouraging and supportive—to guide you.

AN OUTLINE OF THE SIX-STEP PROGRAM

In the early stages of building your new relationship with food and your body, you will need to spend time planning when, how, and what you will eat. The longer you spend doing this—three to six months is probably a good period to aim at—the more likely you are to establish a new eating routine. Then, gradually, you can become less strict with your meal plans, experiment with a wider range of foods, and learn to respond to your experiences of being hungry and full.

Many people confuse meal planning with dieting. A meal plan is not a diet. Meal planning is about making changes in your eating patterns and, later, in the amounts and types of food you eat. It does this by taking away the option of eating less later if (for any reason) you overeat, because you know you will still stick to eating the next meal you have planned. Meal planning can also help you to change some of the common features of chaotic eating patterns—such as leaving long periods between meals or eating very frequently—that can put you out of touch with your feelings of hunger and fullness.

Your new way of eating involves learning to be more mindful of the influences that can lead to over-eating. It is broken down into six steps:

1. Establish a regular eating pattern.

2. Reduce your intake of high-risk foods that trigger overeating.

3. Balance your energy intake with your energy needs.

4. Develop a healthy nutritional balance.

5. Learn to respond to your hunger and fullness.

6. Learn to enjoy food and eating.

Each step will help you learn more about your relationship with overeating. It's best to start with step 1 and work through all the steps at a pace you feel comfortable with. As with any new skill, you should only move on when you feel relatively confident you can manage each step. A good rule of thumb is to move up a step when you can manage it for about five days in a week, and to move back a step if you are struggling for two or three days in a row.

This chapter will take you through the first two steps of the program; the next chapter will cover the remaining four.

Step 1: Establish a Regular Eating Pattern

Let's start with establishing a pattern of eating regularly, because this is a good basis for all the other changes I will introduce. Regular eating patterns tend to reduce the body's urge to overeat and help to balance out high and low levels of blood sugar, which have a powerful influence on your appetite and moods.

If you're going to eat regularly, then obviously this means regulation! And yes, there are five rules for you to follow. If you have struggled with overeating for some time, you'll probably need to stick to these rules for a while:

- Plan when you will eat.

- Eat by the clock.

- Eat every three to four hours.

- Do not skip an eating episode.

- Do not add an eating episode.

These rules may look a bit daunting at first, even a little authoritarian, and perhaps impossible to stick to. But don't worry: it may take you a little time to establish them, but most people do manage over time. Of course, you may need to bend the rules occasionally, but the more quickly you can establish a regular eating pattern, the easier it will be to stop overeating.

At this point, you are not aiming to change the amounts or types of food you eat, just to space out your eating more.

To establish your eating plan and record how you stick to it, you will need to use the eating diary we first saw in chapter 8. As we discussed earlier, reviewing our diaries can unintentionally lead us into a dieting or self-critical mind-set. So do be aware of this potential obstacle and prepare yourself to overcome it by ensuring that you plan your eating and review your diary with your compassionate mind. Begin by engaging your affiliative soothing system using your soothing rhythmic breathing. When you are ready, bring your compassionate self or compassionate image to mind. Focus on your compassionate feelings of wisdom and encouragement throughout this next exercise, which will take you through reviewing your eating diary to drawing up a regular eating plan.

Exercise 12.1 Planning to Eat More Regularly

Start by looking at one day's diary from the perspective of your compassionate mind. Pick a typical day, neither one of your worst days for overeating nor one when you were dieting. What do you notice about the times you eat? Are there gaps of more than three to four hours between the times you eat? Or do you find it difficult to leave gaps in your eating; for example, do you eat every couple of hours or even find yourself grazing all day? If you notice either of these trends, try to use your compassionate self or image to explore these key questions. You can use your compassionate eating formulation, and your analysis of overeating and the three emotional regulation systems from chapter 9 to help you. Always keep in mind that your answers need to come from a perspective of genuinely trying to understand, and kindly and gently support yourself in exploring and making changes in your eating.

Key Questions for Planning Regular Eating

- *Why don't I space out the meals I eat?*

- *How does it help me to eat more (or less) frequently than my body needs?*

- *Would I encourage other people in my life I care about to space out their eating the way I do?*

- *How could I encourage myself to eat more regularly? What could I do or say to help myself do this?*

When you feel ready, try to develop a daily eating plan based on the amount and types of food you currently eat. The aim is to break this down into between five and seven eating episodes during the day. Try to eat every three-and-a-half to four hours, starting with breakfast within about thirty minutes of getting up, and ending with a light snack just before you go to bed. You can use worksheet 12.1 to set up your eating plan.

Again, you can use your compassionate mind to help you with this. Draw on its wisdom to help you set realistic and achievable expectations about when you will eat. It will understand that in these early stages, you may still feel the need to overeat, and will not expect you to give this up until you are ready. So at this stage, if you still need to overeat, for example, to help you manage a difficult feeling, that's okay. However, try to do this in a more planned way. For example, you may really want a big tub of ice cream as a comfort food. Instead of coming home and raiding the fridge an hour before you have planned to eat, try to delay your urge and have your ice cream at a time when you have scheduled a meal and when your body is likely to be hungry.

Worksheet 12.1 Daily Meal Plan

Meal or Snack	Time and Place	Food and Drink to Be Taken	Comments, Including any Problems in Keeping to Meal Plan, any Solutions to These Problems or Changes to the Plan
Breakfast			
Midmorning snack			
Lunch			
Midafternoon snack			
Evening meal			
Evening snack			
Bedtime snack			

Meal or Snack	Time and Place	Food and Drink to Be Taken	Comments, Including any Problems in Keeping to Meal Plan, any Solutions to These Problems or Changes to the Plan
Breakfast	Get up at 7:00 a.m. Eat at 7:30 a.m. with partner	Cereal and milk Two slices of toast Cup of tea	
Midmorning snack	10:30 a.m., at my desk at work, talking to colleague	Cup of tea Five ginger cookies	
Lunch	1:00 p.m., at burger bar, with colleague	Burger meal and milk shake	
Midafternoon snack	4:30 p.m., at work, in staff room with other staff members	Cup of tea Five ginger cookies	
Evening meal	7:15 p.m., at home with partner at the dinner table	Take-out meal Individual tub of ice cream Two glasses of wine with meal	
Evening snack	10:30 p.m., at home with partner, watching TV	Five ginger cookies Two glasses of wine the rest of the evening	
Bedtime snack	None, as went to bed early		

Figure 12.1   Alison's Meal Plan Sheet

Figure 12.1 shows an example from Alison's regular eating plan, based on the day's diary we explored earlier. As you can see, she did not reduce the amount she ate, but just changed how it was spaced out. This gave her a greater sense of control over her eating, and also helped her to learn to tolerate her urges to overeat in the knowledge that she could still do this if she needed to, but at a time that felt more within her control. We also based the timing of her eating on the hours she was awake. Because she got up at 7:00 a.m. and went to bed at 10:30 p.m., Alison had only one evening snack, which meant she had to space all of her eating across six episodes. However, this was still in the target range of five to seven episodes. As you can see, Alison also drank the same amount of alcohol on this day. Clearly, drinking four glasses of wine every night wouldn't be very healthy; however, Alison only drank on one evening a week, and this particular evening was the one night in the week that she spent time with her partner watching a movie. Alison acknowledged that she would rather drink less and, over time, managed to space out her drinking a little more across the week, while still keeping well within recommended limits. However, in the early stages of learning to eat regularly, she did not think she could do this and change her "drinking for fun and relaxation" at the same time. This is not uncommon, and it's always important to use your compassionate mind to guide how far you can go with making changes at any one time.

You may also notice that Alison made changes in not only when she ate, but also where she ate. She had noticed that eating alone placed her at greater risk of overeating and also left her quite vulnerable to the waves of emotion that often accompanied eating. She found that planning to eat with others more often helped to provide her with some emotional support (even though the people she ate with at work were unaware that they did this) and also helped to distract her from very self-critical thoughts she had when she was eating.

Interestingly, Alison found that this level of planning took away a lot of her anxiety about eating and gave her a greater sense of control over her appetite. It also helped her to recognize how different mind-sets during the day influenced her and how the people she was with could also affect her urges to eat.

On its own, regular eating can have a positive impact on overeating for some people, so as you start working on this, you may want to look back over your diary each week to see if your eating has improved.

Some people find it difficult to establish a regular eating plan. This is not surprising, given the obstacles that can arise from having to rearrange when and how we eat, let alone the emotional reasons for eating in the way we've gotten used to doing. The next exercise is designed to help you explore any blocks you may have to eating regularly, and to develop a plan and alternative compassionate thoughts to help you address them.

Exercise 12.2 Managing Blocks
to Eating Regularly

The first step is to imagine that you are going to start eating regularly tomorrow. This can be quite exciting, because it is a practical start to addressing your overeating; however, you might have a lot of "yes, buts" or imagine the problems that might arise when you start. These problems could be practical (for example, *I don't have food in the house*) or related to your thoughts and feelings (for example, *I'm worried that if I can't comfort-eat, I won't be able to cope*). Write them down in the left-hand column of worksheet 12.2.

The next step is to use your compassionate mind to help you. Take a little time to feel compassion for yourself, either from "you at your best" or from your compassionate image. Then allow yourself to feel

Worksheet 12.2 Managing Blocks
to Regular Eating

Practical or Emotional Block to Managing Regular Eating	Compassionate Things I Can Say to Myself or Do to Get Past the Block

compassion for the blocks you may encounter in making these changes. Remember, it's not your fault that these blocks arise; maybe there are very real obstacles in the way of your making changes, or maybe thinking of making these changes has activated your threat/protection system in some way and raising obstacles is your brain's way of trying to protect you from harm. Take a little time to explore why these blocks may have arisen and perhaps try to write down the reasons for your blocks, too, underneath the blocks themselves on the worksheet.

Finally, imagine how you would feel if you could work through these blocks and manage the feelings that might arise as you did so. You may then wish to add in the right-hand column of the worksheet anything you could do or say to yourself to help you overcome these blocks and begin to eat regularly.

There is a completed example of the worksheet to help you in figure 12.2.

Practical or Emotional Block to Managing Regular Eating	Compassionate Things I Can Say to Myself or Do to Get Past the Block
People are always snacking at work, and it's difficult to say no to the cookies or if they bring chocolates in. They might not like me if I refuse.	This is difficult, because eating is a very sociable thing, especially since I have never tried to say no. But I could choose to try to say no. Other people at work do, and people don't think badly of them. I can try to do this one day at a time and see how I feel.
I get so famished, especially if I see food on TV.	This is very understandable. I do tend to get desperately hungry a lot in the evening, sometimes because I have not eaten as often as my body needs. Eating more regularly might make this a bit easier. TV is designed to make us have cravings; otherwise why make commercials! However, before reaching for that unplanned snack, I can take a breath or two and bring on my compassionate smile and image, and consider how I would feel if I resisted.
I'm so busy I don't really stop for lunch; well, few people in the office do.	This is hard, especially when other people at work don't stop. However, I do deserve the time to eat, and I will try to reschedule my work so that I can. Perhaps I could even encourage a few other people to join me.

Figure 12.2   An Example of Managing Blocks to Regular Eating

When you begin to space out your meals more regularly, you may find that this, too, can be difficult at times, or that it may provoke painful thoughts and feelings. Keep a note of these difficulties in your eating diary, because when you review your diary, these notes will help you understand what works in favor of your eating more regularly and what tends to obstruct your progress.

Remember, you are likely to have setbacks along the way. Each new block you encounter is a sign not of failure, but of your courage in making changes and an opportunity for you to learn more about how your eating works.

Step 2: Compassionately Reducing Trigger Foods to Overeating

The next step toward your new way of eating is to reduce your risk of being tempted to overeat out of habit or as a way of managing your feelings. The compassionate element here is to figure out what you can actually manage without triggering your dieting mind, being overwhelmed by feelings, or depriving yourself of these foods as a way of punishing yourself. Though it can be trickier than it looks, this step has the advantage of not requiring you to count calories or plan your meals.

The first thing to do is to identify the types of foods that are most likely to put you at risk of overeating, which may be foods that you associate with comfort eating or that you really enjoy but find it hard to stop eating once you've started.

Returning to Alison's diary, we can see that she had several foods that were associated with emotional comfort (such as ginger cookies) and some foods she really enjoyed (such as burgers or pizza). Some of these foods (for example, burgers) fell into both categories, in that she enjoyed them and also ate them to "treat" herself for having been upset. Sometimes Alison would eat sweets when she felt angry with herself, which didn't really give her comfort and didn't allow her to really enjoy them either. After a while she realized that because she knew they were "bad" for her, she ate these sweets when she felt very self-critical and as if she didn't deserve to eat more healthily or to be happy; in other words, these foods became ways of punishing herself. Of course, this was something she really needed to work on, and gradually she managed to stop doing this as she became less self-critical and more self-compassionate.

You can use your own eating diary to determine the types of food that put you at risk of overeating. You can then list them using worksheet 12.3, putting them into one or more of the four categories according to why you tend to eat too much of them. Figure 12.3 gives you an example of how to do this, using Alison's observations from her diaries.

Next, you can begin to work on reducing the amounts of these foods you eat. Try doing this in four stages.

1. Don't tell yourself you are not allowed to have them. This is really important. Humans have a tendency to want what they can't have the minute they are told they can't have it! Remember back in chapter 3, when I asked you to imagine that I said you couldn't go to the toilet until you'd finished reading the chapter?

This urge to do whatever we're told we can't do becomes even stronger if we feel we are denying ourselves something that's really important to us, such as something that we enjoy, that gives us comfort, or even that punishes us. Again, the kinder we are to ourselves about these urges, the easier it is to manage them.

Worksheet 12.3 High-Risk Foods for Overeating

Food	Comfort Food? Yes/No	Enjoyable Food? Yes/No	Treat Food? Yes/No	Self-Punishing Food? Yes/No

Food	Comfort Food? Yes/No	Enjoyable Food? Yes/No	Treat Food? Yes/No	Self-Punishing Food? Yes/No
Ginger cookies	Yes	Not really	No	No
Burger	No	Yes	Yes	No
Pizza	No	Yes	Yes	No
Sweets	No	No	No	Yes
Wine	No	Yes	Yes	No

Figure 12.3   Alison's High-Risk Foods for Overeating

2. Figure out the minimum amount of this type of food that you can eat. The key here is not to stop eating this food entirely. You may still have the need to comfort-eat for some time and will still want to eat many foods because you enjoy them. As you work on changing your eating habits and learn new ways to deal with your feelings, you will also be gradually working on changing the emotional meaning of foods, particularly foods you habitually use to comfort or punish yourself. However, at this stage we are trying to help you reduce the amount of these foods you eat and at the same time to learn to tolerate your feelings.

To begin with, figure out how much of the food you need to eat to get the emotional response you want. Aim to have only this much of the food available to you at any one time. Of course, you may be tempted to buy more when it has gone. However, this approach will at least mean that you have time to stop and think before you do this, so that you can understand your urges and give yourself some time to work with them.

3. Gradually reduce the amount of this type of food and learn to tolerate your emotions. The aim here is to allow yourself enough of the food to take the edge off your emotions, but to learn to tolerate them a little more.

To see how this works in practice, let's go back to Alison. Alison found that ten cookies tended to be enough for her to feel comforted, and after this she did not feel any more comfort from them, even if she ate another twenty. So initially she decided to keep ten comfort cookies that she could use if she needed them. She could only have ten, so that meant the rest of the package got thrown away. It was a waste of money, but she would have wasted her money on extra cookies anyway, because they did not provide her with extra comfort and overeating by eating them all did not stop her from eating again later.

After several weeks of doing this, Alison felt she could gradually reduce her reliance on cookies for emotional comfort. So she decided to reduce the total by one cookie at a time. Alison managed to do this, and although she felt some distress when she did not have as many cookies as usual, she felt she could cope as long as she had her safety net of a smaller number of cookies.

The extent and rate at which you reduce your comfort eating and switch to a healthier balance of foods will be personal to you. People do vary on this, and determining your own way is very important. It's also important to bear in mind that even when we are eating in a more balanced way, we are still allowed to eat and enjoy foods we used as comfort foods in the past; the key is just to change your relationship with them so that you are not using them to manage your emotional life. We'll be looking in more detail at learning to enjoy food in a balanced way in the next chapter.

4. Increase the delay between the urge to eat your specific food and eating it. This is similar to reducing your intake slowly, in that you are learning to sit with your feelings for a time and to find other ways to manage them. You may recall that we explored mindfulness in chapter 5. This is a good time to become more mindful by learning to notice what your feelings are, not to change them necessarily, but to notice them.

You might also find it useful to write down your feelings. What's going on for you when you turn away from comfort eating or say no to foods you love? Rather than eat your feelings away, you will have written compassionately about them, helping you to understand your feelings better, and becoming kinder and gentler with them. You may also find that writing about your feelings lowers the power of the eating urges.

Alison did not feel she could give up cookies as a comfort food entirely, so when she got down to seven cookies, she worked instead on delaying when she would eat them. Initially she decided she could only manage one minute of feeling distressed before she ate her cookies. Gradually she built this up to five minutes, which gave her time to put other coping strategies in place.

The key issue here is learning to become mindful of what we eat and why we eat it. Minimizing the amount of these foods and delaying when you eat them can help you be more in control of the quantity you eat but, more important, gives you time to reflect on your reason for overeating.

If you eat to treat yourself or because you enjoy a particular type of food, by all means, let yourself have these feelings. But if you do, take time over the taste, texture, and smell of the food, rather than gobble it down. Make time to eat it in a way that's within your control, and only eat the amount you need to eat to have these feelings.

You may have heard people call chocolate their "guilty pleasure." If you feel this way about, say, chocolate, you could work on reducing your feelings of guilt so that chocolate becomes something you can eat and enjoy. You may well find that you get more satisfaction and enjoyment from one chocolate that you eat slowly, focusing on savoring the taste and texture, than you get from eating a whole box while watching TV! What's happening here is that the feeling of being a naughty child has changed to that of being an adult, in control, who is allowed to feel pleasure.

SUMMARY

This chapter has explored the first practical steps you can take toward changing your eating habits. We have explored how you can begin to eat more regularly, and ways to think about and address some of the potential obstacles to doing so. We have also explored how you can allow yourself to slowly reduce the types and amounts of foods that can trigger your overeating. These first steps can help you to manage some of the biological highs and lows that come with chaotic eating patterns, and to tolerate and understand your urges to overeat.

The key here is to be compassionate with your attempts to eat more regularly and your urges to overeat. When you feel that you can manage a regular eating pattern, and have a little more control over and understanding of the foods that can trigger overeating, you are ready to move toward the second phase of addressing overeating: changing the amounts and types of food you eat, and learning to respond to your body's needs. We will look at these steps in the next chapter.

CHAPTER 13

Toward a New
Way of Eating: The Final Steps

In the last chapter we worked through the first two steps of a program to establish new and better-balanced eating habits: spacing out your eating and reducing your intake of foods that are likely to lead to overeating. In this chapter we will move on to cover the remaining four steps: planning what you eat to meet your energy needs, improving the nutritional balance in what you eat, learning to respond to your body's signals for hunger and fullness, and finally, learning to enjoy eating and caring for your body's needs.

THE BENEFITS OF MEAL PLANNING

Meal planning can be tricky to begin with, and I am often asked whether the effort is worth it. It certainly does take some time, but in my experience, meal planning is crucial to resolving overeating. Most people who don't overeat tend to eat regularly, and have a good idea of the types and amounts of foods they will eat and when. If you don't have a sense of this—and many people who overeat don't—then it's certainly worth learning to acquire it, which is what meal planning is all about.

It's important to recognize that meal planning is not an end in itself. None of us wants to have to plan exactly what we will eat and when we will eat it for the rest of our lives! Meal planning is the basis for helping you separate emotional overeating (because you're angry, for example) from biologically driven overeating (because you're hungry). It can also:

- Give you a clear idea of what you intend to eat

- Provide a structure to your eating

- Help you avoid chaotic eating patterns

- Match your energy intake to your energy needs so you are less likely to be hungry

- Give you a baseline from which to make changes in the types and amounts of food you eat

- Help you take into account changes in your daily energy needs

- Help you identify and work with times when you eat "off plan"

- Retrain your body to experience feeling hungry and feeling full

You are likely to need to plan your eating for between three and six months. Gradually you will develop a menu of foods you can eat regularly that will meet your nutritional needs and won't lead to over-eating—this will make planning (and shopping!) a lot easier—and then move toward eating in response to the signals your body gives you, rather than according to your plan. Please remember that your meal plan should be based around foods that you enjoy, help you feel full, and keep you healthy.

POTENTIAL PROBLEMS WITH MEAL PLANNING

Many people encounter problems in developing a meal plan and putting it into practice, potentially including:

- Not knowing how much of a particular food to eat

- Feeling too constrained by the plan

- Difficulty keeping to the plan when other people are around

- Difficulty keeping to the plan when on vacation or visiting others

It's useful to identify any problems you think might crop up, and have some ideas about how to deal with them before you actually start on your meal plan. The next exercise will help you to do this.

Exercise 13.1 Identifying Potential Problems with Meal Planning

In the following spaces, list any problems you think you might face when setting up a meal plan.

-

-

-

-
-

Now write them in the left-hand column of worksheet 13.1. Then, using your compassionate mind to guide you, as you did when you started to plan eating regularly, think about what you might do or say to yourself to overcome these problems, and write your suggestions in the right-hand column of the worksheet. Figure 13.1 shows a sample completed worksheet that may help you.

Practical and Emotional Blocks to Managing a Meal Plan	Compassionate Things I Can Say to Myself or Do to Help Me Manage My Meal Plan
I don't like to plan when and what to eat.	Most people don't like to plan like this. *But* I deserve the opportunity to develop a better relationship with food. I have been able to schedule regular eating a little better. I can live with this for a while to see if it can help me; if it doesn't, I can always stop doing it.
Eating according to a plan makes me feel controlled and brings up unhappy memories of the way people fed me in the past.	It's really sad that people were controlled, by eating in unhelpful and unkind ways in the past. It's also understandable because overeating and dieting often helps you to feel in control. *But* now that I am an adult, I can choose to take control of my eating and learn new ways to take control of my life. I don't really control food anyway; it controls me, because I can't stop overeating when I want to.
I don't know what a normal portion of pizza is.	I can look up what a normal portion is in my calorie-counting book. I can figure out how many calories of pizza I will eat as part of my evening meal and allow myself this.
The plan does not give me any freedom.	If I give myself too much freedom, I know I will overeat. It's worth having some constraints to help me figure out why I overeat. I can choose what I eat on the plan.
It's hard to keep to the plan when other people are around.	Everyone struggles to eat consistently when they are with others. I can plan in advance for the kind of meal other people might eat. I can use this as a chance to practice saying no when people offer me food.

Figure 13.1   An Example of Dealing with Blocks to Meal Planning

Worksheet 13.1 Dealing with Blocks to Meal Planning

Practical and Emotional Blocks to Managing a Meal Plan	Compassionate Things I Can Say to Myself or Do to Help Me Manage My Meal Plan

Meal planning is a "live and learn" process, and you're likely to come up against a number of challenges to sticking to your plan as you go. No one's expecting you to keep to your meal plan all of the time; that would be unrealistic for any of us! The key is to stick to it as much as possible. That way it can serve its purpose as a way of retraining your body to eat *what* it needs to eat and *when* it needs to eat it, and to help you identify the various influences that lead to overeating so you can work on them.

Step 3: Balancing Your Energy Needs

The first thing to do in designing a meal plan is to balance your energy needs so that you are eating approximately the amount of calories your body will use up.

However, first here's a word of caution: There's quite a high risk that putting this step into action may trigger your dieting mind-set. If your overeating has led to weight gain, you're likely to lose some weight as you establish a better energy balance. It's all too easy to become fixed on this as an achievement in itself, or become impatient with the rate of weight loss and try to eat less than your body needs. Also, if you try to reduce your overeating too rapidly, you run the risk of triggering your famine-survival responses described in chapter 2.

So here are some guidelines to help you manage this step, summarized in four key points:

* Know what your needs are now.

* Know by how much you are overeating or undereating.

* Don't reduce your energy intake too quickly.

* Plan your eating at least one day in advance.

Know what your needs are now. We explored your energy and nutritional needs in some detail in chapter 11. You can use this information as the basis of your meal plan.

Know by how much you are overeating or undereating. Again, the information you collected in chapter 11 will help you to calculate this. Remember to look at these needs day to day as well as across the week to avoid the urge to overeat that comes from trying to "make up" for overeating on the previous day.

Don't reduce your intake too quickly. Most of us will be familiar with the notion that diets would only aim to reduce our weight by one to two pounds a week. The evidence suggests that this is the most our bodies can manage healthily. If you tend to overeat as a consequence of getting caught up in a dieting mind-set when you start to reduce the amount you're eating, even this may be too much. A weight loss of one pound represents a negative energy balance of roughly 3,000 calories over a week, which works out at just over 400 calories a day. Ideally, you might aim at reducing your overall energy intake by about 200 calories a day until it roughly matches your daily energy needs so that you are in a neutral energy balance.

Remember, changing your eating is a long-term process, and the goal is to make changes that will last as part of a healthier relationship with food, eating, and your body. This is a little easier if you aim to make smaller, but sustainable, changes in your eating.

Plan your eating at least one day in advance. This does require some forward thinking and you may find it difficult at first, but over time you will get used to having a range of food options you enjoy that meet your energy needs, so that you can make changes at will from day to day without having to start from scratch every time.

The principles of designing a meal plan are basically the same as those you used to establish a regular eating pattern in the previous chapter, and you can use a similar form to set out your plan. This is provided in worksheet 13.2 (more copies of the worksheet are available at http://49776.nhpubs.com, and you can download as many as you need or make your own). The only change is that now, besides eating regularly, you're planning what and how much you will eat to roughly balance your eating intake with your needs.

So meal planning has the same five rules as for planning regular eating, plus new ones:

- Plan when you will eat.

- Plan how much you will eat at each episode.

- Eat by the clock.

- Eat every three to four hours.

- Do not skip an eating episode.

- Do not add an eating episode.

- Drink enough fluid (about eight glasses, or around half a gallon) a day.

In figure 13.2 you will find an example of a day's meal plan to guide you. Remember, we don't initially change the types of foods we eat; rather, we move gradually into healthier options. So view this example as a way to make small changes toward generally healthier, but nondieting, food choices.

Step 4: Developing a Healthy Nutritional Balance

Sometimes when we begin to plan our meals, we can also begin to change the types of food we eat. However, many of us find this a step too far at first, which is why step 3 simply concentrated on planning how much and when you will eat. Once you have established your meal plan, however, and are getting used to aiming at a neutral energy balance, the next step is to work at getting a better nutritional balance as well. You can use the information in chapter 11 (especially table 11.1 and figure 11.1, the "eatwell plate") to guide you on proportions of the various types of food.

One of the problems that can arise with doing this is that we are often brought up to associate healthy eating with having boring meals or feeling forced to eat foods we don't like. The key to improving our nutritional balance is to explore a wider range of foods. This may mean that we need to experiment a little more. For example, you might think you don't like the taste of vegetables, but there is an awful lot of different vegetables, and maybe you were put off by just one or two, perhaps always cooked the same way. So you may need to try a lot of different types, cooked and prepared in quite a lot of ways, before you can really decide what you like.

Worksheet 13.2 Tomorrow's Meal Plan

Day and Date _____

Eating Episode	Time	Food and Drink to Be Taken (Including Type and Amount)
Breakfast	a.m.	
Midmorning snack	a.m.	
Lunch	p.m.	
Midafternoon snack	p.m.	
Evening meal	p.m.	
Bedtime snack	p.m.	

Monday, March 30

Eating Episode	Time	Food and Drink to Be Taken (Including Type and Amount) Please note: Where there is a choice of portion sizes (such as two or three potatoes), women should have the smaller sized portion (such as two potatoes) and men the larger one (such as three potatoes).	
Breakfast	7:30 a.m.	STARCH	1 bowl cereal 2 slices bread
		FATS/SUGAR	butter or margarine jam, honey, or marmalade
Midmorning snack	10:30 a.m.	DAIRY FRUIT	1 yogurt (not diet) 1 apple
Lunch	1:00 p.m.	STARCH	2 slices bread or average baked potato
		FATS	mayonnaise, butter, margarine, or salad dressing
		PROTEIN	1–2 slices meat, 2 eggs, 2 oz cheese, canned fish, or 1 small can beans (men should double these amounts, for example, 2 full sandwiches or 2 baked potatoes)
		VEG DAIRY	salad if wanted 2 scoops of ice cream
Midafternoon snack	4:30 p.m.	FRUIT	1 banana 1 fruit juice
Evening meal	8:00 p.m.	STARCH	2–3 medium potatoes, 4–6 heaping tablespoons of cooked rice or pasta, or 2–3 slices bread
		FATS PROTEIN	oil in cooking, butter, margarine, mayonnaise, or salad dressing 2 slices meat, 2 eggs, 2 oz cheese, small can beans, average serving fish, or 4 fish fingers
		VEG SUGAR	vegetables or salad 1 chocolate-covered cookie
Bedtime snack	11:00 p.m.	DAIRY	milk drink (men should add an extra snack)

Figure 13.2   Sample Daily Meal Plan

This can be quite an exciting time in your process of tackling overeating. Here are a few tips you might want to try to help you.

- Use your meal plan and the information in chapter 11 to explore how your current eating fits with a nutritionally balanced food intake.

- Try to make small changes in your balance and then build on them. For example, you may want to increase your intake of fruits and vegetables by 100 calories a day at first, swapping this number of calories for another type of food (perhaps reducing sugary or higher-fat foods by the same amount).

- Have some fun experimenting with food. For example, you might write the names of twenty types of fruit on pieces of paper, mix them up, and pick one at random. Go and find one of whatever it is. If you really don't like it, try something else.

- Experiment with cooking food as well. For example, my kids really don't like carrots that much, so my wife mashes them with potatoes.

- Learn what you like and don't like, and don't eat what you don't like!

Step 5: Learning to Respond to Feelings of Hunger and Fullness

Meal planning is designed to help us retrain our eating patterns so that we can then move on to deciding what and when to eat on the basis of whether our bodies feel hungry or full, rather than on the basis of our habits and emotions. Within the structure of regular, balanced eating, which your meal plans will provide, you will gradually learn to experience these feelings of hunger and fullness. A healthier nutritional balance will mean that most of the calories you eat come from the types of food that are most likely to help you feel full and satisfied.

Some diets can add to our confusion about how full or hungry we feel, for example, by getting us to drink a lot of water before we eat. Just adding extra fluid to your diet may not be enough to help you regulate your eating or recognize what your body needs. For example, studies do suggest that having a large glass of water before eating can help some older people to feel fuller (van Walleghen et al. 2007) and hence to eat less afterward, but sadly this mechanism does not work for most of us (at least if we are under seventy years old), and indeed the systems that regulate how thirsty or how hungry we are appear to be quite different. Drinking too much before you eat can make it more difficult to determine whether you are full. By all means have a drink when you eat, but try not to drink so much that you feel bloated, as this will make it harder for you to determine what foods help you to feel full and how much of them you need to eat.

Developing a compassionate approach means that we need to recognize this complexity and try to determine what helps us to feel full and satisfied. This can be a little tricky, because at this stage the science is still unclear about all of the mechanisms that can affect our feelings of hunger and fullness. So this section is about helping you to learn about the amounts and types of foods that help you to feel full, and to recognize when you need to eat.

Often the ways in which we eat can obscure our natural feelings of hunger or fullness, or lead us to ignore our bodies' signals. To become aware of them again, we may need to learn to be more mindful of the experience of eating. If we think about which Western countries have the longest life span and most healthy lifestyles, we tend to think of the countries of southern Europe and the Mediterranean diet, which is based around fresh fruits and vegetables; starchy food, such as pasta; and protein from meat and fish.

However, this is only part of the story. The Mediterranean diet is also associated with a very specific way of eating. Eating tends to be a shared family ritual, each dish is savored, and a meal can last for several hours, including the occasional glass of wine, also sipped and savored rather than gulped down. This is in fact the very type of eating we evolved for. The key point is that food is not just fuel that we eat in front of the TV, at our desks or workstations, or even behind the steering wheel. Allowing yourself to eat more slowly, to savor the tastes and textures of food, and to begin to digest one course before you decide whether you want the next one can help you listen to your body and become more sensitive to its signals.

You can add this step at any stage of your journey to a new way of eating. However, the reason I have put it here, toward the end of the six-step program, is that if your eating has become entangled with managing difficult feelings, then being more in touch with feelings of hunger and fullness may also put you in touch with difficult emotional experiences or memories. If this is the case for you, it can be helpful to eat in a *less* mindful way in the early stages of changing your eating. Nevertheless, to beat overeating for good, we do need to become more mindful when we are eating or when we have the urge to eat. You can use your eating diary to help you note any thoughts and feelings you have when you eat more mindfully.

If you feel ready to embark on this step, start by becoming more mindful of the physical experience of hunger, so you can begin to use this as a guide for when to eat and how much you need. Sometimes it's easier to recognize when we have eaten far too much than when we are hungry. So to begin with, spend a little time remembering the last time this happened. How did your body feel? When did you notice you had eaten too much? What happened that helped you to ignore these feelings of becoming full while you were still eating?

Next you may want to think about the last time you were so extremely hungry that you found it really hard to stop eating once you had started. How did this feel in your body? What things had led you to ignore your hunger this much?

Finally, think about the last time you felt you had eaten just enough to feel satisfied (a bit like Goldilocks and her porridge—you got it just right!). This is the sensation you want to experience to guide you in knowing when your body has had enough to eat. Sometimes we will not get this absolutely right; we will have eaten just a little too much or remain just a bit hungry.

Again, using your compassionate mind, try to bring to mind each of these stages, and explore how it felt and what helped you to notice when you had eaten enough or just slightly more than your body needed.

You can practice this skill by rating your hunger and fullness, which we will explore in the next exercise.

Exercise 13.2 Learning to Feel Hunger and Fullness

In this exercise you can work on becoming more mindful of your body's hunger and fullness signals.

To begin with, every time you eat, make a note of how hungry you feel before you eat and how full you feel after you eat. You could do this in your eating diary or meal plan.

When you have a better idea of how hungry and full you are before and after you eat, you can move on to the next stage, which is to track these sensations during the day and when you are actually eating.

As you develop this skill, you can then use the knowledge you gain to decide when you need to eat and when you have had enough to eat. It can also be helpful to make a note of whether other things interfere with your ability to keep an eye on (and respond to) your body's needs, for example, feeling tired, angry, or upset, or becoming too engrossed in other activities.

You can use the following rating scales to help you. The hungriness scale is something you can use throughout the day, perhaps keeping a note of your score every hour or so and every time you eat. If you use it together with your eating diary, it can help you to explore anything that increases your hunger. Such things may include a desire to eat that's triggered by changes in your blood sugar levels when you need food; however, you may also notice associations between certain feelings (such as tiredness or anger) and increased feelings of hunger. The fullness scale is designed to be used while you are eating; perhaps just keep a note of changes in feelings of fullness during your meal and for around thirty minutes after you finish eating.

Hungriness Scale

1 = Extremely hungry, so much so that you will find it very hard to stop eating when you are full or that you can't wait for your next meal.

2 = Moderately hungry; you may still be inclined to overeat or to snack a little before your next meal.

3 = Slightly hungry; you may have strong urges to overeat or snack, and have to work hard to resist.

4 = Ready to eat; you know you are ready for your next meal, but don't have a strong urge to snack and are unlikely to overeat when you have it.

5 = Don't need to eat; you don't feel hungry, and if you were to eat now, you would feel overfull.

Fullness Scale

1 = Not full at all; you are still hungry after your meal and are very likely to overeat.

2 = Moderately full; you are still a bit hungry and want to carry on eating; you may end up overeating.

3 = Full and satisfied; you have eaten enough to feel full and don't want to eat any more.

4 = Overfull; you have eaten more than enough, perhaps having eaten a few bites more than you needed.

5 = Far too full; you feel very uncomfortable with the amount you have eaten, perhaps bloated, even physically unwell.

Ideally, we want to start eating as soon as we start feeling hungry (4 on the hungriness scale) and stop when we reach 3 on the fullness scale, so that we won't overeat. You may need to spend some time learning to do this, because we can all get a little out of touch with our bodies' needs; the key is to try to avoid getting so detached from what your body is telling you that you end up getting very hungry and then overeating as a result. It's also important to remember that your body tends to take a little while to give you signals that you are full; so eating more slowly and with fewer distractions is really important at this stage so that you can become aware of your feelings of fullness gradually growing.

What am I hungry for? Recently I had an interesting discussion with a dietitian colleague of mine who regularly asks her clients an interesting question in relation to eating more mindfully: what are you hungry *for*? Now, as a psychologist, I thought she meant, what emotional needs is your eating helping you with? and, of course, this is an important aspect of this work. However, this wasn't quite what she meant, and her answer was fascinating. She is interested in the body's intuitive wisdom in knowing what it needs and hungering for that thing; sometimes, she said, we need to know what this is in order for our bodies to feel satisfied. The most extreme example of this can be some of the curious food cravings that happen during pregnancy. But let's take a more everyday example. Let's imagine you really want some orange-flavored chocolate, but deny yourself this and have an orange instead. My guess is that no matter how many oranges you eat, you will still be "hungry" for the chocolate. Being aware of this can help you to recognize what it is you want and then be satisfied with a little of it, rather than spend so much time denying your needs that you eat food you don't want and then, having denied yourself and so increased the craving, ending up overeating the thing you wanted in the first place!

Step 6: Learning to Enjoy Food Again

This is your final step along the road to a new way of eating. By this stage you should be able to keep (mostly) to your meal plans, be more in touch with your body's needs, or both. You will also be able to recognize trigger foods and other things that are likely to lead to overeating.

You may also have included in your eating plan some of the foods you enjoy. However, some foods you used to enjoy may now have less-pleasant associations. For example, you may like the taste of cakes but have learned to be afraid of the consequences of eating them. Or you may have always eaten sweets when you overate, but ate so many, so fast that you never really knew whether you liked the taste. You may have eaten so much of a particular food that all you associate with it now is the experience of feeling overfull and bloated.

If certain foods have specific unpleasant associations for you, you may wish to start to weaken and break these links so that you can once again allow yourself to enjoy these foods. The next exercise can help you do this.

Exercise 13.3 Changing Food Associations

Choose a food you have previously been concerned about eating, but think you might enjoy or would like to eat again. Plan to eat some of this food at a time when you don't feel hungry. Then bring your affiliative soothing system into play by practicing your soothing rhythmic breathing or safe-place imagery. When you feel ready, put a piece of the food in your mouth. Take time to experience the smell, taste, and texture of the food. What do you notice? Is the food something you like? Does eating the food trigger any other experiences, for example, unpleasant memories? What might worry you if you allowed yourself to enjoy what you have eaten?

If you notice memories, thoughts, and feelings cropping up that could stop you from enjoying the food, don't eat any more of it just now, but pause and write them down. Now think what your compassionate mind might say or do to help you cope with these thoughts. You could use a version of the compassionate thought balancing form (worksheet 6.1) to help you, though, of course, with new column headings; or you might like to write yourself a compassionate letter (we will explore this skill in the next chapter).

When you feel ready, you can repeat the exercise with another piece of the food, but this time, gently and kindly, imagine, or even actually say out loud, these new compassionate thoughts as you eat. With practice you will learn to associate these new thoughts with these foods and to allow yourself to enjoy them.

As well as returning to foods you used to enjoy, try also to increase the variety of foods you eat so you can learn that you enjoy exploring new tastes, smells, and textures.

Another aspect of learning to enjoy food again is getting used to eating with others. Many people who overeat have come to avoid eating socially, either because they are concerned about what other people might think about what they eat (for example, seeing them as greedy) or because they are more likely to overeat in these situations. Again, this is something you can overcome with practice; after all, you deserve to eat out, and to eat with your friends and family as much as anyone else! This is the time to learn to reclaim eating as a pleasant and normal human social activity that you no longer need to be afraid of. The next exercise will help you to do this.

Exercise 13.4 Enjoying Eating Socially

Again, you can use the thought-balancing form (worksheet 6.1), with appropriate column headings. Begin by writing down in the left-hand column any thoughts or feelings that have stopped you or put you off from eating with other people. Now bring your compassionate mind into play and explore ways in which you could address these concerns from a compassionate perspective. If you have noted that you are concerned about how other people would react to seeing you eat, you might want to think about this from the perspective of your compassionate image; would this part of you see it as fair to stop people from eating socially and enjoying food?

Another way to begin feeling more comfortable eating socially is to gradually build the range of people you eat with or places where you eat. The key word here is "gradually"; for example, you might start by having a meal with just one other person you know, like, and trust, and then try eating with a small group of just two or three people. This will give you the opportunity to practice your new compassionate thoughts and behavior. When you feel comfortable in twos and threes, you could then gradually expand the range of people you eat with and places where you eat.

The key to this last step in the program is to experiment and learn to have fun with foods. Allow yourself to reclaim your relationship with eating so that you enjoy food, safe in the knowledge that you are in tune with your body's needs and have alternative ways of managing your feelings. It is this feeling of pleasure and safety, rather than the rigid (and impossible) rules of dieting, or the chaos of overeating to manage your feelings or overeating from habit, that will make eating a "risk-free" and enjoyable part of your life.

PUTTING IT ALL TOGETHER: CARING FOR YOUR BODY WITH COMPASSION

Our bodies need to be cared for if we are going to get the most out of them, and eating healthily is a big part of this—but it's not the whole story. None of us will have the perfect body, and indeed it's an illusory aim. A more realistic aim is to have a body that's healthy for as long as possible and one that you appreciate and enjoy. To this end, you need to not only eat well but also attend to two other needs: activity and rest.

Physical Activity

Our long-term health has far more to do with how physically fit we are than how much we weigh. The good news is that our evolution means that our bodies are relatively low maintenance compared to, for example, those of a thoroughbred racehorse (or even our pet dogs). We need about one hour of physical activity every day that increases our heart rate and keeps it up, without making us out of breath (a good indicator of this is whether we can still keep up a conversation). It seems that we can even do this in short bursts of five to ten minutes and still get the same health benefits. Sadly, most of us—including me!—don't always do this. We tend to be very sedentary because of the changes in lifestyle that have come with working longer and longer hours in less-physical jobs. Or we engage in intense programs of activity that we find hard to sustain, typically as a New Year's resolution to join a gym.

Our average levels of physical activity, particularly among younger people, are going down year by year. For a whole range of reasons, people who overeat tend to do even less physical activity than the already unhealthily low average. This is not good for our mental or physical health. Lack of activity can lead to low mood, tiredness, and anxiety, and a range of physical problems, as well as leave us weighing more than our genetic makeup intended.

However, many of us also overexercise, usually by setting targets for exercise that are not sustainable, for example, vowing we will go running every day, come rain or shine. We also tend to link exercise with the dieting mind-set: we exercise to lose weight, and we give it up when we give up our diets.

So we need to aim for a compassionate level of physical activity that recognizes and is in tune with our bodies' needs, but that also reflects and responds to our physical health so that, for example, we don't force ourselves to go running when we are ill. We also need to break the link between exercise and the dieting mind-set.

In fact, it can be better not to think of "exercise" at all, but of "physical activity" instead. For many of us, formal exercise can have a whole range of negative connections, for example, with being bullied into cross-country running at school, or feeling humiliated by not being picked for the football or hockey team. For others, exercise simply became "uncool" and was abandoned as they grew older. Many young girls give up formal physical exercise as they reach their teens for this reason.

Starting formal exercise or taking up a sport again can take a lot of courage if you've had any of these types of experience in the past, and it can be even harder if you don't feel good about your fitness level or your size and shape. Many people can and do find going to the gym or taking up a sport a fun and useful way to increase their physical activity. However, physical activity covers a whole range of things that are a long way from gym workouts and exercise classes. It can include dancing around at home, going for a walk, gardening—even housework.

The key to increasing your physical activity is to choose a variety of things you're prepared to do now and a couple you'd like to work toward. Ideally, this will build on things you already do, but remember, variety is the spice of life. An extra hour of housework may increase your activity levels but may not be as much fun as going for a walk with a friend!

Increasing your physical activity will take some planning, and you might want to add it to your meal planning. If you do this, you can use your increased activity to improve your energy balance, but do bear in mind that activity tends to make us hungry, so we need to plan to eat and replace fluid afterward.

Start by increasing your physical activity levels slowly: listen to your body and ease off when it tells you that you're doing too much. Remember, you should still be able to hold a conversation; pushing through pain is not necessary and it's certainly not compassionate. The usual advice also applies: before you begin to increase your activity, check with your doctor that there's no medical reason why you shouldn't.

If you have at least an hour of physical activity a day, then you are meeting your body's needs. Anything over and above this will affect your energy balance for the day. As you get more in touch with your hunger, you are likely to notice this increase in energy need and respond to it appropriately.

Rest

Your body needs time to rest and repair itself just as much as it needs food to fuel it and physical activity to maintain it. We get most of the rest we need when we sleep, but we also need to have some rest during the day, particularly if we have just finished physical activity (and more than usual, of course, if we are unwell).

It's easy to work all day, come home, do housework, and look after other people, or even continue to work from home, right up until bedtime. If we don't get enough rest, we can end up feeling stressed, anxious, depressed, and irritable, all of which can lead to overeating. So we may need to begin to plan in periods of rest during the day, even if it's only a couple of minutes at a time. This can also help us to learn why we don't allow ourselves to rest. It may be that we have just gotten out of the habit, but it may also be that we keep busy to avoid difficult thoughts and feelings or because we feel compelled to stay busy. You might like to use some of the exercises in chapter 6 on dealing with blocks to compassion to help you explore and overcome these obstacles to taking rest.

Many people who overeat also have problems with sleeping. Lack of sleep can directly increase our likelihood of overeating. If we are awake for longer periods, we have more opportunities to overeat; not having enough sleep also lowers our moods, and leaves us too tired to plan eating and prepare food or to keep physically active. It can even leave us craving foods to give us an energy burst, usually those high in fat and sugar!

Sleep problems can be a complicated area. However, the following simple sleep hygiene tips can help:

- Always get up at the same time, no matter how tired you are.

- Don't sleep during the day.

- Only go to bed when you are tired.

- Use only your bed for sleeping: don't sleep elsewhere, such as in a chair or on the sofa.

You may wish to develop a bedtime routine to prepare you for sleep. This could usefully include the following guidelines:

- Cut out caffeinated drinks (such as coffee, tea, and cola) for *at least* four hours before bedtime.

- Avoid drinking alcohol for a couple of hours before going to bed.

- Don't overstimulate your mind by doing mentally challenging work, playing computer games, or watching scary or upsetting TV programs for a couple of hours before bedtime.

- Have a milk drink before you go bed.

- Spend a little time getting ready for bed, getting changed into your pajamas, brushing your teeth, and so forth to give yourself the message that you are going to sleep soon.

- If you like to read in bed, try to choose something that's not too interesting or emotionally stimulating.

- If you can't sleep after ten minutes, get up and repeat your bedtime ritual until you feel sleepy.

This type of sleeping plan may well leave you feeling exhausted for a week or so, but can be very effective in establishing a sleep routine. We all struggle to get to sleep or stay asleep at times in our lives, but usually this phase passes after a day or two. If you have problems with sleeping that last longer than this, have a word with your doctor. You can also find resources to help you work on this on your own in the "Useful Resources" section at the end of the book.

SUMMARY

This chapter has taken you through the final steps toward a new way of eating, which include planning your energy balance and nutritional needs, learning to respond to natural feelings of hunger and fullness, and learning to enjoy food again, both on your own and with other people. We've also explored how to care for your body in other ways by getting appropriate amounts of activity and rest.

It may be that these practical approaches are enough to help you to stop overeating, or at least to improve how often it happens and how severe it gets. Still, however much we plan, our emotions and thoughts can get in the way, and may still trigger overeating from time to time, even when we have established a better structure to our eating. One way of using your compassionate mind to help you with these troublesome thoughts and feelings is compassionate letter writing. In the next chapter we will explore how to go about this, so that you can use it alongside all the practical skills you have learned over the course of the past chapters.

CHAPTER 14

Compassionate Letter Writing

For thousands of years people have found that writing down what they're concerned or worried about can help them get it off their chests and either defuse difficult feelings or put them aside until they are ready to work on them. Writing can be helpful to us for a number of reasons. It slows down our thinking in a way that's difficult to do if we just think in our heads. It helps us to become more reflective and thoughtful. Also, we can read back what we have written, and revisiting our thoughts in this way can give us new insights and ideas about what may help us. In this chapter we will focus on a particular approach to writing things down that takes the form of composing a letter to ourselves in a style that offers us support, understanding, and kindness to help us deal with the challenges of life. This approach is called *compassionate letter writing*.

In compassion-focused therapy we can use letter writing to develop our skills in both offering and receiving compassion. Letters can help us to capture thoughts, feelings, new ways of paying attention, and new ways of acting on paper. They can also help us to identify blocks to compassion that can occur in imagery work or when we are trying out new ways of behaving compassionately. You can use compassionate letter writing in addition to the other skills you have worked on in this book. Ideally, as with each new skill you have learned, you don't want to try it for the first time when you are in the grip of another powerful mind-set that can lead you to overeat. So, initially at least, you will use your letters as a way to plan managing your overeating in the near future. As you become more skilled, you may find that you can use letter writing to help you deal with urges to overeat as they happen, or with other painful emotions or feelings.

We will explore how this kind of writing can help you put together in a structured way the information and analysis you have developed about your overeating and the skills you have learned so far. Many people have found this type of structure very helpful when using the compassionate mind to help them find lasting solutions to overeating.

GETTING STARTED

There's nothing rushed in compassionate letter writing; just take your time. Having said that, once you are ready and in the right frame of mind (more on this later), it's useful to start writing regardless of whether or not you know what you will write. In fact, in many ways it's a good idea not to work things out too far in advance, but to just go with the flow. Sometimes people sit staring at a blank page, going over and over in their heads what to write. This can be linked to the self-critical or judging mind-set, trying to work it all out in advance and make sure you do it "right." But there's no right or wrong here, and it's fine to start and stop; you might have a number of false starts before you get into the flow.

What "getting into the flow" really means is allowing your writing hand, rather than your head, to do the work, so that you're writing as you think rather than thinking first and then writing. The biggest block to this exercise is trying to have too much clarity before you start. If you just start writing, regardless of whether what you're putting down seems sensible or, indeed, makes much sense, then slowly the flow may come.

There's always the temptation to want to write the "perfect letter." I never have, nor ever will; nor has anyone I have worked with—but that's okay! What we are looking for is a "good enough" letter to help bring feelings of compassion to the fore and to get us into the compassionate mind-set. So you may also need to be compassionate with your inability to write the "perfect" letter whenever you attempt the exercise! I have been writing compassionate letters for several years, and I still find it a difficult, although incredibly useful, skill to use when I am dealing with challenging events or painful feelings in my own life.

When you feel more comfortable writing letters, it's likely that you will intuitively know what the feelings and challenges are that you want your letter to help you think about and work with. However, many people who overeat can find this difficult to begin with, not least because overeating often helps us manage difficult feelings, and we may be so used to doing this that we're not even aware of precisely what is behind the distress we are trying to soothe by eating. In my experience these roots of distress become a little clearer when we begin thinking about giving up overeating as a way of helping us to manage things. Compassionate letter writing can help you to look at this distress more clearly but also in a manageable way, to give you an opportunity to explore your feelings and thoughts. It can enable you to practice bringing your affiliative soothing system and compassionate mind together to find new solutions to your difficulties.

SETTING THE SCENE FOR COMPASSIONATE LETTER WRITING

There are a number of key steps in developing a compassionate letter. Before you even begin to write, it's important that you are in the right frame of mind. To do this, you may wish to use your soothing rhythmic breathing or the safe-place exercise introduced in chapter 5. If you are feeling really distressed before you start, you might like to use some of the self-soothing exercises we explored in chapter 6. When you notice your affiliative soothing system coming into play, you can then use compassionate imagery to help you.

There are two ways you can use imagery at this point. The first way is to create a compassionate frame of mind within yourself. When you are ready, imagine yourself as a compassionate person and go through the "You at Your Best" exercise we explored in chapter 5. So you will imagine yourself to have wisdom, strength, confidence, and great kindness. Remember to spend time trying to get into this mind-set, even if only a little way. Try to create a compassionate expression on your face and to focus on what your tone of voice would be if you were to speak. Spend a few moments focusing on what it feels like and sounds like to become "you at your best."

Alternatively, if you prefer, you can imagine your compassionate companion, that person, being, or element that conveys great compassion (involving wisdom, strength, and kindness) to you. Remember, you don't have to have a well-defined image; just a presence you can sense within you that is focused on your well-being and recognizes the nature of the difficulty you are struggling with is fine. Imagine the sound of the voice or any communication that comes from this person as wise and strong, expressed with great warmth and kindness, never judgmental, always understanding and looking for the helpful way forward.

When you can feel that your compassionate mind or compassionate companion is actively with you, you can begin to work though the various steps to letter writing outlined next. Don't feel that you have to go right through the process at once; take your time and only go as far as you're comfortable with in one sitting. You will need a bit of time to work on letter writing: it's a good idea to put aside an hour or so each time you try it. The key is not to rush things, to feel comfortable with the skills in each step before you move on to the next. You can use your compassionate mind to help you work out whether you are ready to move on, and to offer you support and encouragement while you experiment with this new way of working with your thoughts, feelings, and eating.

You may wish to plan for something soothing or distracting to do after you have finished writing your letter, and to allow yourself time and space before and after your writing session to care for yourself.

STEPS TO COMPASSIONATE LETTER WRITING

Step 1: Pay Compassionate Attention to Your Feelings

This step involves both any difficult feelings you are experiencing now and any you anticipate experiencing in a new situation. Start by bringing to mind the changes in your eating that you want to make, or the situation or feeling that you want to work on that may trigger overeating in the near future. This is likely to bring your threat/protection or drive system into action. Notice how thinking about this affects the feelings in your body, and the thoughts and emotions that come up. You only need to stay with this focus for a minute or so, perhaps making a few notes of the thoughts, feelings, and any physical sensations you notice as you go along. The changes or situation you have in mind will be the focus of your letter, but we don't want to stay with the feelings any longer than we need to work out what our letter will help us with. Usually about a minute is enough! As soon as you feel in touch with this, it's time to move on to the next step.

Step 2: Step Outside the Feeling

Having noticed with mindful attention the effects that the prospect of changing your eating (or whatever other situation you have in view) has on your threat/protection or drive system, your aim now is to step outside those feelings a little. You can use the soothing rhythmic breathing and other mindfulness exercises you have practiced to help you to do this. In this way you can experience the emotions you are struggling with, without getting too caught up in them or feeling the need to act on them immediately.

Step 3: Experience Safeness

Of course, if you feel you can tolerate your feelings and move straight into your compassionate image now, you are free to do so. However, if you find it difficult to stay with your feelings—for example, if your threat/protection system becomes too active or your drive system wants you to do something to change your feeling state—then it can be helpful to work on your safe-place imagery first. When you notice that your threat/protection system or drive system has dampened down a bit, but you are still aware of the feelings you may need to work with, then it's a good time to move on to the next step.

Step 4: Activate Your Compassionate Image

The next step is to bring your mind back to your compassionate image. This could be "you at your best" or your compassionate companion. You can do this by working through the process described previously in the section "Setting the Scene for Compassionate Letter Writing." It's best not to begin letter writing until you feel confident you can bring this image to mind, even if only as a fleeting experience.

When you are developing your compassionate image, you want to make it as much of an emotional, bodily, and sensory experience as you can, even if this is only a fleeting sensation. It may also be helpful to have something with you to look at, touch, or smell that reminds you of your image and helps to keep your affiliative soothing system active.

It is the feelings of compassion flowing into us from our images that are so important. You want to try to tone up your affiliative soothing system, not just on an intellectual level but also on an emotional level. When you can feel this compassion, then it's time to begin writing your letter.

The key to writing your letter is to write it from the perspective of the compassionate self. The compassionate self understands, empathizes with, and supports you unconditionally. It is wise, strong, and caring. It will recognize that thinking about doing things differently or understanding ourselves in new ways can be painful, so it won't rush your letter or ask you to make changes you are not ready for.

It can be difficult to activate your compassionate self, and if you find it tricky, don't worry; this happens to all of us. It may be that this is as far as you can get on your first four or five tries at compassionate letter writing. This is perfectly normal; it can take several weeks, even months, of returning to practice before some people are ready to move on to the next stage of their letters.

Step 5: Begin Your Letter

As someone who has always struggled to write the first paragraph of anything, I know that compassionate letters can be tricky to write. I, and many people I have worked with, have found it helpful to have a structure to follow that gives us some idea of where to begin and where to move on to. So the next steps will provide a suggested sequence of themes you might follow. For now, we'll start with a couple of general guidelines.

RECOGNIZING YOUR COMPASSIONATE QUALITIES

In the first part of your letter, it's important to help yourself recognize your own internal wisdom, courage, strength, and resilience. This is because we can often feel overwhelmed by our problems or become locked into a very self-critical way of thinking. If we are stuck in these feelings, it can be hard to recognize these qualities in ourselves that we will need to help us face our problems. So we are aiming, at least, to remind ourselves that we have these qualities, even if we can't feel them.

FIRST PERSON (I) OR SECOND PERSON (YOU)?

Sometimes we find it hard to write directly about ourselves in the first person (for example, "I have been very brave in acknowledging feeling angry this week and in trying to understand why I feel this way"). So it can help to write your letter in the second person to begin with, ideally as coming from your compassionate self or compassionate companion (for example, "You have been very brave." When you feel ready, you can then start to write first-person letters.

Imagine for the rest of this chapter that your name is Kerry and that you are writing your first compassionate letter to yourself. So you'll start by writing in the second person, beginning "Dear Kerry," and then go on to recognize the compassionate, wise, brave, strong, and resilient things you feel that Kerry has done well over the last week and in the past. At this point you're not focusing particularly on your achievements as much as on the qualities of compassion you want to foster. This part of the letter should also include your own (or your companion's) compassionate feelings for Kerry; for example:

Dear Kerry, it has been very difficult to watch you struggle with your feelings over the last week, and it is not surprising that you have ended up overeating. I understand that life has been hard for you in the past and is hard at the moment. However, I am impressed by how courageous you have been in trying to tackle these feelings and to understand how your brain and body work. I am also impressed by the ways in which you have been able to care for others, even though you have been upset, and to carry on with some things at work that you found difficult.

It's really important to try to think about specific examples that your compassionate image would offer you. You may not even believe your compassionate image at this point, but it's important to activate that part of your brain that focuses on your compassionate capacities, your courage, and your ability to tolerate and manage distressing and difficult things.

Step 6: Express Empathy and Understanding

It's important that your letter allow you to express empathy with and understanding of the struggles you have experienced in the past, are having now, or may be facing over the coming days or weeks. There are three important elements to this that we will work through in turn in this step.

RECOGNIZING THAT YOUR STRUGGLES ARE UNDERSTANDABLE

It's really important to understand that the struggles you are having are part of a common human experience, and relate to your history and your current ways of coping. To help you recognize that your struggles are understandable, you can reflect on what you know about your brain and body, your personal history, the situation you find yourself in, and the ways in which you have learned to cope with difficult things. For example, you might continue your letter:

It is understandable that you would be worried about feeling depressed or anxious this week. In the past, people often told you that you weren't capable or good enough, and that is what your body has remembered. When you are struggling with difficult things, often these memories come to the surface, and you can remember when people put you down and criticized you when you tried to do new things. Of course, you would have learned from this that new things were too difficult to manage or that your own feelings of inadequacy were the truth, rather than a feeling that was taught to you by other people. It is also understandable that your brain is very good at helping you make these feelings worse, by spending time ruminating and thinking about them, by pulling in other memories, or by thinking about new situations where things might be difficult, and focusing on how you might be rejected if you don't get things right. Your brain is also very good at helping you be sensitive to threats, particularly threats of being left alone or abandoned, because this is what all animals fear. In the past you found that food often helped you to deal with these painful feelings, or you ate with others to help you to fit in with people you thought would reject you.

Sometimes, in fact, quite often, we will find it hard to understand why we are struggling with things. For example, you may not recall your history in detail or have a full understanding of why you cope in the way you do. When this happens, it can be helpful to focus on what is threatening to you and what your biggest concerns would be if what you feel threatened by were actually to happen now. You can also look at the ways you have coped with these threats in the past. For example, what would worry you about stopping overeating or giving up dieting?

It's very likely that the threats you have experienced are those faced by all humans at some time in their lives, and your way of coping was the best you could find at the time. You may wish to discuss with someone close to you how you came to cope in these ways. If you don't want to, or there's no one suitable to talk to, it's important to recognize that your ways of coping have helped you, at least in the short term, so it's understandable that you would want to keep them until you had better ways of managing your feelings or difficult situations.

UNDERSTANDING THE UNINTENDED CONSEQUENCES OF YOUR WAYS OF COPING WITH THREATS

We do this not to beat ourselves up for doing things that, in fact, haven't solved difficulties for us, but to help us recognize some of the costs and pain these ways of coping have caused us and may cause us in the future. It is part of recognizing our suffering, and it helps to motivate us to relieve it in a way that does not involve food. For example, your letter might continue:

It is understandable that you would struggle with feelings of depression and anxiety. It is also understandable that the way you have learned to cope has been to withdraw, to hide away, to avoid sharing your feelings with anyone in case they might hurt you or put you down, and to comfort eat. This way of coping with things has sometimes helped you get through difficult times in the past, but might stop you from getting the support and care you need from people around you at the moment. It is also understandable that you bully yourself, to remind yourself to keep safe from other people's attempts at attacking you. One of the unintended consequences is that you are now so good at bullying yourself that you end up feeling even more miserable, alone, and isolated. It also stops you from thinking about other ways of dealing with the things in your life that anybody would find difficult and challenging.

UNDERSTANDING THAT IT'S NOT YOUR FAULT, BUT IT IS YOUR RESPONSIBILITY

This is a key principle of compassion-focused therapy. Remember, we didn't ask to be born into the circumstances or relationships we grew up with, and we certainly did not ask to have a see-food-and-eat-it brain, a body that's better at storing food than burning it, and a complex emotional system that can easily get out of kilter! However, we have inherited these things and are responsible for managing them in a way that reduces our suffering and lets us take pleasure and joy in the lives, bodies, and brains we have, and frees us to engage in the world around us.

So, to continue your letter, you might say:

It's not your fault you want to run away and hide; this is very normal for any of us when we are feeling under attack or under threat. Nor is it your fault that you didn't have an opportunity to learn that you are capable and can manage life's challenges. You didn't choose to be here; you didn't choose to have your history; you certainly didn't choose to have a brain that's primed for fear or primed to ruminate on things you find difficult. You also didn't choose a brain that's set up to see food and eat it, or that responds so that food helps you with your feelings. Your overeating was encouraged by other people and the food industry when you were growing up, and it was the only way you could manage the painful feelings you had then and have now. Of course, you overeat when you're socializing with other people—most people do—but for you, this is a way of helping you get closer to other people so you don't feel so afraid that they will not want to be with you.

You do want to find other ways to cope with the threats you experience now, and I know you can and will work to find other ways to cope that are better for you when you feel afraid.

Step 7: Understand What You Need to Help You Cope with Threats

The next step in letter writing focuses on understanding what you need to help you cope with your emotions or the situation you are in. This step has two elements: what you needed in the past to help you find ways of coping, and what would help you to cope differently now.

WHAT DID YOU NEED IN THE PAST?

For example, you might write:

In the past you needed people to support you, to mentor you, to help you feel confident in managing life's struggles, and to help you find ways of dealing with the challenges that all human beings face. This may have included having people around to tell you that you were good at things, to teach you how to do things patiently, to tolerate your frustration when you couldn't cope anymore, and to support you and help take over some of the things that you found too overwhelming. You may have needed people to be there for you when things were hard and to help remind you that you could deal with things as well. You also needed people not to use food to pacify your feelings.

What Do You Need to Help Yourself Cope Now?

What was just written may well be very useful in helping you to identify your emotional and practical needs, but sadly you cannot change the past! However, knowing about these needs can help you to change the present and future by responding to them in a different way. It can help put you in touch with the kinds of things you can say or do differently, rather than use your comfort-food or dieting mind-set to get you through difficulties. So you might write:

The first thing you need to help you cope now is to recognize that you are facing difficult challenges at the moment; on top of the ones that every human being faces, including dealing with your brain and body, you are also struggling with things at work that are difficult just now. You have too much work to do, and you are worried that people will judge you harshly if you can't do it all.

This is not unrealistic, because there is an element of performance-related promotion in your job. However, now you need people to understand the amount of pressure that you are under, and to be supportive and sympathetic with that. You need to find ways to manage your workload differently and perhaps to be more assertive with your managers. Try also to be honest with yourself about the things that make you good at your job, so that you don't feel so threatened when you are struggling with things. You may need to be able to share some of your worries with people at work who will be sympathetic and able to help you recognize that you are not the only one who's feeling under pressure at the moment.

You may need some structure and support to learn to deal with these difficult feelings and situations without using food. It may help to have a better structure to your eating, and to find other ways to deal with this stress so that you are less likely to overeat. You may also need to accept that you will not be able to give up overeating all at once, and to be gentle with yourself when you eat more than you need to.

Step 8: Develop Compassionate Coping Thoughts and Actions

The next part of your letter involves thinking about the ways of thinking and acting that may help you deal with the struggles you face in a different way. Remember that it's okay to allow yourself to keep your old ways of coping until you feel ready to give them up; otherwise this step can feel like making a list of things you *must* do, and you can then easily fall into the trap of beating yourself up if you can't do them straightaway or if some strategies don't work for you. So in your compassionate letter, you might say:

Everybody struggles with work pressures, and you are no different from other people in that; remember how often in the past you recognized that other people struggle at work and tried to help them cope. Your friends and family may listen to your distress, and it is important that you listen to it too. In fact, several people have commented on the fact that you are overworking at the moment, and that if you slowed down, it would be okay. Perhaps you can look at what work you need to do and what you can schedule differently. Perhaps you can arrange a meeting with your manager to reschedule your workload.

You could also choose to eat with other people, because you know you are more likely to overeat at work when you are alone. Perhaps you could start by having lunch with Dave at work, so you are a little less hungry when you come home.

Here you can see that you may need a combination of thoughts and actions to help you cope differently. It can help to write down these thoughts and actions in note form, and keep them somewhere that's easy to get to you when you want to remind yourself of them. People use various ways of doing this, for example, jotting them down on a flash card, or as a text or voice message on their phones. It can also help to remind yourself of these thoughts and actions by saying them to yourself through your compassionate image or even using the mirror with a compassionate tone of voice.

It may well be that these new ways of coping do not feel at all comfortable, or even believable, at this point. That's absolutely normal. Part of the work you're doing in your letter is at least identifying that there are other ways of thinking about and managing threats that are different from the strategies you have learned in the past and used to help you cope.

Step 9: Imagine a Compassionate Future

When you have developed some compassionate ways of thinking and acting differently to manage threats, it's important to think about how life would be if you could put them into practice. This will help you to explore compassionately the reasons why you might want to think and act differently in the future. One way to do this is to write about what your life would be like if you were able to follow the compassionate wisdom in your letter. So we focus on what could change and how things would be different. For example, you could write:

Kerry, I know it's really hard for you to think that you could deal with yourself in a more compassionate way around your mood, worries about work, and comfort eating. However, if you were able to, perhaps you wouldn't feel so anxious and so fearful that other people were thinking critically of you. It might even be that you would feel under less stress at work. You might worry less about what you eat and be able to give up dieting. You might have a better balance between work and home life. You might even be able to enjoy your work more, take pleasure in your achievements there, be content with the things you can achieve, and tolerate the frustration of the things you can't.

Clearly these are all "maybes"; however, it's really important that this part of your letter helps you be open to these new ways thinking or acting. Just play around with them; write down all the possibilities you can think of.

It's likely that you will hear a lot of "yes, buts" in your head when you are writing this part of your letter. Again, this is normal and to be expected; the key is to notice what the objections are but not to engage with them. If you feel that they are getting in the way, you can pause here in your letter and return to focusing on your compassionate image, feeling their concern for you and their real understanding of you, and knowing that they can help you with these concerns a little later in your letter. If need be, take a complete break from your letter at this point, and let your compassionate image help soothe the anxiety that thinking about new ways of being has prompted. When you feel ready, you can continue your letter.

Step 10: Make a Compassionate Commitment to Change

In this part of the letter, your compassionate self will be supporting you and encouraging you to commit yourself to making some of the changes it suggested in step 9. The key here is to commit to these changes without bullying yourself into making them. Your compassionate self is aware of your limitations, so you can use it to help you decide what elements of compassionate thinking and action you are prepared to take on right now, and what may feel too difficult to try straightaway. It's important to remember that you are moving toward these changes in a compassionate way, and that it's best to do this in small and achievable steps.

At this point you may need to reread step 9 from the perspective of your compassionate image ("you at your best" or your compassionate companion) to help identify the things you feel you can move forward with now. Do remember that it takes courage to try new ways of coping, and wisdom to recognize what's possible for you in the short term and then in the longer term. It can help to set out a series of steps that will take you gradually to the point where you can manage your distress in the ways your compassionate image would want you to.

So, for example, you might now write:

Kerry, having reread my letter to you, I recognize that perhaps you are not as compassionate with yourself as you want to be, and a bit of you feels that this is your fault too! Perhaps you could try a couple of things to help you be more compassionate with yourself. Try not to blame yourself as much for the difficulties you have faced at work, and let other people know that you are struggling and that maybe you need their support at this time.

What you could try right now is to phone your best friend, Mark, let him know you have had a hard week at work, and plan to do something more relaxing together. You might talk to your boss, too, but you might need someone to help you do that. Maybe you could talk to Mark about how you could raise the idea with your boss that work has just gotten too difficult? You could also ask Dave to have lunch with you a couple of times in the week and perhaps arrange for Danielle to visit you over the weekend, when you tend to be most likely to overeat when you feel down.

You can practice bringing your compassionate image to mind to help you feel safer with your own feelings, and work on recognizing that they are not your fault.

I would like you to be compassionate with yourself all of the time, but we both know that this is impossible for any of us.

I know that you are going to find relaxing very difficult, because you normally feel driven to achieve things. But I would like you to try to do a self-soothing exercise for five minutes a day, though please don't be too hard on yourself if you find this difficult.

Finally, think about how you can finish off your letter. You might do this by summarizing the main points of the letter, perhaps recognizing your courage for reading it, and wishing yourself well with the time to come.

For example, you might draw the letter to a close by writing:

Thank you for taking the time to read this, Kerry. You have faced some difficult decisions while you've been reading this letter, and explored some difficult feelings. This took a lot of courage on your part, and I am proud of you.

Good luck over the coming week. Please remember, I will always be here for you if you need me.

Step 11: Pay Compassionate Attention to Your Letter

So now you've written your letter—to yourself. The final two steps are to do with you as the recipient as well as you as the writer.

Many people can write a very compassionate letter for someone else or even for themselves, but cannot "feel" it; these next two exercises are designed to help with this common difficulty.

Exercise 14.1 Imagining Offering Compassion to Yourself

The aim of this exercise is to help you "feel" the compassion in your letter, to have the experience of being cared for and supported by another person in a warm, kind, nonjudgmental, and helpful way. This is similar to exercise 5.13; again, you will imagine kindness and compassion flowing from you toward yourself.

When you feel ready, bring to mind your compassionate self. Imagine yourself expanding as if you were becoming calmer, wiser, stronger, and more mature, and able to help.

Now imagine expanding the warmth within your body, and imagine it flowing over and around you. Feel your genuine desire to be free of suffering and to flourish. Focus on your tone of voice. It can help to imagine having a conversation with yourself. Next think about your pleasure in being able to be kind to yourself and to accept your own kindness.

Exercise 14.2 Finding Your Compassionate Voice

It's important to be able to "hear" your letter in the voice you've used to write it. When we are being compassionate with others, it's often our tone of voice, far more than what we actually say, that conveys our compassion. In just the same way, it's not only what you say in your letter that is important, it's also the way you say it. So if you still find it difficult to feel and act on the compassion expressed in your letter, try this exercise, which involves reading your letter out loud to yourself.

Many people find it really helpful to read their letters out loud and listen to them carefully, as if they were being compassionate with somebody else. It can sometimes help to do this in front of a mirror or to a photograph of yourself. If you tend to pick on yourself about size and shape, or how or what you eat, it may be better to look at just a picture of your face, rather than your whole body.

First, though, when you have written your letter, take time to pause and perhaps practice offering compassion to somebody else before you read it aloud to yourself. You might want to try exercise 5.7, focusing on finding your compassionate voice. Notice your tone of voice, the concern, the warmth, and the wisdom that your letter brings to somebody who is in pain and distress and just doing the best he can to get through life, as we all are.

Now try reading your letter aloud to yourself. Sometimes it can be really helpful to record this and then listen to the recording from the perspective of yourself when you need compassion. This can make it a little easier to sort out which parts of your letter are helpful to you. If you feel uncomfortable with this, just practice reading your letter aloud, and notice which parts touch you and help you feel soothed and understood.

Often when we are feeling the need for compassion, we are taken back to a place in our memories where we feel quite young, scared, and unsupported. So you might find it helpful to read your letter to a younger version of yourself, because we tend naturally to be more compassionate toward children. Even so, many people who are highly self-critical can find this to be a struggle. Still, give it a try and see what's the best way to help you use the letter to offer compassion to yourself.

Step 12: Enhance Your Compassionate Letter

As you read your letter to yourself, try to notice your feelings and whether they change as you read. Are there parts of your letter that are harsh or condemning? This is not at all unusual, particularly in the early stages of learning to be compassionate. If this is the case, you may wish to change these parts of your letter. However, as I said at the beginning of this sequence, it's important not to get caught up in trying to write the "perfect letter"; it only needs to be good enough to bring your affiliative soothing system into play and tone down your threat/protection and drive systems enough to allow you to consider other ways of thinking or acting without getting caught up in old coping strategies. No letter you write is ever going to be perfect, no matter how much you practice—and believe me, I have had a fair amount of practice!

Rereading the letter often helps you to see blocks to compassion and to pinpoint things you can't believe or find hard to do. It's important to be compassionate with these blocks and to recognize that they are a normal part of the process. You can use them to develop your letter further.

MAKING TIME TO WRITE YOUR LETTER

Letter writing can be a very time-consuming process while we are learning. As I said at the beginning of this chapter, you'll probably need to set aside about an hour at a time to practice. You may also find it difficult and frustrating at times. However, it's also empowering to discover that you have this ability and can improve it with practice. It's a skill like any other. We can all learn to play the piano; some of us find it harder than others and take a lot more time than others to make progress, but it's something we can all become good enough at. The key message with compassionate letters is that they don't have to be perfect; they just have to be good enough to:

- Help stimulate compassion for yourself and help you to find other ways of feeling safe with your emotions, rather than be driven to do something about them instantly

- Develop new ways of thinking about yourself and about our shared humanity

- Find new ways of coping that fit for you and that have fewer unintended consequences than your old ones that involved food and eating

If your letters are getting in touch with painful feelings, writing them can be quite exhausting, and the feelings may stay around for a little while after you have finished. In this case it's important to practice compassionate behavior toward yourself after you have stopped writing. Try to allow yourself at least half an hour afterward, when you are not doing stressful things. It can also help to have something soothing or distracting to do at this time. You might want to plan for this in advance using some of the techniques we explored in chapter 6.

On the final page of this chapter, I have included a summary of the key steps in compassionate letter writing.

SUMMARY

This chapter has explored using letter writing as a way of helping you to use your compassionate mind to find new solutions to overeating. You may find that this tool helps you to make use of the practical steps to changing your eating outlined in this book.

Of course, many people do not like writing letters, and the structured approach I have introduced here can look a little daunting. Please don't be put off! Once you begin to write letters, you may find that your letter naturally follows the flow I have outlined in this chapter. Indeed, this step-by-step process was developed from analyzing actual letters people have written and seeing what was most helpful. The structure given here is only a suggestion, to provide you with some ways to stimulate your compassionate mind to help you. Indeed, many people have used the steps in the letter-writing sequence to help them in their compassion work without ever writing a single letter! For example, some people develop compassionate letters in their heads, but rather than write them down, they dictate to themselves, or write compassionate poems or songs—or even draw compassionate cartoons! Whatever works for you is absolutely fine; remember, the key to compassion is knowing what's helpful in the moment.

In the next and final chapter is a brief reminder of the key points of a compassionate approach to overcoming overeating.

Before beginning your letter, get into a compassionate mind-set by bringing your compassionate image into mind. Allow yourself at least half an hour to write your letter, and plan something soothing or distracting to do when you have finished.

1. Begin by getting in touch with the feelings or situations you are likely to find difficult. Do this by imagining yourself being in the situation you are going to face. Jot them down quickly; don't stay here for long!

2. Step outside the feelings using mindfulness or your soothing rhythmic breathing.

3. Activate feelings of safety by developing your safe place.

4. Bring to mind your compassionate image, your compassionate companion or "you at your best."

5. Begin your letter by recognizing your courage, your resilience, and the ways you have coped, both recently and in the past.

6. Develop empathy and understanding for your difficulties:
   • They are understandable; be specific about your history and memories of previous ways of coping, and the key threats you were trying to avoid.
   • Understand the unintended consequences of your current ways of managing these difficulties.
   • Remind yourself that these events and ways of coping are not your fault, but they are your responsibility.

7. Consider what you need to help you cope with the difficulty.
   • What did I need in the past?
   • What do I need now?

8. Develop self-compassionate coping thoughts and behaviors to deal with the struggle differently.

9. Think about how your life would be different if you were able to be more self-compassionate.

10. Make a compassionate commitment to the changes you feel ready to make.

11. Pay compassionate attention to your letter:
   • Offer compassion to yourself.
   • Find your compassionate voice.
   • Reread your letter out loud to yourself. Ideally, use an image of yourself, either in the mirror, or a recent or much earlier photo.

12. Listen with your heart and wisdom to anything that could help your letter become even more compassionate.

13. Plan to do something soothing or distracting when you finish your letter.

Figure 14.1   Steps for Compassionate Letter Writing

CHAPTER 15

A Compassionate Focus on Eating: Final Thoughts

This final chapter will bring together some of the ideas that have run through the whole book. To begin with, here are ten key reminders:

1. Our relationship with food and eating can be very complicated. We evolved with a see-food-and-eat-it brain and body, and an emotional system to help us survive in a world full of threats. We did not evolve for a sedentary lifestyle in a world of plenty with a powerful food industry that has created a huge range of easily accessible and highly appetizing foods, many of which are high in fat and sugar. In a modern world where we are subject to far fewer direct physical threats but quite a lot of mental and emotional stress, our emotional systems can become very entangled with our eating.

2. A desire to overeat, therefore, is *absolutely not your fault* but the result of a whole range of factors, many of which you have no control over. So, no matter what you weigh or what you eat, there's nothing to be ashamed about; no matter what society says, remember, in some societies plumpness is a sign of beauty and wealth! However, how you eat, and how you care for your body more generally, *is your responsibility*, and you can learn to eat and look after yourself in new ways that are better for your physical and emotional health than relying on overeating to cope.

3. Learning to be compassionate—gentler and more relaxed about your eating, rather than anxious, depressed, and self-critical—can be the first step on a journey toward these new ways of eating and taking responsibility for yourself.

4. Learning why compassion is so beneficial for you, for example, by understanding the three systems model of our emotions, will help you to see the value of living more compassionately. Remember, compassion is not about being soft or self-indulgent, or about letting your guard down. It's about developing a very important inner quality, related to how your brain works, that will help you face difficulties in your life and cope with setbacks and disappointments.

5. Learning to become more aware, more *mindful*, of the urges to eat and the act of eating, and then of the link between our emotions and our eating, is a key step. This book has given you many ideas for exploring how to become more aware of when and why you eat what you do. It will help you understand how eating might have come to have emotional significance for you, for example, as a comfort eater.

6. Understanding your personal history, in terms of how your eating styles have evolved over time, can be especially useful. You may want to explore these ideas again from time to time. Different things may occur to you at different points on your journey, and as you move on, you may gain different insights into your personal history and its links to your overeating.

7. Getting to understand your personal relationship with food can help you to develop new ways of dealing with food and your feelings, not in an aggressive, forceful way, but in a kind and compassionate way.

8. Learning to stand back from setbacks and being open, curious, and kind about them can help you understand what they were about, what triggered them, and how you might respond differently next time. Getting angry with yourself or becoming depressed when setbacks occur is only likely to lead to further episodes of overeating.

9. Taking practical steps such as meal planning, choosing healthy eating, gradually switching from unhealthy foods to more healthy ones—for example, stopping buying foods you know tend to trigger overeating for you—will help to change your relationship with food. By these means, you can gradually learn to trust your body's responses to eating, for example, its natural signals of hunger and fullness, and allow yourself to enjoy eating again.

10. Developing your compassionate mind, for example, through imagery exercises, will strengthen your capacity for compassion, both toward yourself and others. In working through this book, you have learned how to develop your affiliative soothing system, to manage difficult emotional experiences, and to tolerate and mindfully explore your feelings. The key principle underlying all these changes is the development of a compassion-focused approach to eating. In all kinds of situations from now on, you can practice asking yourself, *What would compassionate attention be focused on here? What would compassionate thinking be in this situation? How can I behave compassionately to myself or others in these circumstances? If I take a breath, slow down, and switch on my compassionate mind, how would it help me?* Compassionate letter writing can be a great help in dealing with the challenges that lie ahead.

There are a lot of ideas in this book; you may even feel that there are too many or that the prospect of change is too complex, difficult, or overwhelming. The key is to go one step at a time. Try things out for yourself and see what you can use; if you only change one or two things, that's still helpful. Few of us follow manuals or recipes to the letter, if we're honest. But we also know that if we want to learn to drive, play a musical instrument, or speak Spanish, the more we practice, the better we'll get. If ever you have thought, *This can't work for me*, wonder why you thought that; treat your response as an interesting question rather than a definitive statement. Remember, your threat/protection system may be used to running your life! Try saying to yourself instead, *Maybe this will work for me; let me give it a try*.

Don't be frightened of asking for help, either; there are increasing numbers of dietitians and organizations you can consult. Sometimes your family doctor can be very helpful in advising you on what's available locally. Many people find that having the support of others is really valuable, although keep in mind that diet groups that focus too much on weight loss, rather than healthy eating and healthy living, may not be such a good idea, particularly if you find that your dieting mind-set leads to overeating (and longer-term weight gain). Nonetheless, sharing your thoughts and experiences with others, and feeling supported and understood by them, can be very helpful, and seeking support is a very compassionate thing to do. If you would like some guidelines on where you might look for support, try the "Useful Resources" section at the end of this book. If you prefer not to meet others in person, there are some options here for making contact on the Internet or over the phone.

The "Useful Resources" section also contains information on where you can find help in becoming more self-compassionate and in working on overeating. Take your time to explore the possibilities, and use your compassionate wisdom to help you decide which ones are likely to be most helpful to you.

I hope that the compassion-focused approach set out in this book will help you learn to change unhelpful eating habits and enable you to enjoy the wonderful tastes, textures, and smells of food, and the opportunity to share these with people you care about and who care for you.

All that remains for me to do is to send you many compassionate good wishes in your new and developing relationship with food and your body. As they say in compassionate practice:

May you be well.
May you be happy.
May you be free from suffering—
And may you be compassionate with your eating!

Useful Resources

BOOKS

Compassion

Germer, C. K. 2009. *The Mindful Path to Self-Compassion: Freeing Yourself from Destructive Thoughts and Emotions*. New York: The Guilford Press.

Hopkins, J. 2001. *Cultivating Compassion: A Buddhist Perspective*. New York: Broadway Books.

Sangharakshita. 2004. *Living with Kindness: The Buddha's Teaching on Metta*. Birmingham, UK: Windhorse Publications.

If you're interested in learning more about the evolutionary approach, take a look at the following:

Davidson, R. J., and A. Harrington, eds. 2002. *Visions of Compassion: Western Scientists and Tibetan Buddhists Examine Human Nature*. New York: Oxford University Press.

Gilbert, P., ed. 2005. *Compassion: Conceptualisations, Research, and Use in Psychotherapy*. New York: Routledge.

——. 2010. *The Compassionate Mind*. Oakland, CA: New Harbinger Publications.

——. 2010. *Compassion Focused Therapy*. New York: Routledge.

Mindfulness

Siegel, D. J. 2007. *The Mindful Brain: Reflection and Attunement in the Cultivation of Well-Being*. New York: W. W. Norton and Company.

Siegel, R. D. 2010. *The Mindfulness Solution: Everyday Practices for Everyday Problems*. New York: The Guilford Press.

Thich Nhat Hanh. 1991. *The Miracle of Mindfulness: The Classic Guide to Meditation by the World's Most Revered Master*. Trans. M. Ho. London: Rider.

Kabat-Zinn, J. 2005. *Coming to our Senses: Healing Ourselves and the World Through Mindfulness*. London: Piatkus.

Mindfulness and Eating

Albers, S. 2006. *Mindful Eating 101: A Guide to Healthy Eating in College and Beyond*. New York: Routledge.

Eating and Dieting

Bacon, L. 2008. *Health at Every Size*. Dallas: BenBella Books.

Booth, D. A. 1994. *The Psychology of Nutrition*. Bristol, PA: Taylor and Francis.

Logue, A. W. 2004. *The Psychology of Eating and Drinking*. 3rd ed. New York: Brunner-Routledge.

Taubes, G. 2008. *The Diet Delusion*. New ed. London: Vermilion.

The Dalai Lama

The Dalai Lama is the spiritual head of Buddhism, which can be seen as both a spiritual and a philosophical tradition. It is particularly valuable for its insights into human psychology, built over thousands of years of meditation and introspective observation.

Dalai Lama. 1995. *The Power of Compassion*. London: Thorsons Publishers.

———. 2001. *An Open Heart: Practicing Compassion in Everyday Life*. Ed. N. Vreeland. Boston: Little, Brown and Company.

The Importance of Affection in Our Lives

Cozolino, L. 2006. *The Neuroscience of Human Relationships: Attachment and the Developing Social Brain*. New York: W. W. Norton and Company.

Gerhardt, S. 2004. *Why Love Matters: How Affection Shapes a Baby's Brain*. New York: Brunner-Routledge.

CDS FOR MEDITATION

Two useful book and CD combinations are:

Dagsay Tulku Rinpoche. 2002. *The Practice of Tibetan Meditation: Exercises, Visualizations, and Mantras for Health and Well-Being*. Rochester, VT: Inner Traditions. This book offers a very useful set of postures and exercises, along with a CD of mantras and instructions.

Kornfield, J. 2004. *Meditation for Beginners*. Boulder, CO: Sounds True.

Some useful CDs that will guide you are:

Brantley, J. 2003. *Calming Your Anxious Mind: How Mindfulness and Compassion Can Free You from Anxiety, Fear, and Panic*. Oakland, CA: New Harbinger Publications.

Gilbert, P. 2007. *Overcoming Depression: Talks with Your Therapist*. London: Constable and Robinson. Two CDs with a range of exercises, some of which (for example, soothing rhythmic breathing and compassionate images) are covered in this book.

Kabat-Zinn, J. 2005. *Guided Mindfulness Meditation*. Boulder, CO: Sounds True.

Pema Chödrön. 2007. *How to Meditate: A Practical Guide to Making Friends with your Mind*. Boulder, CO: Sounds True.

Williams, M., J. Teasdale, Z. Segal, and J. Kabat-Zinn. 2008. *The Mindful Way Through Depression: Freeing Yourself from Chronic Unhappiness*. Boulder, CO: Sounds True.

WEBSITES

Compassion

The Center for Compassion and Altruism Research (http://ccare.stanford.edu): Website of an institution set up by Professor James Doty for international work for the advancement of compassion.

Compassionate Mind Foundation (www.compassionatemind.co.uk): In 2007, Paul Gilbert and a number of colleagues (including myself) set up a charity called the Compassionate Mind Foundation. On this website, you'll find various essays and details of other sites that look at different aspects of compassion. You'll also find a lot of material that you can use for meditation on compassion and links to many other related websites.

Mind and Life Institute (www.mindandlife.org): The Dalai Lama has formed relationships with Western scientists to develop a more compassionate way of living. More information on this can be found on this website.

Self-Compassion (www.self-compassion.org): This website is run by Kristin Neff, one of the leading researchers into self-compassion.

Eating Disorders and Overeating

Academy for Eating Disorders (AED) (www.aedweb.org): Though mainly a website for professionals working with people with eating disorders, this is also a good source of information for the public.

BEAT (Beating Eating Disorders) (www.b-eat.co.uk): Beat is the working name for the UK-based Eating Disorders Association. This charity offers a wide range of helpful information and support for people with eating disorders and disordered eating.

National Center for Overcoming Overeating (www.overcomingovereating.com): A great resource for non-dieting approaches to eating, based in the United States.

National Eating Disorder Information Centre (www.nedic.ca): This is a Canadian nonprofit organization founded in 1985 to provide information and resources on eating disorders and preoccupations with food and weight. One of its main goals is to inform the public about eating disorders and related issues. It also staffs a Canadian-based helpline.

Nourishing Connections (www.nourishingconnections.com): The main focus of this organization is giving up dieting. It has a lot of helpful articles and resources to help you get back in touch with your hunger and satiety system.

Linda Bacon (www.lindabacon.org/resources.html): Linda has pioneered the Health at Every Size (HAES) movement in the United States, a nondieting approach to eating and health that has becoming increasingly popular in the United Kingdom too. This website contains useful articles and downloads for individuals and health care providers.

WIN the Rockies (www.uwyo.edu/WinTheRockies/default.html): This website is a helpful resource for individuals and communities who want to foster acceptance of all people, regardless of body size. It is based on the principles of body-size differences and size acceptance, positive self-acceptance, physically active living, and healthful and pleasurable eating.

References

FOREWORD

On how negative environments increase unhappiness and mental illness, especially in youth: Twenge, J. M., B. Gentile, C. N. DeWall, D. Ma, K. Lacefield, and D. R. Schurtz. 2010. Birth cohort increases in psychopathology among young Americans, 1938–2007: A cross-temporal meta-analysis of the MMPI. *Clinical Psychology Review* 30 (2):145–54.

On the relationship between self-compassion and happiness: Neely, M. E., D. L. Schallert, S. S. Mohammed, R. M. Roberts, and Y.-J. Chen. 2006. Self-kindness when facing stress: The role of self-compassion, goal regulation, and support in college students' well-being. *Motivation and Emotion* 33 (1):88–97.

Leary, M. R., E. B. Tate, C. E. Adams, A. B. Allen, and J. Hancock. 2007. Self-compassion and reactions to unpleasant self-relevant events: The implications of treating oneself kindly. *Journal of Personality and Social Psychology* 92 (5):887–904.

CHAPTER 1: UNDERSTANDING YOUR RELATIONSHIP WITH FOOD

On maintenance of weight loss: National Heart, Lung, and Blood Institute Obesity Education and Innovation Expert Panel. 1998. Clinical guidelines on the identification, evaluation, and treatment of overweight and obesity in adults: The evidence report. *Obesity Research* 6:51S–209S.

CHAPTER 2: MAKING SENSE OF OVEREATING, PART 1: HOW YOUR BODY WORKS

On blood sugar levels and appetite: Logue, A. W. 2004. *The Psychology of Eating and Drinking.* 3rd ed. New York: Brunner-Routledge.

On the starve-eat cycle: Keys, A., J. Broze, and A. Henschel. 1950. *The Biology of Human Starvation.* Vol. 2. Minneapolis: Minnesota University Press.

On the body's natural tendency to increase physical activity to match increased energy intake: Levine, J. A., N. L. Eberhardt, and M. D. Jensen. 1999. Role of nonexercise activity thermogenesis in resistance to fat gain in humans. *Science* 283 (5399):212–14.

CHAPTER 3: MAKING SENSE OF OVEREATING, PART 2: EATING AND YOUR FEELINGS

On how we learn to eat: See Booth, D. A. 1994. *The Psychology of Nutrition.* London: Taylor and Francis. He provides a fascinating review of how we learn to eat, how our eating patterns change as we grow older, and the psychological and biological influences on eating.

On the areas of the brain and hormones that respond to kindness: See references in Gilbert, P. 2009. *The Compassionate Mind,* chapter 5. London: Constable and Robinson.

On the threat system of emotional regulation: Baumeister, R. F., E. Bratslavsky, C. Finkenauer, and K. D. Vohs. 2001. Bad is stronger than good. *Review of General Psychology* 5 (4):323–70.

CHAPTER 10: MOTIVATING YOURSELF TO CHANGE

On psychological research on change: Prochaska, J. O., and C. C. DiClemente. 1983. Stages and processes of self-change of smoking: Toward an integrative model of change. *Journal of Consulting and Clinical Psychology* 51 (3):390–95.

CHAPTER 11: DETERMINING WHAT YOUR BODY NEEDS

On sugar content in processed foods: Information based on UK National Health Service guidelines for healthy eating. For more detailed advice on balanced healthy eating, see www.nhs.uk/Livewell/Goodfood/Pages/Healthyeating.aspx#comments.

CHAPTER 13: TOWARD A NEW WAY OF EATING: THE FINAL STEPS

On establishing a sleep routine: For more detailed help in managing sleep problems, see Espie, C. A. 2006. *Overcoming Sleep and Insomnia Problems: A Self-Help Guide Using Cognitive Behavioral Techniques.* London: Constable and Robinson.

On taking water before meals: van Walleghen, E. L., J. S. Orr, C. L. Gentile, and B. M. Davy. 2007. Pre-meal water consumption reduces meal energy intake in older but not younger subjects. *Obesity* 15 (1):93–99.

Ken Goss, DClinPsy, is a consultant clinical psychologist and head of Coventry Eating Disorders in the United Kingdom. He has pioneered the use of compassion-focused therapy for the treatment of eating disorders. He was a student of Paul Gilbert, author of *The Compassionate Mind* and *Overcoming Depression*, and has worked within the field of compassion-focused therapy since the early 1990s. He is on the board of the Compassionate Mind Foundation and is one of the country's leading experts on using compassion-focused therapy for the treatment of eating disorders.

Foreword writer **Paul Gilbert, PhD**, is professor at the University of Derby in the United Kingdom, Director of the Mental Health Research Unit at Derbyshire Mental Health Trust, and author of *The Compassionate Mind*.